Governmental Strategies and Innovation in Higher Education

Higher Education Policy Series

Edited by Maurice Kogan

Graduates at Work: Degree Courses and the Labour Market
John Brennan and Philip McGeevor
ISBN 1 895302 500 3
Higher Education Policy 1

The Use of Performance Indicators in Higher Education: A Critical Analysis of Developing Practice
Martin Cave, Stephen Hanney, Maurice Kogan and Gillian Trevett
ISBN 1 85302 504 6
Higher Education Policy 2

Degrees of Success: Career Aspirations and Destinations of College, University and Polytechnic Graduates
Chris J. Boys and John Kirkland
ISBN 1 85302 502 X
Higher Education Policy 3

Higher Education and the Preparation for Work
Chris J. Boys, John Brennan, Mary Henkel, John Kirkland, Maurice Kogan and Penny Youll
ISBN 1 85302 505 4
Higher Education Policy 4

Changing Patterns of the Higher Education System: The Experience of Three Decades
Ulrich Teichler
Foreword by Eskil Björklund
ISBN 1 85302 507 0
Higher Education Policy 5

Evaluating Higher Education
Edited by Maurice Kogan
ISBN 1 85302 510 0
Higher Education Policy 6

Academics and Policy Systems
Edited by Thorsten Nybom and Ulf Lundgren
ISBN 1 85302 512 7
Higher Education Policy 8

Major American Higher Education Issues in the 1990s
Richard Miller
ISBN 1 85302 514 3
Higher Education Policy 9

Higher Education Policy Series 7

Governmental Strategies and Innovation in Higher Education

Edited by Frans A. van Vught

Jessica Kingsley Publishers
London

First published in 1989 by
Jessica Kingsley Publishers Ltd
13 Brunswick Centre
London WC1N 1AF

British Library Cataloguing in Publication Data
Vught, Frans van
Governmental strategies and innovation in
higher education. - (Higher education policy
series, ISSN 0954-3716; 7).
1. Higher education. Political aspects
I. Title II. Series
378

ISBN 1-85302-513-5
ISSN 0954-3716

Printed and bound in Great Britain by
Biddles Ltd, Guildford and King's Lynn

CONTENTS

FOREWORD

Frans A. van Vught

This book is the result of a joint effort of a group of scholars and higher education administrators from various countries. Within the context of a project in the programme Institutional Management of Higher Education (IMHE) of the Organisation for Economic Cooperation and Development (OECD) these scholars and administrators worked together to gather insights on the relationships between governmental policy-making in the field of higher education and the behaviour of higher education institutions. In the introduction this project is explained in more detail.

I would like to thank here the colleagues who played an important role in making the project a success. First of all, I thank professor Ulrich Teichler, professor Jacques Guin and professor John Davies for their indispensable theoretical and methodological contributions to the project. I am also indebted to Paul LeVasseur and Peter Lykke of the OECD-IMHE secretariat, who planned and coordinated the project administratively, as well as to the members of the OECD-IMHE Steering Group, especially Ferdinand Mertens, who decided to start the project.

Furthermore, if the project has been succesful, it is primarily because of the efforts of the scholars who participated in it. I thank Karl Alewell, Justus-Liebig Universität, Giessen; Ole Brønmo, University of Trondheim; Denis Carrier, University of Ottawa; Olaf mc-Daniël, Ministry of Education and Science, the Netherlands; Ingrid Engqvist, University of Linköping; Pierre Gauye, University of Fribourg; Jacques Guin, University of Montpellier; Gregor Rensen, Council for Higher Vocational Education, the Netherlands; and Ulrich Teichler, Gesamthochschule Kassel for their precious work.

I am sure that I express the feelings of all project participants in thanking especially the many colleagues and experts in higher education institutions, governmental organisations and intermediary bodies who took the time to inform us and discuss their attitudes and opinions. Without their willingness to contribute, this book could not have existed.

I also owe gratitude to professor Maurice Kogan of Brunel University who, as the editor of the Higher Education Policy Series, gave me much valuable advice.

Finally, I am indebted to Ann Brunskill who helped me in correcting several texts, and especially to Jacinte van Schaik and Ada Krooshoop who typed and retyped drafts and who produced the complete book with admirable professionalism.

INTRODUCTION

Ulrich Teichler and Frans A. van Vught

By the end of the 1980s, the view has spread in various Western industrialised countries that institutions of higher education should take more initiative in shaping the tasks and functions of the higher education system than they did in previous decades. Higher education institutions are stimulated to formulate their own missions and goals and to develop their specific course offerings, research priorities and services to society.

Governmental policies can obviously play a central role in inhibiting or stimulating activities of institutions of higher education. It is generally assumed that the network of governmental regulations and policies regarding higher education grew tighter in many countries during the 1960s and 1970s. The systems of state regulation and the various policies established in these decades tended to favor uniformity within sectors of the higher education system and to discourage specific initiatives on the part of higher education institutions. Recently the question has been raised whether a certain degree of *deregulation*, or a new type of governmental strategy which encourages institutional initiatives, is needed. In fact, some European governments have stated their readiness to change their regulatory and policy system in those directions (see Van Vught, 1988).

In this book the results of a comparative study project are presented. This project was undertaken within the programme of the Organisation of Economic Cooperation and Development (OECD) on Institutional Management in Higher Education (IMHE). The objective of the study project was to analyse the influences of governmental regulation on the behaviour of higher education institutions with respect to designing and implementing innovations in their curricula. In this introduction the context and basic structure of this project are presented.

At their meetings in May and October 1985, the Steering Group of the OECD Institutional Management in Higher Education programme (IMHE) discussed and agreed on a *Comparative Study of State Regulation of Higher Education in Europe* which can be characterised by the following features:

- The study should be organised primarily for senior management staff, both career administrators and academic administrators, at institutions of higher education and other higher education agencies of OECD countries. For these administrators participation in the project was, on the one hand considered to be a training exercise. On the other hand, the administrators were supposed to act as experts in analysing the relationships between state regulations and educational initiatives of the institutions of higher education. The programme should enable participants to exchange ideas on problems, policies and practices related to the major topic of the study, to acquire an in-depth knowledge of state regulations and policies in some countries and to acquire some additional capability in organisational and policy analysis in the context of higher education.

- The study should focus on state regulation and governmental policies concerning higher education in the Federal Republic of Germany, France and the Netherlands. In all three countries a strong role for government regarding higher education and a relatively high degree of homogeneity within respective sectors of the higher education system could be observed in the past. Also in all three countries policies have been emphasised or implemented in the 1980s to stimulate institutional initiatives through changes of the governmental strategies towards the higher education system.
- The study should analyse the impact of state regulation and policy-making on one major area of institutional activities. The area of education (course programmes, curricula, teaching and learning, etc.) was chosen, because this is obviously the area in which specific institutional activities may be considered to be of extreme importance.
- The core element of the study, three one-week field visits, should focus on a small number of institutions of higher education, thus enabling the participants to trace institutional initiatives and views held at institutions of higher education as regards the impact of regulations and policies on institutional behaviour. State and other agencies should be included in the visits in order to put into perspective the experiences gained at institutions of higher education.
- The study should be comparative. This ought to be achieved by making use of the experience of the participants in their own countries, by agreeing to a joint conceptual and methodological framework in a preparatory seminar and by exchanging experiences acquired in the three countries during the respective field visits and in a joint concluding seminar.

Some weeks before the actual field visits, participants were provided with basic documents and reports on higher education policies, legislation and other regulations regarding course programmes in the Federal Republic of Germany, France and the Netherlands. The participants also received fairly detailed explanations of the project in order to familiarise themselves in advance with the topics and the methods envisaged.

The study programme as such was arranged in three phases:

- During the first phase, the participants and some other experts met for three days in an orientation seminar (19-21 November 1987 at Chateau de Morigny in Etampes near Paris) in order to prepare for the subsequent field investigations. The seminar served as an opportunity:

- to get acquainted in detail with issues related to the basic concepts of the project, i.e. theories regarding governmental steering of higher education, the underlying assumptions of the project and the outline of the visiting programme;
- to get briefed in detail by governmental representatives of the respective countries about state regulations and policies regarding the educational tasks of higher education institutions in all three countries under consideration and to raise questions helpful for in-depth understanding;
- to develop an investigative framework for the field studies, whereby both general conceptual and methodological guidelines for inquiries were treated and lists of possible questions to be raised were established.

- During the second phase (22-28 November 1987) participants were divided into three groups, each of which visited one of the countries under investigation. During this phase, the participants were able to gain first-hand, in-depth knowledge of how regulations and policies were perceived and applied and of how innovations of studies were realized. Information was obtained by personal and group interviews, presentations, group discussions and through the analysis of documents. Participants visited institutions of higher education, governmental agencies and other co-ordinating agencies.

  Efforts were made to arrange a similar range of visits in each country. Participants met rectors and other high-level administrators of institutions of higher education as well as representatives of basic units for teaching and research in various disciplines (notably law, engineering and certain fields of humanities and social sciences). In some cases, participants met representatives of the same institutions again at the end of the visiting programme. They also had an opportunity to discuss the findings with representatives of government and other co-ordinating agencies.

  On the other hand, deliberate choices were made to enable participants to observe specific characteristics of the respective countries. In France, three universities were visited in one region which reacted differently in a period of legislative transition. In the Federal Republic of Germany, two different *Länder* as well as various co-ordinating agencies were visited in order to analyse the impacts of federal structures on innovations. In the Netherlands, both universities and non-university institutions of higher education were visited, because the latter were recently upgraded and incorporated in a steering system almost identical to that of the

universities.
- In the third phase, all participants met again for a final seminar (28 November - 1 December, 1987) at the University of Twente in Enschede, the Netherlands, in order to compare and discuss their respective findings and to write a first draft of their reports.

The basic question of the study project was how governmental regulations and policies inhibit or enhance initiatives of higher education institutions with respect to the design and implementation of innovations in their curricula. This basic question pointed to three major areas of investigation:
- The nature and character of governmental regulations and policies potentially affecting actions on the part of the institutions of higher education regarding their educational tasks.
- The nature of institutional behaviour regarding their educational tasks, especially the nature of institutional responses to external pressures and institutional efforts to create innovations.
- The outcomes of governmental regulations and policies on the one hand and of institutional behaviour on the other hand in terms of the number and the appriopriateness of innovations of curricula.

Each of these three areas of investigation will now briefly be elaborated upon.

In order to examine the influence of government regulation and policies on educational initiatives of higher education institutions, various elements and aspects regarding regulations and policies in the three countries under study had to be examined. In the conceptual framework several important aspects were distinguished:
- The actors of external regulation and policy-making and their relative influence in the overall system of external regulations and policies. What role does national government play as compared to non-governmental authorities (and/or to state authorities in the context of a federal system)? To what extent are regulations and policies determined by parliament, executive governmental agencies or courts? In which way do other ministries than those directly in charge of education and science interact with institutions of higher education? Do councils, committees and/or 'buffer-organisations' exist, and what is their function and influence? What is the relative influence of other actors, such as employers, unions, professional organisations, 'consumers', and how do they interact with government and with institutions of higher education?
- Factors influencing the general steering approach of government. The steering approach of government (as well as of other external actors) does not necessarily have to be completely attributed to the general inclinations and behaviour of those actors, but is also related to other

factors, such as changing social and economic conditions, prevailing views regarding the socio-political role of government and regarding the need and potential of planning, cycles of governmental expenditures, etc. Such factors were addressed in the study as far as they seemed to be helpful in explaining changes in the patterns of steering higher education in the last two or three decades.

- Styles of interaction between government and institutions of higher education. To what extent does government influence higher education institutions with the help of laws, decrees and specific administrative regulations, policy papers, organised communication through regular meetings or occasional conferences, inspection, executive supervision, informal advice, etc.? Which styles of interaction between government and institutions of higher education are promoted by government? Do formal mechanisms prevail or are informal practices stimulated? Are tight or loose frameworks set for institutional actions? To what extent does the initiative for interaction rest with the institutions of higher education or with government? Do direct or indirect modes of control of institutional behaviour prevail?
- The frameworks, guidelines and rules regarding the educational tasks of institutions of higher education. Are there specific guidelines from government regarding curricula, selection, examinations, duration of courses, workload of students, etc.? Are these guidelines formulated in laws, general decrees or specific orders for each institution and course programme? Are there limited lists of recognised fields of study? What role does government play in the approval of individual course programmes? Are there specific consultation procedures? Are there specific frameworks for experimentation and innovation of curricula?
- The regulatory and policy modes and styles indirectly affecting course programmes and curricula. Obviously, steering of the educational tasks of higher education does not only take place through guidelines and other regulations directly addressing forms and contents of course programmes. Therefore, other ways of steering, notably those of funding and resource allocation as well as those of appointment and supervision of teaching staff, had to be taken into consideration.

Regarding the behaviour of the institutions of higher education, the investigations focussed on two aspects: the perception of the external regulations and policies and the institutional policies and efforts with respect to the innovation of courses and curricula.

- With regard to the perception of external regulations and policies, the questions were: how are state regulations and policies perceived? Do these perceptions differ from the governmental intentions? To what extent are external regulations and policies considered to be restrictive?

To what extent are they considered to be inhibiting or stimulating for innovation of curricula? What role do government regulations and policies play vis-à-vis other external influences according to the views of the actors at the institutions of higher education?
With regard to the institutional policies and efforts regarding curricula, the questions were: what are the typical formal and informal processes of decision-making regarding courses and curricula, both at the central institutional level and at the departmental or faculty level? How are external steering efforts handled in this framework? Do specific traditions, resources and environmental conditions shape a specific institutional mission? Is this mission consistent with external expectations? What efforts are made on the central institutional level to stimulate innovations? What procedures and mechanisms - such as resource control, setting up of new organisational units, personnel policies etc. - are applied in this context? What internal factors inhibiting or stimulating educational innovation are perceived at the institutional level? What kind of innovations have been envisaged or realised recently? What were the reasons for pursuing such innovations and who initiated those activities? What kind of processes for implementation were chosen and to what extent was support or resistance met? What was the role of the institution of higher education and what was the role of the various external actors in shaping the processes and outcomes of innovation?

According to the underlying assumptions of the general conceptual framework used in this study, state regulations and policies on the one hand and the behaviour of higher education institutions on the other would have been successful, if indeed a growing number of appropriate innovations could be observed. In this study these were the outcomes on which the attention was focussed.

It was not possible, however, to acquire a sufficient overview of this kind of 'success' in the framework of this study, because the study could only be based on visits to a few institutions of higher education within a limited time-span. The study had to refrain from far-reaching conclusions in this respect. It was rather used to develop an empirically based model of the relationships between governmental regulations and policies on the one hand and institutional efforts to create innovations on the other. In later studies this model can be tested on a broader basis.

As was indicated before, the project included three case studies on the influence of government regulation on institutional behaviour with respect to the design and implementation of innovations of curricula within higher education institutions. The three case studies were carried out in the

Federal Republic of Germany, France and the Netherlands. These case-studies are presented in Part II of this book.

The project has been coordinated by a team consisting of Jacques Guin (professor of economics, Université de Montpellier I), Ulrich Teichler (professor of higher education and director of the Wissenschaftliches Zentrum für Berufs- und Hochschulforschung, Gesamthochschule Kassel), Frans van Vught (professor of public administration and director of the Center for Higher Education Policy Studies, University of Twente), John Davies (professor of higher education, Danbury Park Management Center) and Paul LeVasseur and Peter Lykke (OECD-IMHE-secretariat). Van Vught, Teichler and Davies were asked to work out concepts, methodologies and procedures of the projects. Guin, Teichler and Van Vught were asked to serve as rapporteurs of the visiting groups in the Federal Republic of Germany, the Netherlands and France. Van Vught agreed to take the responsibility of writing a general publication on the project.

This book contains the results of the study project, put in the broader perspective of governmental strategies and processes of innovation in higher education. Part I contains the theoretical and empirical analyses. In Chapter 1 two basic general governmental strategies are distinguished and an inventory is made of the various instruments a government may use to influence (parts of) society. Chapter 2 addresses the subject of innovations in higher education. It discusses the literature on this subject and gathers from it a set of theoretical expectations regarding the relationships between governmental policies and instruments on the one hand and the innovative behaviour of higher education institutions on the other. In Chapter 3 the recent developments in government regulation of higher education in Western industrialised countries are discussed. More specifically, attention is focussed on governmental approaches to the processes of curriculum development in higher education. Chapter 4 contains the conclusions which are drawn from the three case-studies. In this chapter the general lines of the foregoing chapters are brought together to confront the theoretical analyses with some recent empirical experiences.

As was already mentioned, Part II contains the three case studies which were carried out in the project. In the Chapters 5, 6 and 7 the detailed information on the respective countries can be found.

It is the hope of all the authors that this book will provide the readers with as many powerful insights as were gained during the study project.

PART I

THEORY AND ANALYSIS

Chapter 1

STRATEGIES AND INSTRUMENTS OF GOVERNMENT

Frans A. van Vught

1. Government regulation

During the past decades government regulation has become an increasingly important issue, both in political debates and processes, and in the theoretical studies of these debates and processes. Much of the attention has been focussed on private sector regulation. Economists have analysed the effects of government regulation on the affected market sector organisations and industries (for instance: Kahn, 1971; Stigler, 1975).

The effects of public sector regulation have also attracted some attention. In the fields of public administration and policy studies, public sector regulation has fruitfully been studied as an issue of compliance or noncompliance. The literature on implementation processes in particular has offered some interesting results with respect to the identification of factors explaining why specific government policies have or have not succeeded (Pressman and Wildavsky, 1973; Van Meter and Van Horn, 1975; Dunsire, 1978; Rein and Rabinovitz, 1978; Barrett and Fudge, 1981). However, the studies of the effects of government regulation of public organisations have so far not resulted in a clear 'body of knowledge' from which relevant policy-advice can be drawn.

In this book we will focus on the processes and effects of government regulation in the context of higher education. We will especially try to analyse the relationships between types of government regulation and the innovative behaviour of higher education institutions. Limiting ourselves to this already very complex field, we hope to be able to throw some light on some of the fundamental aspects of government regulation of public sector organisations.

Generally speaking, regulation has to do with the influencing of behaviour, i.e. with trying to steer the decisions and actions of others according to certain objectives and by using certain instruments. Mitnick has defined 'regulation' as 'the intentional restriction of a subject's choice of activity, by an entity not directly part to or involved in that activity' (Mitnick, 1980, 5). Government regulation can be described as the efforts of government to steer the decisions and actions of specific societal actors according to the objectives the government has set and by using instruments government has at its disposal. There are three basic categories of rationale for government regulation: efficiency (usually pertaining to correcting market failures); distribution; and stimulating or protecting social and cultural objectives (Skolnik, 1987, 60).

Government regulation can be interpreted as a 'framework of rules within which other decision units can make decisions without the high transaction costs of maintaining private force for the purpose of protecting their belongings or of maintaining threats to enforce the carrying out of agreed upon contracts. As a framework, the government simply delineates the boundaries within which other units determine substantive choices, the government making its own forces available to defend the established boundaries' (Sowell, 1980, 145).

Following Sowell's viewpoint, government regulation can be studied from the perspective of decision-making. Societal decision-making processes may be thought of as the dynamics of collections of decision-making units, engaged in making certain classes of choices. Decision-making units seldom have complete control over a decision-making process. They may relate to one another in all kinds of ways and their patterns of relationships may be expected to have a substantial influence on the outcomes of the decision-making processes. Government regulation can be understood as the structuring of these patterns of the relationships between decision-making units from the viewpoint of government.

From the perspective of decision-making, government regulation may be analysed by asking what pattern of decision-making is appropriate in the light of the specific characteristics of the context in which it will be used. Crucial aspects of such a question have to do with the level of consensus between the units involved in a specific pattern, with the power of one or several units to enforce certain choices and with the balance of benefits and costs for the various units. We will address the question of the appropriateness of a decision-making pattern within the context of higher education. More specifically, we will explore the relationships between strategies of government regulation and the innovative behaviour of higher education institutions, especially in the field of curriculum development.

It should be remembered that, seen from this perspective, government regulation is a category basically different from the market (in its pure form). A crucial aspect of government regulation has to do with the efforts of government to influence the behavior of other actors. When regulating, government tries to be in charge. 'The market form is . . . . a type of interaction in which, in pure form, no one is in charge and matters are disaggregated' (Clark, 1983a, 30). Sowell makes very clear where the differences between government regulation and the market can be found: 'The government is . . . . an institution, but the market is nothing more than an option for each individual to choose among numerous existing institutions, or to fashion new arrangements suited to his own situation and taste'. In the market, decision-making processes are not deliberately structured. No effort is made to design, implement and maintain a specific framework of rules, which sets boundaries for non-governmental (as well as governmental) decision-making units. In the case of government regulation such frameworks are the most crucial characteristics. Government regulation implies the structuring of decision-making processes by setting objectives and using governmental instruments. 'The government establishes an army or a post office as the answer to a given problem. The market is simply the freedom to choose among many existing or still-to-be-created possibilities . . . . . . The market is no particular set of institutions. Its advantages and disadvantages are due precisely to this fact. Any comparison of market processes and governmental processes for making a particular set of decisions is a comparison between given institutions, prescribed in advance, and an option to select or create institutions ad hoc' (Sowell, 1980, 41).

At the end of Chapter 4 we will come back to this issue of the market form of decision-making. Noting that the market, in its pure form, is very different from the concept of government regulation, we will explore the possibilities of the coordinating capacities of the market-mechanism in a framework set by government.

In this chapter we will focus on governmental strategies of public sector regulation. We will first explore this topic from the point of view of decision-making processes. We will then describe two extreme cases of governmental strategy and we will make an inventory of the instruments government can use for regulation. In the following chapters these governmental strategies will be analysed in the context of higher education.

2. Perspectives of decision-making

The literature on decision-making is extremely broad and differentiated. Also, this literature is spread over several academic fields and disciplines. However, in all these fields and disciplines a few general theoretical conceptions of decision-making can be recognised. Let us first explore the two most important theoretical concepts, so that we can later characterise two extreme cases of governmental strategy with respect to public sector regulation.

2.1. *The rationalist perspective*

The rationalist perspective offers first and foremost a theoretical conception of decision-making. The rationalist perspective has an impressive history. Its roots can be traced to the empiricist philosophers of the eighteenth century and even further back through the later Middle Ages to the Ancient Greeks, where the Olympic gods claimed to be far more rational than those other less civilised gods who had more affinity with primitive beliefs (Russell, 1971, 51). From the period of the Enlightenment onwards, the rationalist perspective has attracted philosophers and politicians who have tried to argue for a hypothetical rule of reason. As Mannheim states: 'The role of reason in human affairs and the idea of the free individual as the seat of reason are the most important themes inherited by twentieth-century social scientists from the philosophers of the enlightenment' (Mannheim, 1968, 168).

In its simplest version the rationalist perspective is rarely doubted. The thesis that a man acts to maximise his values under the constraints he faces has hardly ever been challenged.

The rationalist perspective is met in two fundamentally different versions: the positive version and the normative version. In its positive appearance the rationalist perspective consists of a set of assumptions for explaining or predicting how actual empirical decision-processes proceed. In its normative appearance, the rationalist perspective consists of a set of statements on how decisions ought to be made. In government regulation the normative appearance of decision-making prevails. Rational governmental decision-making is generally assumed to consist of a set of rules indicating how governmental agencies should act to reach the goals it has set.

The most general postulate of the rationalist perspective holds that an individual decision-maker will try to maximise his values given the constraints of the situation. A rational decision-maker defines his values, analyses his information and selects that alternative from his set of options which provides him with the maximum value.

Behind these general postulates of the rationalist perspective, a number of more specific assumptions can be found which have often been the object of heated debates. Let us explore some of the more fundamental discussions. The normative appearance of the rationalist perspective provides a good starting-point for such an exploration.

What are the philosophical reasons for accepting the rationalist perspective as a normative guideline? To answer this question we address ourselves to Karl Popper, who clearly indicates that a choice for this perspective is a moral choice: 'The rationalist attitude is characterised by the importance it attaches to argument and experience. But neither logical argument nor experience can establish the rationalist attitude; for only those who are ready to consider argument or experience, and who have therefore adopted this attitude already, will be impressed by them'

(Popper, 1966, 230). Popper also argues that the rationalist perspective is related to a secular view of man as maker of himself: 'Instead of posing as prophets we must become the makers of our fate' (Popper, 1966, 280).

A choice for the normative version of the rationalist perspective thus is a moral choice for a Promethean view of man. The normative version of the rationalist perspective incorporates a view of man as gaining mastery over himself by power of his faculty of reason.

But there is more to this normative rationalist attitude. In the rationalist vision a decision may only be called rational if it is the result of an evaluation of all consequences of all alternatives. If we want to take a rational decision we thus need a complete image of all the possible consequences of all the available alternatives. Besides that, we should be able to allocate weights to all these consequences and alternatives, for only then are we able to select our 'optimal' solution. For reasons of briefness let us follow Camhis' stylistic presentation of the requirements of the rationalist perspective:

1. A general set of values expressed as goals and objectives.
2. Generation and examination of all alternatives open for achieving the goals.
3. The prediction of all consequences that would follow from the adoption of each alternative.
4. The comparison of the consequences in relation to the agreed set of goals and objectives.
5. The selection of the alternative whose consequences correspond to a greater degree with the goals and objectives (Camhis, 1979, 30; see also Allison, 1971, 29, 30).

Many authors have argued that trying to come to rational decisions in this way is unrealistic. One well-known argument is that of Braybrooke and Lindblom (1970). They attack the rationalist perspective on some of the basic requirements mentioned above. They argue that formulating a coherent set of values is impossible, due to their fluidity and due to the fact that conflicts among values will always exist. Regarding the analysis of all alternatives and all consequences, they point at the inadequacies of theories and information gathering. Braybrooke and Lindblom's conclusion is that the rationalist perspective is fruitless and unhelpful as an ideal because it does not 'take into account the manifold difficulties . . . . . that beset social analysts and evaluators in the real world' (Braybrooke and Lindblom, 1970, 16).

This is a positive argument against the rationalist perspective. Braybrooke and Lindblom describe a number of practices which differ widely from the normative rationalist ideal and which prove to be fruitful to their users when coping with the difficulties of decision-making. This makes their work very important, particularly since several studies have endorsed their conclusions about the actual practices of decision-making (Wildavsky, 1974; Bailey and O'Connor, 1975; Schulman, 1975).

But the question is whether the finding that many actual decision processes do not resemble the rationalist ideal implies that the ideal therefore is not worthwhile. On this question opinions diverge. On the one hand there is a group of authors who seem to be convinced that the rationalist attitude should be done away with as soon as possible. Braybrooke and Lindblom are convinced that the rationalist attitude should no longer be regarded as a normative guideline (Braybrooke and Lindblom, 1970, 22, 23). On the other hand, there is a group of authors who, although accepting the criticism on the rationalist perspective, are not willing to abandon the perspective as a normative ideal. Etzioni, for example, has argued that the necessary calculations assumed in the rationalist perspective cannot be carried out. Firstly, the decision-makers do not have all the relevant information they would need to examine all consequences of all alternatives. Secondly, they do not know how much of the information they have is really necessary and/or valid (Etzioni, 1968, 265).

But Etzioni does not seem to completely reject the rationalist perspective as a normative ideal. He presents his model of 'mixed scanning' as an adaptation of the rationalist perspective (Etzioni, 1968, 282) and seems to hold on to what he feels is a less unrealistic rationalist ideal. In his own way Etzioni seems to express the same view as Simon, who calls his 'satisfising man' a modest cousin of the 'maximising man', this modesty being the result of the fact that the satisfising man does not select the best alternative among all those available to him, but looks for a course of action that is satisfactory or 'good enough' (Simon, 1976, xxix).

Both Etzioni and Simon, and with them many other advocates of the rationalist perspective, frankly admit that the ultimate requirements of this perspective may be unrealistic. But they nevertheless want to hold on to the ideal, simply because it serves the process of justification of decisions (Solesbury, 1974, 141).

A special problem with the rationalist perspective comes to the foreground when it is applied to the process of collective decision-making and policy development. When more than one actor is involved in a process of decision-making, the rationalist requirement of formulating and integrating values must be shared by all those participating in the process. Also, the rationalist analysis of all consequences of all alternatives should take place in such a way that every participating actor can agree. However, there is more than one way of perceiving reality and there are many values an individual actor can pursue. In a process of policy development the various subjective preferences and images therefore can differ widely (Ackoff and Emery, 1972).

The rationalist view of collective decision-making and policy development addresses this question of coordinating individual preferences and images in a special way. It states that a process of social communication should eventually lead to a unanimous and rational consensus concerning the selection of the optimal policy. This view can be traced back to the basic rationalist attitude, described by Popper as the attitude of saying: 'I may be wrong and you may be right, and by an effort we may get nearer to the truth' (Popper, 1966, 225).

The rationalist view of collective decision-making involves the possibility of criticising both factual and value propositions. In an open process of social communication, the consequences of every proposition should be discussed so that finally an agreement can be reached on the policy which should be adopted. As such, the rationalist process of adopting a policy in a process of social communication may be compared to the process of adopting a proposition in scientific research. ' . . . . both propositions, which state facts, and proposals, which propose policies, including principles or standards of policy, are open to rational discussion. Moreover, a decision - one, say, concerning the adoption of a principle of conduct - reached after the discussion of a proposal . . . . may be in many respects very similar to a decision to adopt, as the best available hypothesis, a proposition which states a fact' (Popper, 1966, vol. II, 384, 385).

Following Popper, Collingridge (1982) comes to the conclusion that a rationalist approach to collective decision-making should be based on the fundamental conception that preference judgments, although impossible to justify, may be assessed by exposure to criticism in a rational discussion. 'Making a social choice is not finding some reasonable compromise between the fixed values of the individuals concerned. On the contrary, disagreement is resolved by some of the people involved in the decision changing their views about what their interests are, realising that their original opinions about what the group should choose were mistaken. Each person tries to convince those in opposition to him that the option which really serves their individual interests is the one which he thinks serves his own. Thus debate and not compromise is the key to the making of social decisions' (Collingridge, 1982, ix).

It may be concluded that in the rationalist view of collective decision-making and policy development two conditions should be met. The first is that there should be a 'community of discourse' embracing all those concerned. The second is that this discourse should lead to an agreement concerning the selection of the optimal policy (Faludi, 1986, 101).

Again, opinions diverge as to whether this rationalist view of collective decision-making and policy development is an ideal that should be strived after or done away with. On the one hand there are, as Elster indicates, many authors who differ strongly in many respects, but who agree on the need for 'purging the private, selfish or idiosyncratic preferences in open and public debate'. They all agree on the central assumptions of the rationalist view of politics and policy-making: 'The goal of politics should be unanimous and rational consensus, not an optimal compromise between irreducibly opposed interests. The forum is not to be contaminated by the principles that regulate the market, nor should communication be confused with bargaining. From these contrasts it is easy to identify the writers I have in mind. They include Rousseau and Hegel, Hannah Arendt and Jürgen Habermas . . . .' (Elster, 1983, 35).

On the other hand are the authors who think that the rationalist view of collective decision-making and policy development is unrealistic and useless. Steinbruner, for instance, concludes that there are formidable logical barriers to extending the rationalist analysis of individual decision-making to the collective level (Steinbruner, 1974, 36). In criticising Habermas' ideal of discourse, Weinrich explains that the formulation of the ideal itself can stimulate the participating actors in a decision-making process to develop special strategies which make the ideal both unrealistic and unattainable and which eventually lead to the 'dictatorship of the rear' (Weinrich, 1971).

Nevertheless, we may agree with Steinbruner's conclusion that the rationalist perspective is a theoretical conception which can be given real empirical content and which also offers scope for a valid normative argument (Steinbruner, 1974, 45). The rationalist perspective offers us analytical schemes for the study of government regulation, as well as tools to design such regulation.

2.2. *The cybernetic perspective*

As was indicated before, the rationalist perspective has often been criticised for not being in accordance with the practical processes of decision-making in the real world. However, to many authors the rationalist perspective still appears to be plausible and worthwhile. Although they doubt whether the rationalist conception of decision-making is realistic, they often nevertheless hold on to the normative idea of rational decision-making.

The only serious challenge to the hegemony of the rationalist perspective has come from cybernetics. Cybernetics offers a set of alternative assumptions for the processes of individual and collective decision-making. Therefore, the cybernetic perspective can be seen as a serious substitute for the rationalist conception.

Wiener has defined cybernetics as the science of 'control and communication in the animal and the machine' (Wiener, 1948). In *The Human Use of Human Beings* Wiener explains his thoughts behind this definition: 'In giving the definition of cybernetics in the original book, I classed communication and control together. Why did I do this? When I communicate with another person, I impart a message to him, and when he communicates back with me he returns a related message which contains information primarily accessible to him and not to me. When I control the actions of another person, I communicate a message to him, and although this message is in the imperative mood, the technique of communication does not differ from that of a message of fact. Furthermore, if my control is to be effective I must take cognisance of any messages from him which may indicate that the order is understood and has been obeyed' (Wiener, 1967, 24, 25).

Wiener indicates that especially the cybernetic principle of feed-back offers an important conceptual framework for the analysis of the processes of communication and control. According to Wiener feed-back is a method of controlling a system by reinserting into it the results of past performance. 'If . . . . the information which proceeds backwards from the performance is able to change the general method and pattern of performance, we have a process which may well be called "learning"' (Wiener, 1967, 84). Sowell argues that the principle of feed-back is a crucial element in decision-making processes. 'This feed-back is not only additional knowledge, but knowledge of a different kind. It is direct knowledge of particulars of time and place . . . .' (Sowell, 1980, 41).

Ashby in particular has offered a conceptual cybernetic framework which has been developed into a serious substitute for the rationalist perspective on decision-making. According to Ashby a decision-maker is neither a 'maximiser' nor a 'satisfiser'. Decisions should instead be interpreted as the outcomes of non-purposive, adaptive behavior (Ashby, 1952).

The focal point of cybernetic decision-making is the reduction of variety by maintaining a set of 'critical variables'. This reduction of variety is realised by an information-processing behaviour which can be understood by paying attention to the principles of feed-back and recipe. Feed-back is a process of monitoring and reporting performances on certain (feed-back) variables. The principle of recipe points to a specific repertory of operations which an actor performs when he is confronted with a certain set of conditions.

Referring to Simon (1969), Steinbruner explains the cybernetic perspective of decision-making by combining these principles of feed-back and recipe: 'Simon notes the difference between a state description of reality and a process description of reality. The former constructs a blueprint or model of the environment as the focus of decision, and specific action is taken in accord with the model. The latter, which he argues is like a recipe rather than like a blueprint, details a sequence of operations which when performed do produce the object or actual situation desired, but which works without any clear picture of the actual product. Roughly speaking, the mechanism of decision advanced by the cybernetic paradigm is one which works on the principle of the recipe. The decision-maker has a repertory of operations which he performs in sequence while monitoring a few feed-back variables . . . . The cook, in this model, does not construct the relative preference for sweetness or tartness for an average range of customers in baking his pies. Rather, he follows established recipes and watches attendance at the restaurant and the rate at which his pies disappear' (Steinbruner, 1974, 55).

From this description it may be understood that the cybernetic conception of decision-making is very different from the rationalist perspective. The cybernetic decision-maker does not calculate possible consequences of alternatives of action. Neither does he express his general set of values and compare these values to the various action alternatives. The only thing the cybernetic decision-maker does, is monitoring a small set of 'critical variables' which he tries to keep within tolerable ranges. When a critical variable exceeds its tolerable range, a repertory of operations is performed, the effects of which are fed back to the decision-maker.

The conception of decision-making using the perspective of the cybernetic mechanism is very different from the conception of decision-making in the rationalist perspective. Instead of the rationalist assumptions (or prescriptions) to formulate objectives and preferences, to examine as many alternatives and consequences as possible, and to value these alternatives and consequences in the light of the objectives and preferences, the cybernetic mechanism offers a fast and simple procedure of monitoring feed-back variables and performing recipes.

Because of this simple procedure, the cybernetic perspective is able to avoid the problems that have given the rationalist perspective its image of a worthwhile but not very realistic conception. In the cybernetic perspective the central assumptions of the rationalist perspective are rejected. No effort is made to try to formulate a comprehensive set of potential outcomes and their consequences; no effort is made to specify values and preferences; and consequences and values are not compared.

The cybernetic perspective is based rather on the assumption of the reduction of variety by focussing on only a few variables. 'The decision-maker is assumed to have a small set of responses and decision rules which determine the course of action to take once he has received information to which he is sensitive. That is, decision rules associate a given action with a given range of values for the critical variables in focus. The responses are action sequences, of the character of a recipe, established by prior experience. They are programs which accept and adjust to very specific and very limited kinds of information' (Steinbruner, 1974, 66).

The cybernetic perspective also offers its own solution to the problem of collective decision-making. Where the rationalist perspective has to assume the two conditions of a 'community of discourse' and of the reaching of consensus concerning the selection of an optimal choice (see before), the cybernetic perspective puts an emphasis on the fragmentation and decentralisation of decision-making processes. The assumption is that in a complex decision environment the basic simplicity of the cybernetic decision-mechanism can be preserved if the number of decision-makers is increased. When a complex problem is fragmented into a large number of subproblems, each decision-maker can address his own relevant variables and produce his own recipes. Within the cybernetic view on collective decision-making no effort is made to integrate the images, opinions and preferences of the various units in a decision-making process. Instead, the cybernetic perspective assumes the existence of multiple actors, each of them operating as cybernetic decision-makers.

Collective decision-making in this perspective is not so much a process of integration as of separation of actors. Cyert and March indicate that the cybernetic conceptualisation of organisational decision-making implies the fragmentation of organisations into separate units (Cyert and March, 1963). Within organisations certain levels of acceptable performance are formulated, which can be used by separate units to monitor their specific critical variables. Recipes are performed routinely (by 'standard operating procedures') as long as these variables are kept within the acceptable ranges. Only when a routine procedure fails to achieve the acceptable levels, a tendency to develop new response repertories will arise.

Generally speaking, the cybernetic paradigm proposes to interpret collective decision-making as a process in which decisions are fragmented into small segments and in which these segments are treated separately. Separate actors or units are given their own responsibility. From the viewpoint of the costs of decision-making such a delegation of responsibility to separate units has important advantages. It relieves the central decision-making unit of the task of acquiring a comprehensive knowledge. And it replaces this task with the opportunity to use, at lower costs, the direct knowledge of particulars of time and place, which can be found in the many decision-making units which together form a specific decision-making pattern.

Also, the cybernetic paradigm offers the idea of the loose coupling of separated actors or units. As Aldrich (1979) has indicated in the context of the loose coupling of organisations, this idea of '. . . loose coupling allows portions of the organisation to persist and evolve independently of other parts. This is advantageous for organisational change . . . . Second, loose coupling provides an organisation with a selective sensing mechanism, in the same way that sand is a better medium to display wind currents than rocks . . . . Third, ... loose coupling may be an excellent system for allowing local adaptation of organisational subunits facing environments that in the aggregate pose conflicting demands . . . . Fourth, loosely coupled systems permit the retention of a greater number of mutations and novel solutions than do tightly coupled systems, as they survive in out-of-the-way units or rarely involved practices . . . . Fifth, loose coupling permits the confinement of a breakdown in one part so that it doesn't affect the rest of the organisation . . . . Sixth, loose coupling may permit greater self-determination by persons in organisational subunits, thus raising levels of involvement and generating a greater sense of efficacy among them . . . . Seventh, a loosely coupled organisation could be relatively inexpensive to run, as administrators could save the time and funds that would otherwise be devoted to ensuring tight coupling' (Aldrich, 1979, 83, 84). In short, loose coupling offers the advantages of a high level of robustness, flexibility and innovativeness and of a low level of information, transaction and administration costs.

The general conclusion is that, because the cybernetic perspective on decision-making offers its own logic and its own set of assumptions, it is able to formulate a serious challenge to the often considered hegemony of the rationalist perspective. Therefore, the cybernetic perspective, like the rationalist perspective, provides both an analytical scheme for the study of government regulation and a set of tools for the design of such regulation.

3. Two governmental strategies

Having explored the two most important general theoretical conceptions of decision-making, we now address ourselves to the strategies government may follow with respect to public sector regulation. For an overview of these strategies, we will look at the literature on (governmental) planning. We will present an analytical overview of this literature and distill from it two extreme cases of governmental strategy, which will be explored later in the context of higher education. The two extreme cases of governmental strategy will be related to the two general theoretical conceptions of decision-making presented in paragraph 2. It will be argued that the strategies differ in their fundamental assumptions about decision-making and that these differences have important consequences for the usefulness of the strategies in specific contexts.

3.1. *Planning conceptions*

The literature on planning consists mainly of normative guidelines and recommendations on 'how to plan'. Theories which might explain what kind of factors influence specific aspects of planning processes or what kind of variables produce specific planning outcomes are hardly available. Most publications on planning, be it in the field of urban planning, of public administration or of management sciences, are pleas for certain approaches. Often a specific planning methodology is presented which is claimed to be superior to one or more other methodologies.

Here these methodologies and approaches will be called 'planning conceptions'. A planning conception can be defined as a more or less coherent opinion to be found in the literature on planning, on the desirability and/or the significance of the shape of the process of planning. A planning conception is a set of normative statements on how, according to the advocate(s) of that conception, a process of planning should be given shape.

It is not easy to get a more or less overall picture of the many planning conceptions which the literature has to offer. We nevertheless have tried to make an inventory of some of these conceptions. Moreover, we have tried to characterise these conceptions using some specific angles of incidence.

dimensions of analysis	categories		
1. presumed knowledge of the object of planning	firm	—	uncertain
2. presumed control over the object of planning	complete	—	incomplete
3. self-image of the planning subject	holistic	—	atomistic

Figure 1 : *Instrument for the analysis of planning conceptions (based on Faludi, 1973b).*

To formulate our analytical instrument we have made use of Faludi's 'positive theory of planning' (Faludi, 1973b), which we have given the form of three dimensions on which planning conceptions can be assessed. Figure 1 depicts this analytical instrument.

The first question we have asked looking at a planning conception is whether in this conception knowledge of the object of planning is presumed to be certain or uncertain. An image of (more or less) certain knowledge offers a description of the object from which (if the level of control is presumed to be high) precepts may be derived for manipulating it to reach objectives with certainty. An image of uncertain knowledge at the most gives an indication of the type of intervention which might lead to desired effects. It leaves room for flexibility and caution.

The second question refers to the scope of control the planning organisation thinks it has over the object of planning. At one extreme the image exists of (nearly) complete control, leaving (nearly) no room for the object to act in other ways than those set by the planning subject. The other extreme offers an image of very limited capabilities to control for the planning subject, leading to the necessity to bargain with others or to respond to opportunities that arise.

The third question concerns the image the planning organisation has of itself. On the one hand it may see itself as something with a clear standing of its own (the holistic image). On the other hand it may see itself merely as an aggregate of actors and units (the atomistic image).

By way of example in figure 2 a number of planning conceptions is scored using the analytical instrument presented above. These conceptions have been distilled from the planning literature. The classification of figure 2 has been produced by assessing the opinions and suggested approaches in these publications to the dimensions of our analytical instrument. Of course such a classification is coloured by the subjective interpretations of the literature by this author. Besides, the classification is certainly not complete. It may, however, serve as an indication of the width and the differentiation of the planning literature.

3.2. *The strategy of rational planning and control*

An extreme case of a planning conception (or, in terms of our exploration, of a governmental strategy) is the one in which the knowledge of the object of planning is assumed to be firm, the control over the object of planning is presumed to be complete and the self-image of the planning subject is holistic. Referring to governmental regulation of organisations in the public sector, we will name this conception the governmental strategy of rational planning and control.

planning conception	presumed knowledge of planning object	presumed control over planning object	self-image of planning subject
comprehensive planning (Meyerson and Banfield 1955)	firm	rather complete	holistic
incremental planning (Braybrooke and Lindblom 1970)	uncertain	incomplete	atomistic
process planning (Faludi 1973a)	uncertain	incomplete	
systems planning (Jantsch 1972)	firm	rather complete	holistic
adaptive planning (Benne 1962)	uncertain	incomplete	
advocacy planning (Davidoff 1965)			atomistic
mixed scanning (Etzioni 1967)	rather firm but multi-levelled	incomplete	
communicative planning (Van Gunsteren 1976)	uncertain	incomplete	atomistic
transactive planning (Friedmann 1973	uncertain	incomplete	atomistic
participatory planning (Bolan and Nuttall 1975)	uncertain		atomistic

Figure 2 : *An assessment of a number of planning conceptions*

A fundamental assumption of this strategy is that it should be performed as the normative ideal of the rationalist perspective on decision-making suggests: by comprehensively evaluating all conceivable consequences of all conceivable alternatives.

The authors who can claim to have stated this strategy first in the planning literature are probably Meyerson and Banfield (Meyerson and Banfield, 1955). However, from their publications it also can be concluded that they want to see the strategy of rational planning as basically a normative ideal which is worthwhile to pursue but which cannot completely be realised in reality (Banfield, 1959; Meyerson, 1956). '. . . . no choice can ever be perfectly rational, for there are usually a great - perhaps an infinite - number of possible actions open to the actor and the consequences of any one of them would ramify ad infinitum. No decision-maker could have the knowledge (or the time!) to evaluate even a small fraction of the actions open to him. It is possible, however, to be more or less systematic in the canvass of alternatives and consequences, so that the conception is not an entirely useless one. For practical purposes, a rational decision is one in which alternatives and consequences are considered as fully as the decision-maker, given the time and other resources available to him, can afford to consider them' (Banfield, 1959).

Lindblom especially has strongly criticised this strategy, variously called by him the rational-deductive or the synoptic ideal, (Lindblom, 1959; Lindblom, 1965; Braybrooke and Lindblom, 1970). Lindblom argues against the rational planning ideal from the assertion that it cannot be followed in actual practice and that the attempts to do so distract decision-makers from a more feasible strategy (called by him the strategy of 'disjointed incrementalism'). He argues that the 'synoptic ideal' is not adapted to man's limited intellectual capacities, nor to his inadequacy of information or the costliness of analysis. 'In actual fact, therefore, no one can practice the rational-comprehensive method for really complex problems, and every administrator faced with a sufficiently complex problem must find ways drastically to simplify' (Lindblom, 1959).

Perhaps the most crucial aspect of Lindblom's criticism is his conviction that, given the limited knowledge a planner can acquire, comprehensive control of an object of planning should not be strived after. A complete or nearly complete control cannot but harm the object of planning and will eventually result in the imposing of decisions and in the commanding of their implementation. According to Lindblom, decisions should rather be taken by a large number of decision-making units, each of them free to pursue their own interests. It is this conviction that leads Lindblom to speak of 'disjointed' incrementalism. 'Analysis and evaluation are disjointed in the sense that various aspects of public policy and even various aspects of any one problem or problem area are analysed at various points, with no apparent co-ordination and without the articulation of parts that ideally characterises subdivision of topic in synoptic problem solving . . . . Disjointedness has its advantages . . . . chief among them the advantage of preserving a rich variety of impressions and insights that are liable to be 'co-ordinated' out of sight by hasty and inappropriate demands for a common plan of attack' (Braybrooke and Lindblom, 1970, 105, 106).

It may be concluded from Lindblom's criticism that the strategy of rational planning and control is not only based on the fundamental assumption of the rationalist perspective on decision-making, but also implies the centralisation of the decision-making process and a large amount of control both over the actual choice to be made and over the implementation of the chosen policy. As such, the strategy of rational planning and control rejects the rationalist ideal of collective decision-making. It denies the possibility of a 'community of discourse' which should lead to a sincere consensus concerning the selection of the optimal alternative. As an extreme case of a planning conception the strategy of rational planning and control takes its point of departure in the ideal of rational decision-making, but confronted with the limitations of this ideal in actual practice, it takes refuge in an element very much rejected in this ideal: confidence in centralisation and control.

The strategy of rational planning and control is an approach to governmental regulation in which much confidence is put in the capabilities of governmental actors and agencies to acquire comprehensive and true knowledge and to take the best decisions. Also, it is an approach in which these governmental actors try to steer a planning object by using stringent rules and extensive control-mechanisms. When government uses the strategy of rational planning and control, it sees itself as an omniscient and omnipotent actor who thinks himself able to rightfully steer a part of society according to his own objectives.

3.3. *The strategy of self-regulation*

The strategy of self-regulation is basically the opposite of the strategy of rational planning and control. Instead of the assumption that the knowledge of the planning object can be firm, comes the recognition that such knowledge is highly uncertain. Instead of the wish to control the object as completely as possible, comes the conviction that such a control should to a large extent be avoided. Instead of a holistic self-image of the planning subject, comes the assertion that an atomistic self-image offers important advantages.

The strategy of self-regulation incorporates the logic and the assumptions of the cybernetic perspective on decision-making. It puts an emphasis on the principles of monitoring feed-back variables and of performing recipes. It accepts the idea that a decision-maker should only pay attention to a small set of 'critical variables' which he should try to keep within tolerable ranges. And perhaps most importantly, it underlines the assumption that the fragmentation of complex decision-making processes offers the benefits of a high level of robustness, a high level of flexibility, a high level of innovativeness and a low level of information, transaction and administration costs.

From the field of management sciences St Beer has indicated that a choice for the cybernetic perspective on decision-making is a choice for the strategy of self-regulation. 'Every manager, whether he runs the family business or a small department in a firm, whether he runs the firm itself or a major department of government, whether he runs the country or an aspect of international affairs, faces an identical problem. He faces, that is, the need to maintain a viable system far more complicated than he personally can understand. And the beginning of wisdom for management at any level is the realisation that viable systems are, in large measure, self-regulating and even self-organising' (Beer, 1975, 105, 106). Beer makes it clear that the principles of feed-back and recipe imply the idea of self-regulation. A cybernetic decision-making unit is able to regulate itself. When the feed-back loops are working and when a repertory of operations is available, a decision-making unit hardly needs regulation from outside. Moreover, a complex system with many interrelated decision-making units, is able to realise a high level of stability. Such a system has the capacity of 'homeostasis', i.e. the capacity to hold the critical variables at the level of the overall system within acceptable ranges. Confronted with such a system, the task for an external regulator is to monitor these critical variables making sure that they do not exceed the tolerable ranges, and to evaluate the criteria by which the critical variables and the tolerable ranges are chosen.

In the context of the strategy self-regulation, the role of an external regulating agency or actor is a role at another, higher level. '. . . . the role . . . . is to remain above the homeostatic fray, and to consider what is happening in terms of a higher level understanding' (Beer, 1975, 112). Beer explains this higher level role with the following illustration from the world of games. 'Suppose that as a higher manager you have the responsibility to ensure that team A wins in a game which is already being played between team A and team B, where the scoring is already even. You could dress yourself in the appropriate regalia and charge onto the field of play. The players would recognise you. Your own side might defer to your tactics . . . . while the other side would do their level best to put you out of action. This is not the way to behave at all . . . . the clever action would be to change the rules of the game so that your side must win it' (Beer, 1975, 112).

In the strategy of self-regulation emphasis is put on the self-regulatory capacities of decentralised decision-making units. The complex interrelations between these units are respected. The external regulating activities are limited to monitoring the performance of the overall system of the interrelated self-regulating decision-making units and to evaluating (and if judged necessary, changing) the rules which to a large extent define this performance.

Compared to the strategy of rational planning and control, the strategy of self-regulation is far more modest. It acknowledges the limitations of acquiring knowledge and exercising control over an object of planning which, in itself, already consists of a complex set of mechanisms of decision-making. It tries rather to incorporate the benefits of this complex set of mechanisms by limiting itself to setting broad frameworks and by providing facilities for the behaviour of decentralised units. When government uses the strategy of self-regulation, it sees itself mainly as an arbiter. In this strategy government is the actor who watches the rules of a game played by relatively autonomous players and who changes these rules when the game is no longer able to lead to satisfactory results.

4. The instruments of government

In this paragraph we will present an overview of the instruments government can use in the context of its strategies with respect to public sector regulation. These instruments will be described, so that in the final paragraph of this chapter we will be able to indicate how the various instruments can be related to the strategy of rational planning and control or to the strategy of self-regulation.

In principle every government has a number of instruments at its disposal to perform the tasks that have been appointed to it. If government wants to 'produce' certain outcomes, it employs certain tools. Without such tools governmental policies would be no more than abstract ideals or fantasies.

In the public administration literature the concept of 'governmental instruments' recently has gained renewed interest. Important theoretical concepts have already been developed in the classical publications of Dahl and Lindblom (1953) and Etzioni (1968). Dahl and Lindblom distinguished four sociopolitical processes which, in their opinion, should be used by 'any society intelligently bent on using its resources efficiently' (Dahl and Lindblom, 1976, 172). These four processes are: the price system (control of and by leaders), hierarchy (control by leaders), polyarchy (control of leaders) and bargaining (control among leaders). Etzioni makes a distinction between three types of social relationships: coercive, utilitarian and normative relationships. According to Etzioni, in any concrete case there is a mixture of these three forms, leading to different kinds of social interaction (Etzioni, 1978).

Mitnick (1980) takes Dahl and Lindblom's analysis as a starting point to develop a categorisation of the instruments of government. A crucial distinction in his work is the one between 'regulation by directives' and 'regulation by incentives'. Regulation by directives is defined as 'the interferences that occur by circumscribing or directing choice in some area - i.e. making rules for behaviour that may be transmitted as instruction'. Regulation by incentives is described as 'the interferences that occur by changing the perception of the nature of the alternatives for action subject to choice - i.e. changing the relative attractiveness of alternatives' (Mitnick, 1980, 342, 343). Mitnick develops an overview of 'some common regulatory means' which he classifies in his two broad instrumental categories. Figure 3 contains this overview.

Regulation by : directive	public enterprise (extreme case) common law administrative rules or standards
Regulation by : incentive	tax incentives effluent/user charges subsidies promotion campaign laissez faire (extreme case)

Figure 3 : *Mitnick's categorisation of governmental instruments. (source: Mitnick, 1980, p. 346).*

It seems that Mitnick's presentation of governmental instruments is based on the criterium of the level of restriction by government of the behaviour of societal actors. Directives are more restrictive than incentives, and strong incentives are more restrictive than weak incentives.

Another important publication on governmental instruments is Hood's *The Tools of Government* (1983). Hood distinguishes four categories of governmental instruments. The categories vary depending on the 'basic resources' used by government in trying to reach the objectives set. For each category of 'basic resources' a specific set of governmental instruments can be indicated. For the sake of understanding the broad scale of governmental instruments, we will present a slightly modified interpretation of Hood's categorisation (see figure 4).

Instruments of information	:	responses messages
Instruments of treasure	:	contracts bounties transfers bearer-directed payments
Instruments of authority	:	certificates approvals conditionals enablements constraints
Instruments of action	:	operational activities

Figure 4 : *An overview of the instruments of government (modified from Hood, 1983)*

The first category of instruments concerns the provision of *information.* From its specific position in society, government has the advantage of being 'a store of information'. Compared with other institutions, governmental agencies often have extra possibilities to develop rather broad, panoramic overviews of societal conditions. Hence, government can use the information it has at its disposal, to try to reach its policy-objectives.

There are various ways government can 'send out' information. It can provide informed responses tailored to questions from outside; it can direct standard messages without being asked to specific groups ('targeting information'); it can send out general messages to the broad public. What type of information outlet government uses, depends on various factors such as the size of the informed population, the degree of attention manifested by the informed population, and of course the content of the message. A crucial factor is the political and legal framework government operates in.

In general, it can be said that the providing and propagating of information offers government a set of instruments with rather low or even non-existing 'authority costs'. When information-oriented instruments can be used, government does not have to lay its authority on the line. It can send out the information judged to be necessary or significant, and it can wait and see if the information is accepted.

A second category of governmental instruments concerns 'the power of *treasure*'. Treasure is what enables government to buy favours, to court popularity, to hire mercenaries, etc.; the power of treasure is the power of signing cheques. Hood therefore speaks of the instruments of 'cheque book government'.

Government can use its treasure in two main ways. It can 'exchange' it for some good or service. Or it can 'give it away', that is: it can transfer payments without requiring any 'quid pro quo'.

According to Hood, the two main instruments of the exchange of treasure are 'contracts' and 'bounties'. Contracts are governmental payments made to specific individuals or organisations, under the condition that the recipient supplies a specified product or service. Contracts are payments 'with strings attached'. A governmental contract-payment is only made when the recipient of such a payment accepts the conditions which government requires. Like contracts, bounties also are payments made in exchange for some 'quid pro quo', but in the case of bounties the individual or organization which is to provide that 'quid pro quo' is not specified. A bounty is awarded to anyone who produces the product or service asked for. Bounties are assumed to be especially useful to encourage or discourage specific types of societal behaviour.

The two main governmental instruments of the other method of using the power of treasure (the 'give it away' option) are 'transfers' and 'bearer-directed payments'. Transfers are exchanges of treasure without a requirement of a 'quid pro quo'; transfers are 'gifts', made to specific individuals or organisations for specific purposes or reasons. Bearer-directed payments also do not involve a clear 'quid pro quo'. But, unlike transfers, bearer-directed payments are made to all those who, by some token, are eligible for them.

The instruments of 'cheque book government' can be used directly by government or indirectly through intermediaries. Intermediary organisations are an often used alternative for direct governmental allocation of resources, especially when government wants to avoid getting too closely involved in highly specialized budget-decisions (e.g. in the allocation of resources to scientific research).

In general, the instruments of 'cheque book government' are costly, in the sense that financial resources can only be spent once and the renewal of treasure implies the use of the mechanism of taxation. On the other hand, as has been argued many times before, treasure is an elegant category of instruments, often capable of achieving the kind of societal behaviour government sets out to reach.

The third category of governmental instruments is formed by the instruments of *authority*. The instruments of authority are intended to command and to forbid, to commend and to permit.

Instruments of authority vary depending on the degree of restriction they seek to introduce into the behaviour of the targeted subjects. Least constraining in this sense are 'certificates' and 'approvals'. Certificates are authoritative declarations by government about the properties of a specific individual or object. Approvals are authoritative declarations in a general sense; approvals apply to the world at large or to whomever it may concern. Both certificates and approvals are instruments requiring no compulsive action at all from government.

A subcategory requiring more (but still not extreme) compulsive action is formed by the instruments called 'conditionals' and 'enablements'. Conditionals are the promises by government to act in a certain way when certain conditions arise. A well-known example is the governmental guarantee which is provided as a kind of safety-net for certain circumstances. Enablements are the tokens which permit certain activities. Modern governments use a large variety of enablements. Licences, quotas, warrants, coupons, vouchers and permits are all types of enablements. They all allow (but do not compel) the undertaking of certain activities.

The instrument of authority which asks for compulsive action is the instrument called 'constraint'. Constraints, in contrast to certificates, approvals, conditionals and enablements, demand or prohibit certain activities. Constraints can be positive (commanding) and negative (forbidding). In both cases, they imply a compulsory restriction by government of societal behaviour.

Generally speaking, the instruments of authority depend on the willingness of the public to accept them. A low level of respect for and acceptance of government can make these instruments rather ineffective. As history has shown, governments sometimes in these cases take refuge in the authority-instruments with the highest level of constraint. On the other hand, when government is widely respected and accepted, the low-constraint instruments of authority may be very effective in producing the outcomes government thinks to be relevant.

Hood's fourth and final category of governmental instruments is the category of (direct) *action*. Within this category fall all kind of operational activities by government which directly influence the citizens, their property or their environment. Government can use 'its own' individuals, buildings, equipments and stocks of lands to directly produce certain outcomes or to perform certain tasks. It can for instance act as a national banker; it usually operates a system of involuntary detention; it sometimes holds a monopoly on the production of a certain good; and it of course often takes care of defending the country, controlling crime, treating sewage, controlling traffic, lighting streets, controlling floods, etc.

The governmental instruments of action to a large extent are related to the traditional monopoly on the use of violence and the enforcement of law. As such these instruments tend to be restricted to some specific areas of governmental control. Next to these areas the instruments of action are often used for providing 'collective goods' (like defence and dikes).

In general, it should be noted that the governmental instruments of direct action are rather expensive. They should be reserved for the governmental monopoly on the use of violence, for emergencies and for activities which might otherwise not be performed.

It may be concluded that, as in Mitnick's categorisation, Hood's presentation of governmental instruments is also to a large extent based on the criterium of the level of restraint the instruments try to produce with respect to the behaviour of societal actors.

The instruments of information are hardly at all restrictive. They are used without the explicit goal to directly limit the range of behavioural options of other actors. The objective of the use of information instruments is to try to influence the behaviour of others by providing them with significant information.

The instruments of treasure are more restrictive. In particular when government acts as the most important funding agent of the activities of other actors, these actors may be strongly influenced to adapt their behaviour to the ideas and wishes of government. 'Cheque book government' in this sense can be very restrictive, although the restraining potential is often used in an indirect way. The power of treasure offers governmental agencies the opportunity to design and implement financial incentives and disincentives, strongly urging actors to behave according to government's wishes.

The instruments of authority range from mildly restrictive to completely restraining. The 'certificates' and 'approvals' are only mildly restrictive. These specific instruments provide governmental agencies with the possibility to approve or disapprove. As such they can limit the behavioural options of other actors. Especially when the approval of government is sought after (for instance because such an approval offers the right to acquire financial resources), these mildly restrictive instruments may become very effective in influencing the behaviour of non-governmental actors. The instruments called 'conditionals' and 'enablements' have a higher level of restrictive potential. They allow or do not allow actors to behave in a certain way, usually by providing or denying financial resources or licences. The instruments called 'constraints' are extremely restrictive. These are the instruments a government can use to command and forbid and by using them government can compel other actors to behave completely according to its wishes.

The instruments of direct (governmental) action are also, generally speaking, rather restrictive. Because these instruments are based either on the governmental monopoly on the use of violence, or on the political decision that government should provide a certain collective good, these instruments tend to strongly influence the other actors' behaviour.

However, Hood's presentation seems to imply more than one criterion for the categorisation of governmental instruments (the level of restraint). A second criterion concerns the distinction between the particular and the general use of instruments. 'Particular applications are those that are directed at specific and named individuals, organisations or items . . . . General applications are those that are beamed at the world at large and thus apply to whomever it may concern' (Hood, 1983, 17). Other criteria which seem to be important in Hood's categorisation are the question whether societal actors should or should not themselves try to obtain the benefits of a certain instrument, the question whether societal actors have or have not to provide a 'quid pro quo' and the level of permanence of an instrument (for instance the instruments of authority are more durable than the instruments of treasure).

5. Instruments and strategies

The presentation of the instruments of government has made it clear that these instruments vary according to the level of restraint they try to produce with respect to the behaviour of societal actors. This variation in the level of restraint allows us to relate some specific categories of instruments to the two governmental strategies which were distinguished before. Generally speaking, it may be expected that the instruments that are highly restrictive are more easily applied in the strategy of rational planning and control, while the less restrictive instruments are more appropriate in the strategy of self-regulation.

In the strategy of rational planning and control a government sees it as its task and its capability to influence other societal actors according to its own objectives. In this strategy government judges it to be its prerogative to restrain the behavioural options of other actors in order to reach the goals which are thought to be relevant. In such a strategy, highly restrictive instruments will be assumed to be the most effective. The highly restraining instruments of authority ('constraints') or the indirect but nevertheless often rather restrictive instruments of treasure will be applied to give concrete form to the confidence in centralised control.

In the strategy of self-regulation government puts its confidence in the self-regulatory capacities of decentralised decision-aiming units. Governmental activities are limited to gathering information so as to be able to watch the overall system of activities and to providing and, if judged necessary, changing frameworks to enable and stimulate such a system. The instruments which may be expected to be relevant in this strategy are the instruments of information (responses and messages) and the mildly restrictive instruments of authority (certificates and approvals). A special set of instruments may be formed by the indirect instruments of treasure which may be applied at the systems level to install mechanisms that may influence actors to change their behavioural patterns without reducing their self-regulatory capacities.

It should be stressed that the instruments of government are seldom used in isolation. The categories of instruments which have been presented above can only be distinguished analytically. In reality governmental instruments are used in combination and through all kinds of linkages. An example is the combination of 'enablement' (a specific instrument of authority) and 'bearer-directed payment' (a specific instrument of treasure): the licence for a certain activity may immediately make a person eligible for a certain transfer of payment without a 'quid pro quo'.

Nevertheless, every specific combination of instruments has its own characteristics, which will influence its effectiveness and efficiency. Also, every specific combination of instruments may lead to different results, depending on the context in which it is used.

One of the most crucial tasks in modern governmental management is to try to match governmental strategies and instruments to the circumstances in which they are applied. A crucial task with respect to the study of the relationships between government and society is to design a theory about such a matching of governmental strategies and instruments to specific contexts, and to deduce from this theory hypotheses about the effectiveness of strategies and instruments under specified circumstances which can be tested in reality.

In the coming chapters we will explore the effectiveness and appropriateness of governmental strategies and instruments in the context of higher education. We will particularly address the question of how these strategies and instruments influence the behaviour of higher education institutions with respect to innovations of curricula.

Chapter 2

INNOVATIONS AND REFORMS IN HIGHER EDUCATION

Frans A. van Vught

1. Introduction

In this chapter we will present an overview of the literature on innovation in higher education. In the light of our concern with the relationships between governmental strategies and the innovative behaviour of higher education institutions, we will pay particular attention to government reform policies in higher education and to the factors that appear to explain the success or failure of such policies.

We will first explore the general concept of innovation and the various theoretical frameworks that can be used to study this concept. Next we will make an inventory of the fundamental characteristics of higher education institutions to be able to judge the appropriateness of certain governmental approaches with respect to stimulating innovations in these institutions. Finally we will explore the theoretical and empirical literature on innovations and reforms in higher education and deduce from this literature some insights about factors that may be of relevance for the success of innovations in higher education.

2. Innovation as an object of study

2.1. *The concept of innovation*

In the 1950s and the 1960s there was a strong belief in the social sciences that the construction of a comprehensive theory and methodology of innovation would only be a matter of time. There existed a certain optimism and enthusiasm about the possibilities and the usefulness of such a theory and methodology. The general social theory of innovation would soon enable planners and policy-makers to design and implement successful changes and to create a happier society.

Since then doubt and disappointment have grown. The comprehensive theory and methodology did not arise. The growing number of empirical studies offered a picture of extreme variance among its findings. The conceptual frameworks remained vague. As Downs and Mohr concluded in 1976: ' . . . . the record in the field of innovation is beyond interpretation. In spite of the large amount of energy expended, the results have not been cumulative. This is not to say that the body of existing research is useless . . . . Perhaps the most straightforward way of accounting for this empirical instability and theoretical confusion is to reject the notion that a unitary theory of innovation exists' (Downs and Mohr, 1976, 701).

One of the factors contributing to the theoretical confusion in the field of innovation research is that the concept of 'innovation' appears to be used in two different meanings: innovation as a product and innovation as a process.

When innovations are conceptualised as products, attention is focussed on a specific object (a program, a course, etc.) which will or will not be adopted by individuals or organisations. Usually the innovation is seen as a result of a process of creation or problem solving. However, such a process is not the main focus of attention.

When innovations are conceptualised as processes, the attention is focussed on the decisions of and interactions between the various actors who can be identified in the arena where a new idea or approach is developed, discussed and (possibly) implemented. Not so much the final product of a process of innovation, but the process itself is the object of analysis.

The present opinion in the literature appears to be that a thorough analysis of innovation should pay attention to both the product and the process aspects. The adoption of a specific object can only be understood when the decisions and interactions of the various actors involved are taken into account.

The literature on innovation is very extensive and covers several fields of study. In the field of organisational behaviour, research has been undertaken to try to identify some important variables which are related to the tendency in organisations to adopt innovations. Variables like 'degree of decentralisation', 'degree of formalisation', 'degree of specialisation' and 'complexity' are frequently mentioned (Hage and Aiken, 1967). In the field of social-psychology several variables are suggested, which are assumed to be related to the development of an innovation process. These variables include: the level of motivation of the innovator, the degree of compatibility with existing values and practices, and the level of organisational support (Davis et al., 1982).

In the literature on higher education the concept of innovation has also received some attention. Several rather creative and elegant analyses have been performed from which some interesting insights about innovation processes and outcomes in higher education systems can be deduced (Levine, 1980; Cerych and Sabatier, 1986). Further on in this chapter these studies will be used to formulate some theoretical insights about the relationships between governmental strategies and innovations in higher education institutions.

The conceptual approaches to innovations and innovation processes are numerous. Besides, it is not always clear how these various conceptual approaches can be related in order to try to gain some increasing understanding of the state of the art in the literature on innovation.

Dill and Friedman (1979) have tried to identify the major theoretical frameworks in the conceptual approaches to innovations and innovation processes, with a special focus on the study of higher education. In the next paragraph each of the four frameworks distinguished by them will be discussed.

2.2. *Theoretical frameworks for the study of innovations*

The *complex organisation framework* is the framework most closely related to the conceptualisation of innovations as products. The emphasis in the complex organisation framework is on the analysis of correlations between the 'innovativeness' of an organisation with other organisational variables. Organisational innovativeness is interpreted as the rate at which new products (programs, procedures, etc.) are added to an organisation. This 'rate of product addition' is expected to be explained by variables characterising the specific organisation under study.

Hage and Aiken (1970) discuss seven variables which they found to be significantly related to organisational innovativeness: complexity, centralization, formalisation, stratification (all 'structural' variables), production rate, efficiency and job satisfaction (all 'functional' variables). According to Hage and Aiken only complexity and job satisfaction are positively related to innovativeness; all other variables are negatively related. Zaltman et al. (1973) have stipulated that the influence of the variables differs depending on the different stages of an innovation process. They especially claim that complexity is positively related to the initiation phase and negatively related to the implementation phase of an innovation process.

The focus of the *conflict framework* is on the inequalities in organisations or social systems (especially the inequalities in power), which are supposed to lead to the formation of power blocks or interest groups. Changes in organisations or systems are interpreted as the results of the conflicts between these interest groups.

In his political model of change in organisations Baldridge (1971) emphasises the articulation of conflicting interests, leading to the formulation and implementation of policies. In this perspective, innovation processes can be conceptualised as the conversion of the pressures of various interest groups into the formulation, acceptance and implementation of a policy. Lindquist (1974) states that innovation processes can be analysed as a series of interest-driven considerations on a proposed change (by an initiator) by all the bodies involved in the governance of an organisation.

The *diffusion framework* is probably the most widely used framework concerning innovations in organisations. In the diffusion framework emphasis is placed on the course of the adoption process (or non-adoption process) by the 'adopter units' in a social system or organisation. The course of the (non)adoption process is related to specific characteristics of both the units and the innovation itself, leading to an explanation of the (non)adoption.

In the diffusion framework literature several variables are presented which appear to be related to the adoption of an innovation. Important variables related to the adoption rate are: perceived relative advantage of the innovation, level of complexity of the innovation, compatibility with current practice and triability (ability to implement a small-scale trial of the innovation) (Rogers and Shoemaker, 1971).

Crucial for the *planned change framework* is the emphasis on intervention and implementation. The basic goal is to manipulate conditions and processes to bring about desired changes. The most frequently cited theoretical guidelines are those of Lewin (1957) who has suggested that an organisation should first break loose of existing barriers to change ('unfreeze') before it can change ('move') and construct the support structures to benefit from the change ('refreeze').

Research results in this framework are rather limited. Most planned change literature is prescriptive, indicating process-phases and instruments which are supposed to lead to the designed results. The research publications are mainly historical and/or autobiographical reports of intervention processes. Besides, a certain preoccupation with psychological and emotional aspects can be found. An exception is the finding by Rogers and Shoemaker (1971) that the success of change agents is positively correlated with the degree of value similarity between change agent and client.

Reviewing the four frameworks presented above, Dill and Friedman (1979) come to the conclusion that the theoretical and methodological problems related to the study of innovation processes are still quite large. The theoretical frameworks appear to be both too complex and insufficiently specified to enable researchers to undertake clear analyses. Measuring the many variables mentioned in the frameworks and paying attention to their validity and reliability is an enormous task. Dill and Friedman propose to try to develop less comprehensive theories involving only 'a subset of the panoply of variables' presented in the four theoretical frameworks. Such smaller theories could then be tested on a practical scale.

In the remainder of this chapter Dill and Friedman's warning will be kept in mind. We will limit ourselves to an exploration of the relationships between possible governmental strategies directed towards creating and stimulating innovations in higher education institutions and the processes and outcomes of innovation in these institutions. We do not claim to be able to develop a complete theory on these relationships. We will be satisfied with exploring some of their more important aspects.

3. Fundamental characteristics of higher education institutions

Kerr (1982) has pointed out that, looked at from without and comparatively, higher education institutions (especially research universities) have hardly changed at all during the past centuries. 'About eighty-five institutions in the Western world established by 1520 still exist in recognisable forms, with similar functions and with unbroken histories, including the Catholic church, the Parliaments of the Isle of Man, of Iceland and of Great Britain, several Swiss cantons, and seventy universities. Kings that rule, feudal lords with vassals, and guilds with monopolies are all gone. These seventy universities, however, are still in the same locations with some of the same buildings, with professors and students doing much the same things, and with governance carried on in much the same ways' (Kerr, 1982, 152).

This striking permanence of higher education institutions has to do with some of the most fundamental characteristics of higher education. As in the first medieval universities of Bologna, Paris and Oxford, higher education can still be seen as a social system in which the handling of knowledge is the most crucial activity. In higher education systems knowledge is discovered, conserved, refined, transmitted and applied (Clark, 1983a, 12). If there is anything fundamental to systems of higher education, it is this handling of knowledge.

The primacy of the handling of knowledge is related to some other fundamental characteristics, which can be found within higher education institutions.

A primary characteristic concerns the authority of the professional experts. In higher education institutions many decisions can only be made by the professional experts. These are the decisions regarding the detailed knowledge-oriented academic activities of research and teaching. In all those specialised knowledge-fields, which are held together in a higher education institution, decisions on what and how to investigate, and on what and how to teach come, to a large extent, under the direct supervision of the academic experts. Only they are able to oversee their specialised fields. Only they are able to stimulate the enthusiasm of students for specific objects of study. This is why professional autonomy is so important in higher education institutions and this is why these institutions are called 'professional bureaucracies' (Mintzberg, 1979).

Clark makes it clear how the professionals in higher education organisation work with and upon knowledge. 'The factory floor in higher education is cluttered with bundles of knowledge that are attended by professionals. The professionals push and pull on their respective bundles. If they are doing research, they are trying to increase the size of the bundle and even to reconstitute it. If engaged in scholarship other than research, they are conserving, criticising, and reworking it. If teaching, they are trying to pass some of it on to the flow-through clientele we call students, encouraging them to think about its nature, how it may be used, and perhaps take up a career devoted to it. If engaged outside the 'plant' as advisors, consultants, or lecturers, academics further disseminate knowledge to try to draw out its implications for practical use' (Clark, 1983b, 20).

Of course, not all decisions in higher education institutions are taken by professionals. There is a category of purely 'administrative' decisions (for example, regarding financial administration and 'support services') which to a large extent is beyond the professional influence. There is also a category of decisions which are mainly taken by 'clients' (students, research contractors). And there is an important category of decisions mainly taken by 'outsiders' (government, funding agencies, evaluating committees). Nevertheless, the influence of the professional experts on the decision-making processes in higher education institutions is extensive. In many decisions taken at these institutions professionals play an important role.

A second important characteristic is the organisational principle that in higher education institutions the knowledge areas form the basic foci of attention. The knowledge areas are the 'building blocks' of a higher education organisation and without some institutionalisation of these knowledge areas a higher education organisation cannot exist. This principle leads to the typical organisational structure of higher education institutions. Fragmentation is abundant in these organisations. Throughout the organisation specialised cells exist which are only loosely coupled. Higher education institutions are 'loosely coupled systems' (Weick, 1976). The crucial knowledge oriented activities take place within the rather autonomous cells. Specialists in specific knowledge fields group together to teach and undertake research. To a large extent insulated from the rest of the organisation, these specialists use their autonomy and expertise to perform the basic activities of the higher education institution. '. . . .

specialised professionals have little need to relate to one another within the local shop . . . . They can produce on their own . . . . Producing separately for the most part, the many groups become an extreme case of loosely-linked production. The university is a gathering place for professionalised crafts, evermore a confederation, a conglomerate, of knowledge-bearing groups that require little operational linkage' (Clark, 1983b, 21).

According to Clark it is this organisational fragmentation that explains the miraculous adaptability of higher education institutions. This adaptability consists of 'the capacity to add and subtract fields of knowledge and related units without disturbing all the others'. Clark argues that 'it is the peculiar internal constitution of universities that allow them . . . . to bend and adapt themselves to a whole variety of circumstances and environments, thus producing diversity among universities . . . . and, at the same time, to maintain an appearance of similarity that allows us to recognise them in all the guises which they take' (Clark, 1983a, 186, 187).

Hardy et al. (1983) have pointed to two mechanisms which appear to be essential to the fragmentation of higher education institutions and to the high level of adaptability of these institutions: 'pigeonholing' and 'standardisation of skills and knowledge'.

Pigeonholing is the process of dividing an organisation's activities into a series of standard components or programs which are applied to predetermined situations or contingencies. A higher education organisation partitions its tasks through pigeonholing. Courses and programs are isolated from one another, thereby minimising the need for coordination across tasks and maximising the discretion of the specialists who carry out these tasks.

Standardisation of skills and knowledge takes place through the training of the specialists and through communication and affiliation with their colleagues and peers. Through their often long years of training specialists are programmed to approach their fields in generally accepted terms. Through communication with their colleagues these professional norms are enhanced. 'Professors choose books that tend to be well regarded by their colleagues, they design their courses in ways that reflect their own training, they adopt teaching methods acceptable in their disciplines . . . ., they research subjects that can be funded by the granting agencies (which in turn are subject to professional influence), and they write articles in styles acceptable to the journals referred to by their peers' (Hardy et al., 1983, 413).

A further fundamental characteristic of higher education institutions is the extreme diffusion of the decision making power. In an organisation where the production processes are knowledge-intensive, there is a need to decentralise. When besides that, such an organisation is also heavily fragmented, the decision-making power will be spread over a large number of units and actors. A higher education institution therefore becomes a federal system; 'semi-autonomous departments and schools, chairs and faculties act like small sovereign states as they pursue distinctive self-interests and stand over against the authority of the whole' (Clark, 1983a, 266, 267).

A final characteristic, which is typical for higher education institutions in Europe, is the way authority is distributed within these institutions. Traditionally this authority has been (and still is) located at the lower levels of the organisation, that is: with the academic professionals. At the level of the institutional administration the authority is rather weak. Institutional administrators only have a very limited capacity to steer 'their' organisation. The weakness of the authority at the institutional level in European higher education institutions becomes especially clear when institutional decisions have to be taken. Very often such decisions can only be made when, after long deliberations, agreement can finally be reached.

Reviewing the fundamental characteristics of higher education institutions just mentioned, it may be concluded that the context of higher education confronts government with some specific problems when it wants to develop and implement a policy-strategy directed towards influencing higher education institutions. The extreme professional autonomy within these institutions and the rather limited administrative authority, as well as the organisational fragmentation and the diffusion of the decision-making power make it very difficult to completely control these institutions from an external position. Higher education institutions appear to be very complex associations of largely autonomous cells. Besides, in higher education institutions the traditional guild-culture, rooted in the Middle Ages, is still very much alive. Higher education institutions cherish the traditional norms and values of the 'republic of science' (Polanyi, 1962), which enable them to perform their highly professional tasks.

The fundamental characteristics of higher education institutions suggest that these institutions can only be controlled from outside, when the organisational variety is greatly reduced and when the professional autonomy is largely restrained. However, when such an external control is imposed, it should be realised that the professional tasks these institutions perform may be severely damaged. Confronted with detailed regulation and with an extreme restriction of their behaviour, the scientists and teachers within the higher education institutions may feel the disillusionment of not being able to explore the paths their professional consciousness stimulates them to go. They may become uninterested in new developments, get bored by the routine activities they have to perform and lose their interest in innovations.

4. Formulating insights about the success of innovations in higher education institutions

Now that we have some understanding of the processes of innovation in general and in the context of higher education, we can try to develop some theoretical insights about the relationships between governmental strategies (directed towards the creation of innovations) on the one hand, and innovation processes in higher education organisations on the other hand. In this paragraph these theoretical insights will be deduced from the literature on innovation processes, especially in higher education.

To present the theoretical insights we will classify the (rather extensive) literature on innovation processes in two broad categories. These categories can be described as 'the organisational variables assumed to be related to success or failure of innovations' and 'the characteristics of innovation processes assumed to be related to the success or failure of innovations'. We will discuss the present state of the art in the literature regarding both these categories.

4.1. *Organisational variables related to success of innovations*

4.1.1. Governmental reform policies

In their impressive research-overview of the principal organisational variables that have appeared to influence the success or failure of innovation processes in organisations, Hage and Aiken (1970) offer seven factors which are related to the rate of change in an organisation. These factors can be described as follows:

- the greater the formalisation (i.e. the greater the degree of codification of jobs, the greater the number of rules specifying what is to be done, and the more strictly these rules are enforced), the lower the rate of organisational change;
- the higher the centralisation (i.e. the smaller the proportion of jobs and occupations that participate in decision-making and the fewer the decision-making areas in which they are involved), the lower the rate of organisational change;
- the greater the stratification (i.e. the greater the disparity in rewards such as salaries and prestige between the top and bottom ranks of an organisation), the lower the rate of organisational change;
- the greater the complexity (i.e. the greater the number of occupations/specialities of an organisation and the greater the degree of professionalism of each), the greater the rate of organisational change;
- the higher the volume of production (i.e. emphasis on quantity versus

quality in organisational outputs), the lower the rate of organisational change;
- the greater the emphasis on efficiency (i.e. concern with cost or resource reduction), the lower the rate of organisational change;
- the higher the job satisfaction, the greater the rate of organisational change;

Hage and Aiken's factors are discussed by Levine (1980) in the context of innovations in higher education. Levine suggests that higher education organisations are low in formalisation, low in centralisation, low in stratification, high in complexity, high in the emphasis on quality of outputs, low on efficiency and high on job satisfaction. The author therefore comes to the conclusion that 'institutions of higher education might be classified as low in innovation resistance relative to organisations in general' (Levine, 1980, 173).

Our presentation of the fundamental characteristics of higher education institutions seems on the one hand to lead to the same conclusion. The high autonomy of the professionals within these organisations, the organisational fragmentation, the diffusion of the decision-making power and the limited administrative authority indicate that higher education organisations are *not* very formalised, centralised, stratified and directed towards efficiency, but *are* very complex and by their specific nature offer the possibilities for a strong emphasis on quality of production and a high level of job satisfaction.

However, as has been indicated by Kerr (see above) and many others, it should also be remembered that higher education institutions by nature are conservative and that in these organisations innovations are not likely to occur. According to Hefferlin (1969) for instance, innovations will only occur in higher education institutions, when the level of instability in these institutions is high, i.e., when conditions arise like changing faculties because of expansion or turnover, low rates of tenure, rotating department chairpersons, etc.

It seems that we are confronted with two contradicting theoretical observations. Let us look at this subject from another perspective.

Clark (1983a) has argued that change is far more crucial in higher education institutions than conventional wisdom would suggest. 'Despite the belief of many observers that academic systems change significantly only when pressured by external forces, such systems increasingly exhibit innovation and adaptation among their bottom lines. Invention and diffusion are institutionalised in the work of the departments and counterpart units that embody the disciplines and professions . . . . Such change is widely overlooked . . . . It occurs in segments of the operating level . . .

In a bottom-heavy knowledge institution, grassroots innovation is a crucial form of change' (Clark, 1983a, 234, 235). Clark points once more at the characteristics of higher education institutions. Innovations take place through the professional activities in the various semi-autonomous units in the organisation.

Kerr (1982) seems to agree with this point of view. According to him a distinction should be made between a perspective from within and a perspective from without. 'Looked at from within, universities have changed enormously in the emphases on their several functions and in their guiding spirits, but looked at from without and comparatively, they are among the least changed of institutions' (Kerr, 1982, 152, 153).

Bok (1986) makes clear how the two theoretical observations which seem to be contradictory, can be combined. He underlines Levine's conclusion that, because of their fundamental characteristics, higher education institutions in principle are low in innovation resistance. However, he also points out that these very factors make it difficult to keep innovations alive. 'Universities are large, decentralised, informal organisations with little hierarchical authority over teaching and research. These characteristics favour innovation by making it easy for any of a large number of faculty members to experiment in search of better ways of educating students. Unfortunately, the very factors that aid experimentation make it harder for successful initiatives to spread throughout the institution or from one institution to another' (Bok, 1986, 176). Innovations are created easily within higher education organisations and (as Clark indicates) they may even spread among their bottom levels. But this diffusion of innovation only takes place by virtue of the professional belief that certain innovations are worthwhile. Faculty members will only adopt innovations when they judge them to be worthwhile for their own activities. As Bok observes '. . . . the most promising innovations can languish unless some effective force causes them to be emulated widely' (Bok, 1986, 176). And the most effective force is probably the conviction of professional colleagues that an innovation is an effective solution to a common problem.

This point of view leads to an important conclusion: innovations in higher education institutions may arise easily and often, but their diffusion will be difficult and will mainly take place through communication between colleagues.

Clark points at another aspect of the processes of change within higher education institutions. He indicates that innovations in higher education institutions are mainly incremental adjustments, building up to larger flows of change. Major, sudden and comprehensive changes are rare in higher education institutions. Exactly because of the fragmentation of tasks and the diffusion of power such changes are extremely difficult to effect.

It should be realised that the ideology of the academic profession incorporates a basic resistance to comprehensive changes, especially when these are launched 'from above'. The organisational fragmentation and the diffusion of the decision-making power demand that a relatively large number of people and groups with a wide variation in values and opinions tend to discuss a launched comprehensive reform, the result of which will often be that the reform strands in debates and political fights. Becher and Kogan (1980) argue that, because of the fundamental characteristics of higher education systems, innovation processes are localised and specific. '. . . . we are not dealing with a hierarchical system, where change can be decreed from above, but rather with a negotiative one, in which individuals, basic units and institutions each regard themselves as having the right to decide what is best for them. It follows that any innovative proposal has to be finally sanctioned by those who are in a position to put it into effect' (Becher and Kogan, 1980, 121).

This argument has brought many authors to the conclusion that, generally speaking, government-initiated reforms in higher education systems must fail.

Referring to the study of Cerych and Sabatier (1986) (see below), Kerr (1987), for instance, comes to the conclusion that 'intentional changes' have sometimes perhaps been partially successful, but most often have been a failure. Curricular reforms and changes of governance, generally speaking, cannot be called a success (Kerr, 1987, 185).

A possible explanation for this observation can again be found in the fundamental characteristics of higher education institutions. Kerr (1982) stresses that most decisions concerning the dynamics of a higher education system are taken outside the formal system of governance. 'Most decisions about teaching, about curriculum, about research topics and methods, about amount and form of public service are made by individual faculty members. Most decisions made about majors selected, courses taken and time spent on study are made by individual students' (Kerr, 1982, 178). Besides, Kerr indicates that, when intense competition exists among higher education institutions (as in the U.S.), specific arrangements of governance have only minor implications.

Also Bok points out that educational reforms in higher education institutions are seldom the result of external influences (including governmental policies). According to him, external pressures can only be successful when they link up with initiatives or opinions inside a higher education institution. '. . . . no external influence offers a reliable way of initiating constructive change or eliciting new ideas to improve the quality of education. The vital task ultimately rests within the university itself' (Bok, 1986, 183).

Becher and Kogan (1980) have presented an elegant analysis of innovation processes in higher education systems by differentiating between four levels of these systems: the system as a whole, the institution, the basic unit (within the institution) and the individual. According to these authors innovative attempts often fail because they are unable to accommodate to existing structural constraints. 'Academic structures and regulations for the most part evolve to protect the legitimate interests of researchers and teachers. They help to define, and also defend, the main areas of professional concern within an institution. But once established, they can prove surprisingly intractable. Even when an innovative idea is generally accepted on intellectual grounds, it may face severe difficulty if it appears to conflict with conventional practice, or to cut across some existing organisational arrangement' (Becher and Kogan, 1980, 146, 147). Becher and Kogan therefore also put a heavy emphasis on the specific organisational characteristics of higher education institutions as important barriers to innovation. They argue that the often mentioned conservatism of higher education institutions 'mainly stems from contextual, rather than from personal factors' (Becher and Kogan, 1980, 147).

Others have tried to take up the challenge of the 'policy failure theme'. Referring to his analysis of the Swedish higher education policy which led to the reforms of 1975-1977, Lane (1985) has argued that policy-driven changes in a higher education system are possible. But, like the authors just mentioned, he also points out that, to be able to be successful, reform policies should pay attention to the basic characteristics of higher education institutions. 'Indeed organisational transformation of higher education work and higher education institutions is feasible, as long as basic features of the differentiation of work and the structure of authority inherent in the conduct of higher education activities are not threatened. Whereas public policy may effect institution-building and redefinition, it cannot do away with the bottom-dominated nature of the organisation of higher education life' (Lane, 1984, 107).

Premfors (1984) disputes Lane's 'optimism', but he does not conclude that the Swedish higher education reform policy was a complete failure. '. . . . Swedish higher education policy is a mixed bag of success and failure when judged in terms of the initial intentions of central policy-makers . . . . To an important extent . . . . these outcomes have been predicated on basic features of higher education organisation in Sweden' (Premfors, 1984, 47, 48).

The same kind of conclusion (but in a broader perspective) is drawn by Cerych and Sabatier (1986), who studied a number of policy-driven reforms in higher education systems in Europe. Cerych and Sabatier examined the levels of success and failure of nine rather comprehensive reforms which were all largely initiated and developed by government and implemented in a higher education system through the interaction between governmental organisations and higher education institutions. The four main goals set forth with respect to these reforms were: to widen the access to higher education; to stimulate the regional relevance of higher education; to develop short-cycle and vocational higher education; and to integrate distinct types of higher education into one comprehensive system. As their object for study Cerych and Sabatier selected the Swedish 25/5 Scheme (a new admission policy which makes higher education accessible to students of twenty-five or older and having a minimum of five years work experience), the Polish Preferential Point System (favouring access to higher education from workers and peasant families), the British Open University (like the two former oriented towards the goal of widening access to higher education), the French '*Institutes Universitaires de Technologie*' (IUTs), the Norwegian Regional Colleges (both new, short-cycle and vocational types of higher education), the development of the fourth Norwegian university (the University of Tromso) (oriented towards providing regional service) and the German '*Gesamthochschule*' (a structural reform through which the universities and the technical '*Fachhochschulen*' should be integrated.

In their comparative analysis Cerych and Sabatier present a general picture from which it can be concluded that both successes and failures can be distinguished. With respect to the objective of widening access, it is concluded that the reforms aimed at favouring access to adults and to geographically disadvantaged students (the British Open University, the Swedish 25/5 Scheme and the University of Tromso) were rather successful. On the other hand, the success of the reforms aimed at widening access to the educationally disadvantaged (the British Open University, the Swedish 25/5 Scheme) is modest, while the social equalisation effects of reform (the Polish Preferential Point System, the Swedish 25/5 Scheme) can hardly be traced. Regarding the objective of stimulating the regional relevance of higher education, on the one hand success is reported: in some respects the regional enrolments have risen, the enrolments of students of lower social origin have increased, and the influences on the regional developments are judged to be positive. However, it appears that regionally oriented higher education institutes are confronted with the problem of how to fulfil the traditional academic functions and to apply the traditional academic criteria. The creation of new, short-cycle and vocational types of higher education is judged to be only partially successful. The French IUTs and the Norwegian Regional Colleges were not able to replace already existing institutions; they were only received as an addition to the system. Moreover and especially in the case of the German '*Gesamthochschule*' and to a lesser extent also with respect to the IUTs, the new institutions appeared to look for academic recognition. This phenomenon is known as *academic drift* and it indicates the attempts of new institutions in a higher education system to assume the features and educational patterns of traditional institutions, thereby moving away from the specific (vocational) profiles they were created for. Finally, with respect to the German '*Gesamthochschule*' Cerych and Sabatier report that two alternative procedures existed for the integration of the universities and the '*Fachhochschulen*'. Either the curricula, staff and student body could be blended, or a closer cooperation could be created. The authors conclude that the first procedure was tried, but on a limited scale and with very limited success; the second procedure was not executed at all (Cerych and Sabatier, 1986, ch. 10).

The differentiated picture reported by Cerych and Sabatier appears to underline Premfors' conclusion (mentioned earlier) about the Swedish higher education reforms. Apparently reforms initiated and developed by government can be judged as 'mixed bags of success and failure'. An important question of course concerns the factors that might influence the levels of success and failure of these reforms. In paragraph 4.2. we will elaborate on some possible factors. Two important points of view will be presented in the next two sections.

4.1.2. Mechanisms of integration in higher education

An important viewpoint can be found in Clark's analysis of the integration mechanisms in higher education systems. Clark argues that the complexity of higher education systems may lead to some important observations concerning the potential success or failure of externally initiated innovations. Generally speaking, the development of a social system implies a growing institutionalisation and an increase of both the constraints upon change and the imperatives for change. 'The mature social system compared to the emerging one is like the adult compared to the newborn or young child: it has greater stability of character and hence of response; it is much less dependent than when recently emerged from the womb (of society)' (Clark, 1983a, 183). A mature higher education system is often characterised as conservative by nature and not very open to external influences. On the other hand higher education systems are also characterised as surprisingly adaptive (see above). Clark explains this contradiction by pointing at one of the fundamental characteristics of higher education institutions which were mentioned before (organisational fragmentation). 'Adaptability . . . . lies in the internal variety of amalgamated, conglomerate organisation' (Clark, 1983a, 187).

Higher education systems and higher education institutions have a rather high level of complexity, being extremely fragmented and diffused and having a large variety of tasks and activities. According to Clark, various forms of system integration can be distinguished in these complex systems, each with their own ways of promoting as well as constraining innovation: bureaucratic, oligarchic, political and market integration.

Bureaucratic integration concerns the governmental or quasi governmental attempts to control a higher education system with formal and administrative procedures. When this form of integration prevails, innovations are generally formally planned and launched from above, and implementation processes are programmed in detail and hierarchically controlled.

In oligarchic integration an emphasis is put on the personal initiatives of academics and on the processes of collegiate decision-making. Individuals (especially professors 'holding baronial power') may undertake initiatives and bring these initiatives into the oligarchic arena of collegial decision-making. However, this form of integration often develops into a change resistant mechanism, guarding particularistic interests and 'guild territories'.

Political integration mainly takes place by means of the struggles of interest groups. Both external and internal interest groups try to create innovations that would favour their own interests. Political integration is a power game in which equilibria are created by the confrontation of interests and in which innovations to a large extent are the result of the introduction of new interests or specific changes in the power structure.

Market integration results from competitive behaviour among actors. Through the mechanism of market coordination each higher education institution tries to create its own evolutionary niche, each attracting its own clientele and each responding in its own way to external influences.

Clark assumes that, generally speaking, market integration has the strongest adaptive capacity. It stimulates higher education institutions to be responsive and creative and therefore incorporates an influential incentive for innovations. Bureaucratic integration is too formal and rigid, especially in the context of higher education. Oligargic and political integration tends to influence higher education systems to develop into change resistant and closed collections of interest groups (Clark, 1983a, 200-204).

From Clark's analysis it may be concluded that the integration forms in a higher education system provide important indications for the potential success of a reform strategy. Innovations initiated from outside a system may only be expected to have a chance of being successful, when the specific balance of integrating forms of that system is taken into account. Every form of integration, and every specific combination of forms, may be expected to have its own set of constraining and facilitating factors with regard to innovations. From the perspective of creating or stimulating innovations from outside the system, an analysis of the integrating mechanisms therefore is of extreme importance.

4.1.3. Responsiveness to external influences

Another important viewpoint which might help us to discover factors that might explain the levels of success and failure of externally initiated innovation in higher education, can be found in the *finalisation thesis*. The finalisation thesis implies the idea that scientific disciplines move through different phases and that during these different phases a certain discipline is more or less receptive to external influences. The hypothesis is that when a discipline is in a phase during which a paradigm is being established and articulated, the developments of that discipline are to a large extent the result of the functioning of internal norms. When, on the other hand, a discipline is still in a pre-paradigmatic phase, it lacks a strong internalist determination and is therefore more open to external influences. Also, when a discipline has come into a post-paradigmatic phase, it becomes less oriented towards its inner norms and thus more receptive to external criteria of relevance (Schäfer, 1983). Elzinga (1985) has argued that the finalisation thesis may be interpreted as a possible epistemological explanation of 'the unwillingness or incapacity of researchers and academic institutions to bow to governmental and managerial prescriptions'. It would also explain why certain disciplines are more receptive to reforms and governmental policies than others (Elzinga, 1985, 208, 215).

Becher and Kogan have suggested a more or less similar explanation for possible differences in responsiveness to external influences. They suggest that institutions and basic units with offers of courses and programmes that are relatively low on 'the pecking order of recruitment', are relatively open to external influences. 'The other side of the same coin is that the higher up the ladder of disciplinary prestige a particular group of teachers may be, and the more reputable their institution, the less likely they are to want to institute any far-reaching innovations in curricula or teaching methods' (Becher and Kogan, 1980, 143). In a recent publication (Kogan and Youll, in Boys, et al., 1988) the same hypothesis can be found: 'The ways in which institutions respond to external pressures are affected to a large extent by their status and history. The high status institutions are concerned with maintaining academic positions . . . . Less confident and well esteemed higher education institutions . . . . are more likely to assess their present and potential sources of support and change their offerings accordingly. The lower the status, the more the change is concerned with recruiting external, industrial or commercial recognition or support, and in making sure that undergraduate preparation is "relevant" to the labour market' (Kogan and Youll, 1988, 174).

Henkel (1988) has developed this hypothesis further and has, moreover, tried to test it by confronting it with the development of a number of disciplines and fields. The elaborated hypothesis is formulated as follows:

'subjects are likely to be less responsive to external influences:

- the nearer they are to having developed a shared paradigm or overarching theory or set of theories which structures their exponents' thinking about what they know, what they can explain and how to set about extending systematic understanding of their subject;
- the more they rely on an exclusive language or specific techniques in the execution of their work;
- the clearer they are about the rules for the admission of knowledge and the criteria of determining merit in their subject' (Henkel, 1988, 185).

Henkel's analysis underlines the point that disciplines and fields can not only be seen as forms of knowledge, but also as social communities having their own history, their own language, their own values and norms. Academic communities also have their own sense of identity and their own intellectual authority. These communities will judge the acceptability of innovations from their social perspectives and these judgments will to a large extent be influenced by the circumstances and conditions in their disciplines or fields.

From this elaboration of the finalisation thesis it may be concluded that the specific characteristics of disciplines and fields, in the sense of social communities, may be important factors explaining the level of success or failure of a reform strategy in a higher education system. When innovations are initiated from outside, they may be expected to be potentially more successful when they are adjusted to certain social characteristics of the disciplines and fields. Variables like the (epistemological) status, the dominant pattern of values, the sense of identity and the level of intellectual authority are important factors to take into account when reform strategies are designed and implemented.

4.1.4. Conclusion

Reviewing the points of view and analyses of the various authors mentioned above, the general conclusion is that government initiated innovations in higher education institutions and systems can only be successful when certain conditions are met. These conditions have to do with the specific characteristics of higher education institutions. Innovations in higher education institutions can only be brought about by governmental strategies, when attention is paid in these strategies to the basic values and mechanisms of academic life.

More particularly, it may be expected that innovative strategies will be more successful when they are better adjusted to the forms of integration prevailing in a higher education system, as well as to the social characteristics of the disciplines and fields.

We now have presented an overview of the theoretical insights with respect to the organisational variables in higher education systems that may be expected to be related to success or failure of innovations. In the following paragraphs we will focus on the characteristics of the processes of innovation themselves that are assumed to be related to such success or failure.

4.2. *Innovation characteristics related to success of innovations*

4.2.1. The adoption of an innovation

In a study which has become widely known in the field, Rogers and Shoemaker (1971) have analysed more than 1500 studies regarding the characteristics that determine an innovation's success or failure. The authors present five critical characteristics:

- the compatibility of a new idea (i.e., the degree to which an innovation is perceived as consistent with the existing values, past experience and needs of the receiver) is positively related to its rate of adoption;
- the relative advantage of a new idea (i.e., the degree to which an innovation is perceived as being better than the idea it supersedes) is positively related to its rate of adoption;
- the complexity of an innovation (i.e., the degree to which an innovation is perceived as relatively difficult to understand and use) is *not* related to its rate of adoption;
- the triability of an innovation (i.e., the degree to which an innovation may be experimented with on a limited basis) is positively related to its rate of adoption;
- the observability of an innovation (i.e., the degree to which the results of an innovation are visible to others) is positively related to its rate of adoption (Rogers and Shoemaker, 1971, 350-352);

In Levine's analysis (1980) some important observations can be found concerning the importance of these general characteristics in the context of higher education. This study especially focused on the 'institutionalisation or termination stage' of innovation processes. This state is supposed to follow the stages of 'recognition of the need for change', 'planning an innovation' and 'implementing the innovation'. In the institutionalisation or termination stage attention is concentrated on 'the ways in which innovations prosper, persist, decline and fail after they have been adopted' (Levine, 1980, 10).

Levine has developed a theoretical model of the ways innovations can be handled in an organisation. He suggests that in principle two mechanisms can be used. The first mechanism is called *boundary expansion*: '. . . . an acceptance by the host [organisation] of some or all of the innovation's differences'. This mechanism essentially indicates a process of acceptance (which may be more or less comprehensive). Levine indicates that this acceptance can involve diffusing the innovation through the organisation or establishing it as an enclave. 'Diffusion is the process whereby innovation characteristics are allowed to spread through the host organisation, and enclaving is the process whereby the innovation assumes an isolated position within the organisation'.

The other mechanism of handling an innovation in an organization is called *boundary contraction*: '. . . . a constriction of organisational boundaries in such a manner as to exclude innovation differences'. This mechanism labels an innovation as illegitimate or deviant. Again, two forms can be distinguished. 'Resocialisation occurs when the innovative unit is made to renounce its past deviance and institute the acceptable norms, values and goals . . . . Termination occurs when the innovation is eliminated' (Levine, 1980, 14, 15).

Which of the four possible outcomes of the institutionalisation/termination stage of innovation processes (diffusion, enclaving, resocialisation, termination) will occur depends, in Levine's theoretical model, on two variables: compatibility and profitability. Like Rogers and Shoemaker, Levine sees compatibility as the degree to which the norms, values and goals of an innovation are congruent with those of the organisation which has to adopt the innovation. Profitability is a subjective concept, rather similar to Rogers and Shoemaker's 'relative advantage'. It indicates the degree to which an innovation satisfies the adopter's needs or satisfies him better than the existing mechanisms.

Levine has studied fourteen innovation processes with regard to the introduction of the 'college concept' at the State University of New York at Buffalo. His conclusions are that compatibility and profitability are both crucial variables for explaining the success or failure of the adoption of an innovation. An innovation appears to fail (i.e. is resocialised or terminated) when the levels of compatibility and profitability of the innovation decline. Profitability is an especially important variable. When the profitability of an innovation is not disputed, an innovation can still get accepted, even when the compatibility of such an innovation is low. However, when the profitability is seriously questioned, an innovation will fail, even when the compatibility is high.

4.2.2. Compatibility

The argument that the compatibility of an innovative idea is positively related to the rate of adoption of an innovation is frequently found in the literature. We already noticed that for instance Bok (1986) stresses this point. Becher and Kogan (1980) argue that structural reforms of a system as a whole can only succeed when they relate to the fundamental values in higher education. The case of the British Open University clearly illustrates this argument. The introduction of this new institution in the British higher education system succeeded because for its development of the new course materials the Open University applied the quality standards of the conventional universities (Becher & Kogan, 1980, 125).

Concerning the relationship between compatibility and rate of the adoption of an innovation Cerych and Sabatier (1986) introduce an interesting amendment. Cerych and Sabatier propose a three-dimensional framework for the conceptualisation of the 'scope of change'. '*Depth of change* indicates the degree to which a new policy goal implies a departure from existing values and practices of higher education . . . . *Functional breadth of change* refers to the number of functional areas in which a given policy is expected to introduce more or less profound modifications: admission, teacher qualifications, internal structures, curriculum, and so forth . . . . *Level of change* indicates the target of the reform: the system as a whole; a particular sector or segment of the system (group of institutions); a single institution or an institutional sub-unit'.

Reviewing the various comprehensive reforms that were the object of their analysis (see above), Cerych and Sebatier draw several conclusions. Regarding the interconnection between depth of change and functional breadth of change they claim that reforms that postulate a radical departure of existing rules and values, can nevertheless be successfully implemented when they are limited to a few functional areas (of the higher education institution or of the higher education system as a whole) and if at the same time most other prevailing traditions and standards are rigorously accepted. According to Cerych and Sabatier the case of the British Open University shows that innovations which are great in depth but narrow in functional breadth are possible. With respect to the level of change, the authors conclude that, generally speaking, a reform succeeds more easily if it affects an institutional or sub-institutional process, rather than a system as a whole (Cerych and Sabatier, 1986, 244-247).

It appears that Cerych and Sabatier, although they agree with the general conclusion of Rogers and Shoemaker that the more a reform is consistent with existing values the more likely it will be implemented, also notice that a low level of compatibility does not necessarily mean that an innovation cannot be successfully implemented. An important question then is what other factors may stimulate or hamper innovations.

4.2.3. Profitability

We already noticed that Levine has suggested that the concept of profitability is of crucial importance for the explanation of the acceptance of innovations in higher education institutions. The concept of profitability is also often mentioned in the literature as an important variable positively related to the rate of adoption of an innovation. Becher and Kogan underline their view that externally initiated innovations can be successful in higher education, provided that they are acceptable in terms of intellectual substance (compatibility) and that they establish their merits (for instance in terms of student recruitment) (profitability) (Becher and Kogan, 1980, 132). With regard to the analysis of the outcomes of innovation processes, Clark uses the metaphor of a seesaw, 'a long board on which reform-supporting and reform-opposing groups sit at different points in relation to the centre of balance'. According to this author, a decision whether an innovation will or will not be accepted, is the result of the distribution of power among the groups involved in the decision-making process. And the behaviour of each group and individual in the decision-making process is guided by the subjective interpretation of self-interest. 'Innovations typically "fail" because the innovators cannot acquire enough power fully to protect their new ways. They are allowed to start, even to acquire a clientele, but unless they attach the interests of various groups to their own interests and persuade potential opponents at least to be moderate in their resistance, they can be tightly bounded - resocialised or terminated - as others raise their own level of concern, clarify their own self-interest with respect to the reform, and increase the bearing of their own weight' (Clark, 1983a, 226, 227).

Clearly, like Levine, both Becher and Kogan and Clark combine the concepts of compatibility and profitability. In both their analytical interpretations of the potential success of an innovation the two concepts are interrelated.

The concepts of compatibility and profitability offer us the possibility to formulate some further expectations about the appropriateness of governmental instruments in the context of higher education. If we follow the conclusions of the studies just discussed and if we take into account that the higher education context is characterised by a large professional autonomy, a large organisational fragmentation, a diffusion of the decision-making power and a limited administrative authority, we may expect that governmental strategies and instruments which pay attention to compatibility and profitability will be more effective in creating innovations than instruments in which these concepts are not taken into account.

4.2.4. Complexity

Our discussion of innovation characteristics that are supposed to determine the success or failure of an innovation has so far concentrated on two of the five characteristics presented in the survey of Rogers and Shoemaker: compatibility and profitability (relative advantage). However the authors mentioned three other factors: complexity, triability and observability.

Concerning the complexity of the innovation Rogers and Shoemaker themselves suggest that no relationship exists with the rate of adoption. According to them the degree to which an innovation is perceived to be difficult to understand or use, does not really influence the process of acceptance or refusal of an innovation.

However, in the field of higher education another conclusion should be drawn. Cerych and Sabatier argue that a reform that is both 'deep and broad' will tend to fail. Both the German '*Gesamthochschule*' and the French 1968 reform-law are judged to have aimed at too radical changes in too many areas at once (Cerych and Sabatier, 1986, 145). When complexity is defined as the combination of the degree to which an innovation is a departure from existing values and practices with the number of functional areas aimed at by the innovation, the level of complexity of an innovation process in higher education may be expected to be negatively related to the rate of adoption of the innovation. The more complex an innovation, the less successful that innovation will be in getting adopted.

4.2.5. Observability

The observability of an innovation is another factor presented by Rogers and Shoemaker as having a positive relationship with the rate of adoption: the more the goals and results of the innovation are visible and clear, the more likely it is that the innovation will be accepted.

In the field of higher education research Becher and Kogan (1980) come to the conclusion that the observability of an innovation is indeed of some influence. Taking the same position as Cerych and Sabatier (1986) with respect to depth and breadth of innovations (see before), they argue that 'innovations which manage . . . . to challenge certain accepted ideas while reinforcing others have a fair chance of success, provided that they also meet two other prerequisites: that their merits are reasonably visible and that they do not appear seriously to undermine the existing patterns of freedom and control' (Becher and Kogan, 1980, 146). Becher and Kogan's second prerequisite can be translated in terms of profitability. It may be interpreted as the inclination to guard the self-perceived interests of academic groups, often expressed as the conservation of the academic definitions of legitimate activities. The first prerequisite has to do with observability: to be able to be successful the merits of innovations have to be visible.

Cerych and Sabatier also suggest that in theory a high level of clarity and consistency of the objectives of an innovation facilitates the implementation of innovations. However, from their case studies they also conclude that in practice vagueness and ambiguity of objectives appear to prevail, especially because otherwise a consensus on the proposed innovation would not have occurred (Cerych and Sabatier, 1986, 13, 14, 243).

Taking the arguments by Becher and Kogan and by Cerych and Sabatier into account, we could argue that observability as such can hardly be called an important factor for the success or failure of an innovation. At most the level of observability of the objectives and expected results of an innovation is a strategic element in presenting an innovation as compatible with existing values or as profitable for certain groups and interests. Following Levine (1980) we could conclude that, when the objective is to guarantee that others have an accurate or positive picture of an innovation, this factor has more to do with compatibility and profitability than with observability per se. Guaranteeing an accurate or positive picture implies preventing the innovation from appearing incompatible and/or unprofitable (Levine, 1980, 187).

4.2.6. Triability

This leaves us with triability as a last innovation characteristic which is supposed to be positively related to the rate of adoption. Triability concerns an organisation's ability to try an innovation within a limited period and on a limited scale. Moreover, it has to do with the condition that if, after trying an innovation, the conclusion is that the results are disappointing, the situation is reversible without severe damage.

Cerych and Sabatier have found that the assumptions on which reforms are based often are erroneous. This observation should not surprise us. As is the case with every process of policy-design, so too the process of the design of innovations in higher education has to face the basic human impotence in accurately foretelling the future. Our knowledge can only be incomplete and things may change while a policy is designed and implemented (Van Vught, 1987).

Triability is a prudent strategy for those who do not want to overrate the level of knowledge incorporated in the assumptions which form the basis of a certain reform policy or innovation. This is especially the case because it may be expected that scientists and scholars are particularly sceptical about these kinds of assumptions. It is because of this that Bok (1986) pleads for implementing innovations in higher education institutions by means of experiments. Referring to an example of the Harvard Medical

School he argues: 'This tactic has obvious advantages. It relies entirely on volunteers and hence makes few, if any, demands on unwilling faculty members. It costs less than an institution-wide reform. It minimises the risks of failure by leaving traditional programs intact. These virtues are often decisive in holding open the chance of making a substantial change' (Bok, 1986, 187, 188). The major problem with the experimental strategy is of course the spreading of a successful experiment through the entire institution. As we noticed before, the diffusion of an innovation will only take place by virtue of the professional belief that the innovation is worthwhile. Regarding this issue the concepts of compatibility and profitability have provided us with some theoretical insights. Nevertheless, a strategy of experimenting with innovations must be judged to be especially suited to higher education systems. Therefore, governmental strategies that pay attention to triability may be expected to be more successful in creating innovations in higher education institutions than strategies in which the idea of triability is absent.

4.2.7. Conclusion

In paragraph 4.2. we have explored several innovation characteristics that are assumed to be related to the level of succes of an innovation in higher education. We conclude that an innovative strategy can be expected to be more successful when in such a strategy attention is paid to the compatibility and the profitability of the innovation. The compatibility of an innovation (i.e. the degree to which the innovation is perceived to be consistent with existent values and practices), is generally speaking, positively related to the rate of adoption of the innovation. However, a reform that implies a radical departure of existing values and practices can nevertheless be successful when the 'functional breadth of change' is limited, that is, when the reform is limited to a few functional areas while at the same time some other prevailing values and practices are rigorously accepted.

The profitability of an innovation is also positively related to the rate of adoption of the innovation. The relative advantage of the innovation (compared to the idea or practice it supersedes) should be clear to those who are supposed to accept it. The behaviour of each group and individual confronted with an innovation, is guided by the subjective interpretation of self-interest. The outcome of an innovation process to a large extent depends on the distribution of power among the self-interested actors involved in the decision-making process regarding the innovation.

The complexity of an innovation was found to be negatively related to the rate of adoption of the innovation. When complexity is defined as the combination of the degree to which an innovation is a departure from existing values and practices with the number of functional areas aimed at by the innovation, it may be concluded that the higher the level of complexity of an innovation, the less likely it is that the innovation will be accepted.

With respect to the observability of an innovation (i.e. the degree to which the objectives and expected results are clear) it was argued that this factor should be interpreted as a strategic element in presenting an innovation in terms of compatibility or profitability.

The triability of an innovation (i.e. the degree to which an innovation may be experimented with) was judged to be of great importance in higher education. Experimenting with innovations is a prudent strategy, especially because the professionals in higher education institutions will be particularly sceptical about the policy-assumption on which these innovations are based.

Chapter 3

RECENT DEVELOPMENTS IN THE GOVERNANCE OF HIGHER EDUCATION AND HIGHER EDUCATION CURRICULA

Denis Carrier and Frans A. van Vught

1. Introduction

In this chapter we will explore the recent developments in the attitudes and approaches of the governments in various Western industrialised countries with regard to higher education. We will refer to the structural reforms which took place in many countries in the 1970s and early 1980s and we will indicate how these reforms have resulted in the dominance of the strategy of rational planning and control.

However, we will also argue that new governmental policies with regard to higher education are recently being established in several countries, which may very well develop into the strategy of self-regulation. We will analyse some of these recent policies and indicate a basic choice for the future of higher education governance.

In the second part of this chapter we will concentrate on the governmental influence on the processes of design and development of higher education curricula. We point to some important factors related to a growing governmental influence on curricula and we explore three crucial forms of this influence. Finally, we formulate a question regarding the relationships between the two governmental strategies and the innovations of curricula within higher education institutions.

2. Structural models and reforms

Government interest in higher education and scientific research is by no means new. For example, the need to promote scientific research as a means of aiding the expansion of industry and trade was stressed back in 1915 in a British White Paper. And the same concern prompted the Canadian federal government at that time to set up an advisory committee for scientific and industrial research.

However, it was especially after World War II that governments in most Western industrialised countries came to play an important role in higher education. The increasing importance of the role of government is very much related to the fast expansion of most Western higher education systems. Many governments have developed and implemented policies to provide an answer to the increasing 'social demand'. Many governments also designed and implemented policies that were supposed to match the production of the higher education system with the expected future 'manpower demand' and the requirements of the labour market.

In the context of these developments several structural models have been presented which have had an important influence on the processes of government-led restructuring of higher education, especially in Western Europe (see Furth, 1973; Cerych, Furth and Papadopoulos, 1974; Clark, 1977; Trow, 1984; for an overview, see Teichler, 1988). One of the important dimensions on which the models which can be found in the literature appear to differ is the dimension of 'integration'. Referring to the well-known OECD-study on short-cycle education (OECD, 1973), Neave (1983) distinguishes three structural models in higher education. 'Least integrated of all is the *binary model* found in the English higher education system. There, the Polytechnics are legally separate, founded on a different basis than the universities. . . . . The term 'binary' implies, in effect a fixed and irreconcilable alternative: either university or polytechnic with no possibility of crossover from one to the other at undergraduate level. The *multipurpose model*, represented in the form of the Norwegian Regional Colleges and, to a lesser extent, the French University Institutes of Technology, stands on a further step along the road to integration through the building of network courses enabling students to pass from one sector to the university, from short cycle to long cycle education, whilst maintaining the specific mission of both. Finally, we have the *comprehensive model*, in which physical integration between short and long cycle education takes place inside one overall administrative body. It also implies a considerable degree of curricular integration and the 'redrawing of the map of knowledge in such a way that the historic divisions between academic knowledge and vocational applicability are broken down' (Neave, 1983, 263, 264).

Hermanns and Teichler (1983) make a major distinction between the integrated and the diversified model. 'The *integrated model* advocates the admission of students with different prerequisites and abilities to the same institutions, even to a certain extent to the same course of studies'. According to the *diversified model* 'there was to be a multitude of separate institutions within the tertiary area, which were distinctive both in terms of their specific goal orientations and their academic standards . . . . At the same time the diversified system was supposed to guarantee interchange between institutions and between courses of study by means of corresponding entry and transfer regulations (Hermanns and Teichler, 1983, 4, 5).

Hermanns and Teichler indicate that, although many international discussions were held regarding the various structural models of higher education, no structural policy, in the sense of completely implementing one of the models, has been developed anywhere. Rather, in the individual countries the idiosyncratic features of the specific higher education systems to a large extent, survived. '. . . . there is little sign of there being any education system anywhere which nearly matches the ideal types of the models . . . .' (Teichler, 1987, 23).

Nevertheless, the structural models have had an important influence on the governmental attitudes towards higher education and on the various policies that have been designed and implemented, particularly in Western Europe. The objectives of 'opening up' the higher education systems, of bringing and keeping these systems within certain ranges of effectiveness and efficiency and of optimising the relationships of these systems with the labour market have brought many governments to sometimes rather drastic structural reforms. And nearly always this implied an increase of the role of government in higher education.

Especially during the 1970s and the first half of the 1980s the public policies in the field of higher education in Western Europe show a growing penetration of government into higher education. During those years various governments in Western Europe designed and implemented policies which have decreased the autonomy of higher education institutions and of the academic professionals working within them. Most governments continued to stimulate the expansion of the higher education systems. But the growing financial stringencies and the idea that the relationships between higher education and the labour market should be optimised brought governments also to the conclusion that higher education systems should be more rationally managed. To attain such a rational management most governments decided to implement systems of planning and control.

The results of the growing influence of government on higher education can be found in the various reforms that many European systems experienced during the 1970s and the beginning of the 1980s. New structures were invented and more or less successfully implemented. Well-known examples are the 25/5 Scheme in Sweden, the '*Gesamthochschule*' in Germany and the new subsystems in Britain (the Polytechnics), France (the University Institutes of Technology) and Norway (the Regional Colleges). New laws were imposed such as the '*Hochschulrahmgesetz*' in Germany (1976), the Higher Education Reform Act in Sweden (1977) and the new Higher Education Guideline Law ('*Loi Savary*') in France (1984). New budgetary systems were introduced, leading on the one hand to tighter budgets and on the other hand to the need for higher education institutions to look for other funding sources than government. And, last but not least, the administrative structures of higher education systems expanded, notably resulting in various forms of 'meso-administration' (for instance: the 'University Grants Committee' and the 'National Advisory Body' in Britain, the 'Standing Conference of '*Länder*', Ministers of Education and the West

German Rector's Conference in Germany, the University Council in Norway, the Conference of University Presidents in France and the Regional Committees in Sweden).

By the beginning of the second half of the 1980s the grip of government on higher education systems, both in Europe and in other Western industrialised countries had tightened. In many countries higher education systems came to be seen as 'knowledge generating engines sandwiched between the corporatism of the industrial state and the exigencies of business' (Neave, 1985, 120). In the eyes of government, higher education systems became crucial instruments for the attainment of economical goals. And because of the financial stringencies the governments were facing, these instruments had to be used efficiently and professionally. To most governments this meant that higher education systems had to be centrally planned and extensively controlled.

3. The dominance of the strategy of rational planning and control

The governmental orientation towards the strategy of rational planning and control can be clearly recognised in many Western countries. In the Federal Republic of Germany government planning of higher education has been called extremely strong. According to Teichler the 'orientation towards quantitative planning of higher education as well as the governmental concern about the future of graduates have been stronger in the Federal Republic of Germany than in any other market-oriented industrialised country' (Teichler, 1987, 113). The German governmental strategy of planning and control can be found in the attempt to merge the universities and the '*Fachhochschulen*' into the '*Gesamthochschulen*', a policy which to a large extent has failed because it contained a too simple compromise between conflicting goals. Perhaps even more explicitly this strategy of governmental planning comes to the fore in the '*Hochschulrahmgesetz*' which, among other things, called for the establishment of study reform commissions in which representatives of higher education institutions, government and industry should work together to develop innovations in course programmes that would take the changes in the occupation system into account. Teichler (1987) mentions two other examples of the strong governmental orientation towards the strategy of planning and control in the Federal Republic of Germany. One is the fact that in this country more forecasts regarding requirements of highly qualified manpower have been commissioned and published than in other comparable countries. The other concerns the fact that 'the Federal Republic of Germany developed very detailed mechanisms of quantitative planning of higher education: for example, the Science Council - an advisory body comprised of federal and state representatives as well as of scholars and representatives of the public - recommends major ways and directions of the quantitative development of higher education in a very detailed way. As 50 per cent of higher education construction costs are borne by Federal subsidies to the individual state in charge of the respective university, no single university building will be constructed without the Science Council's support' (Teichler, 1987, 113).

In France also a clear governmental orientation towards the strategy of rational planning and control can be found. Traditionally, in French higher education nearly all matters are regulated and controlled by central government. The conditions of access, the financing of institutional activities, the accreditation of courses and diplomas, the distributions of posts, all these matters are under the authority of central government. Besides, in the beginning of the 1980s the issue of efficiency has induced government to implement various policies to steer and control the French higher education system centrally. The instalation of the '*Comité National d'Evaluation*' (in the '*Loi Savary*' in 1984) is often seen as a clear example (Bienaymé, 1984; Lamoure and Lamoure, 1988).

In the 1970s and the first half of the 1980s the Netherlands also experienced several major government imposed restructuring and retrenchment operations, which together clearly indicate a governmental orientation towards the strategy of rational planning and control. The university sector has been restructured into a 'two tier system' in which both the duration of courses and the maximum stay allowed at the university have been shortened. The sector of higher vocational training has been confronted with an enormous operation of scale enlargement and task reallocation in which more than 300 schools eventually merged into less than 50. Also, two major financial cut-back operations have been imposed on the higher education system, leaving higher education institutions with no other choice than to follow government's central steering approach.

In many other countries, both in and outside Western Europe, a similar orientation towards the strategy of rational planning can be found and it is only very recently that a change in this orientation appears to have broken through. Finland witnessed two decades of central government planning (based on the so-called 'Development Act' for the period 1967-1986) (Hölttä, 1988). In Spain the Directorate of Higher Education exercised a rigid type of central control until the introduction of the '*Ley de Reforma*' (1983) (Villanueva, 1984; Pedro, 1988). The Swedish reforms of the 1960s and the 1970s were clearly comprehensively and centrally planned (Lane and Fredriksson, 1983).

The United Kingdom offers a very peculiar picture. Since the beginning of the 1980s the influence of government appears to have been growing strongly in this country (see for instance; Maclure, 1987). Traditionally the

British universities enjoyed a large amount of autonomy. The coordination in the British higher education system was not reached by central governmental planning and control, but rather by 'a system of pragmatic negotiation by means of an intermediary body, the University Grants Committee, acting on behalf of the universities and presenting their requirements to government in a collective manner' (Neave, 1988a, 12). Since 1979 things have changed drastically. Severe budget cuts were imposed in 1979 and 1981 (Kogan and Kogan, 1983). The Jarratt Report on University Management introduced the idea of 'managerialism' (Kogan, 1987, 180). The Education Reform Act (1988) has reformed the University Grants Committee into an instrument in the hands of government and industry (the University Funding Council). The Polytechnics and Colleges are confronted with the Polytechnics and Colleges Funding Council. The result is an extension of the 'juridification' of the British higher education system (Neave, 1988a, 13) allowing central government to steer the system more in accordance with the objectives it judges to be worthwhile. However, as Kogan notices, these objectives do not imply an assault on the values of academic work. 'Our government is schizoid in wanting both a move towards instrumentally useful courses and the retention of elite traditional education, but for a smaller number. The traditional elite, reading any of the traditional subjects, are still snapped up by employers and government where they preside over a robust economy. In this sense higher education continues to be legitimised by employers who want good generalists. . . . . The attack has not been on the power of the academy to determine what it will regard as good academic work. It has been on the subject balances, the resources used and on the uses to which academic evaluation are put' (Kogan, 1987, 184, 185).

In the United States the interests of the various states in their higher education systems have grown. In all 50 states some form of commission or blue-ribbon committee has examined the state's future and in all states the higher education system has been identified as an important factor in creating such a future (Newman, 1987, 6). In nearly all states some type of formal statewide board of higher education has been installed (Berdahl, 1983). At least half the states are involved in continuous strategic planning in higher education (McGuinnes, 1986).

In the U.S. the autonomy of higher education institutions and their separation from regular government processes have always been respected values. However, during recent years it has been suggested in several debates that the government's role in higher education should increase to enable higher education systems to innovate and to meet public needs. In several states policies and mechanisms have been developed to strengthen the university-industry relationships by means of research and development consortia (California, North Carolina, Ohio, Pennsylvania, Rhode Island,

Texas) (Botkin and Dimancescu, 1986). In many states the calls for accountability have become louder.

In the context of this book it is impossible to present a valid and detailed analysis of the developments in higher education governance in the U.S. It may be noticed, however, that in some states the increased political intrusion of government in higher education justifies the conclusion that in the U.S. also an orientation exists towards the governmental strategy of rational planning and control. Many types of sometimes rather detailed regulations are found. There is regulation with respect to the allocation of resources and with respect to the adherence to a state imposed salary structure. There is regulation regarding admission procedures and regarding the substance of course programmes. And there is regulation concerning accountability and quality control. The discussion in the U.S. appears to concentrate on the question how the differentiation and distribution of authority between the higher education institutions and government has to be organised. 'A successful system . . . . depends not on the choices of either centralisation or decentralisation. Rather, it depends on centralising (and decentralising) the right things' (Newman, 1987, 57).

In Canada also, the influence of provincial government has been growing. In Canada the provincial governments control the processes of degree granting and the levels of tuition. They provide the universities with the advantages of a public monopoly, thereby making sure that the universities are not likely to challenge governmental intervention (Skolnik, 1987).

In Canada higher education is to a growing extent considered to be a strategic instrument for governmental policy-making. In Ontario the general disposition to reduce the amount of governmental funding has been translated into a clear policy of governmental planning and control (Rea, 1987, 168). In several provinces the traditional block grants are being replaced by designated and regulated programme grants (Southern, 1987, 46). Most provinces exercise a rather detailed control on community colleges (Dennison, 1987).

Australia offers more or less the same picture. Harman (1987) notices that over the past decade and a half four shifts of power can be found in Australian higher education: 'at the institutional level, from departments and faculties to central administrations . . . .; from individual institutions to government; within government, from state governments to the Federal Government; and at both federal and state levels of government from special coordinating agencies to Ministers, Cabinet and central departments' (Harman, 1987, 193). The 1980s have brought enormous changes in Australian higher education. In 1981 the Commonwealth Government decided that there were too many small institutions. Threatening to end their funding, the Commonwealth forced these institutions into amalgamations. As a result the number of institutions decreased during the 1980s and the average size rose. Moreover, the per capita grants to merged institutions were substantially reduced. In 1989 the binary system was abolished (by the introduction of the Unified National System) and tuition fees were reintroduced. Government also decided to replace the semi-autonomous Tertiary Education Commission by a department of the Commonwealth Government and to introduce the concept of 'contracting' (between the Commonwealth and the institutions) (Taylor, 1989). The growing influence of government has brought an increased degree of different kinds of regulation. Both the state governments and the Commonwealth Government apparently put their confidence in the strategy of planning and control. On the other hand, it should be mentioned that the Australian universities still enjoy their academic freedom. ' . . . . they have a large measure of control in areas which are central to the academic enterprise - the selection of students; the selection of staff; control over what is taught and how it is taught' (Harman, 1987, 205).

Overseeing the developments in the area of higher education policy making in the various countries just mentioned, it may be concluded that the governmental strategy of rational planning and control has been widely used in higher education in the Western industrialised countries in the 1970s and the first half of the 1980s. However, especially on the European continent, a new strategy appears to be developing.

4. A growing emphasis on the strategy of self-regulation?

In the second half of the 1980s in most Western countries the political discussions concerning the societal role of higher education are still focussed on the functions of higher education system in triggering and stabilising economic and industrial innovations. The main objective for higher education systems is to be creative and excellent, both in producing the necessary scientific and technological breakthroughs and in educating the professionals who must be able to handle and organise the innovations that will follow these breakthroughs.

But, although this objective has not changed compared to the basic goals of the 1970s and the first years of the 1980s, a new governmental attitude appears to be arising at the same time. The financial retrenchment operations that could be found in nearly all countries in the Western world at the beginning of the 1980s, may very well be developing into a new governmental strategy towards higher education. The short-term financial cutback policies may be changing into a new, long-term strategic policy.

Neave (1988a) has called this new, developing governmental attitude with respect to higher education the 'Rise of the Evaluative State' and he argues that this new attitude is accompanied by two major shifts in the timing, purpose and location of the idea of evaluation in the processes of policy-making. 'The first is the linking up between "routine" evaluation with "strategic evaluation". The second is a clear shift towards a posteriori [instead of a priori] evaluation' (Neave, 1988a, 9).

However, the recent changes in the governmental attitudes towards higher education, especially on the European continent, suggest a more fundamental development. Neave is right in emphasising the rise of the strategic aspects of present governmental policy-making. But, concentrating on the aspects of evaluation, he may have overlooked the change in the general strategy which several governments have begun to use in the context of higher education.

Most important in this change of strategy is the increase of the autonomy of the higher education institutions. In several Western European countries government seems to want to deregulate its detailed control of higher education. In several countries initiatives have been developed to design new ways of steering the higher education system. In these new steering conceptions the relocation of power within the system is an important aspect.

In the Netherlands the government has officially launched such a new steering conception in the so-called 'HOAK'-paper (1985). Government has proclaimed that it will step back from its strategy of detailed rational planning and control and will only exercise a 'remote control' function. The autonomy of the higher education institutions is strengthened and the self-responsibility of the institutions is emphasised. By doing so, government hopes to create the best conditions for an increase of creativity and excellence in higher education (Maassen and Van Vught, 1988).

Also in Belgium, Finland, Spain and Sweden a more or less identical governmental position can be found. In Belgium the so-called 'Saint-Ann Plan' (1986) has given the universities a larger degree of autonomy, be it within the limits of less financial resources (Wielemans, 1988). In Finland the higher education budget for 1988 appears to stimulate academic self-regulation and institutional leadership (Hölttä, 1988, 100). In Spain the new trend towards more autonomy (which started with the *Ley de Reforma Universitaria* of 1983) has clearly changed the balance between the state and the universities and stimulated the regionalisation of Spanish higher education (Pedro, 1988). In Sweden the government and *Riksdag* have allowed more autonomy to the higher education institutions, by introducing among other things, a new, less detailed budgeting system and by limiting government influence on the contents of course programmes (Bauer, 1988).

In France discussions have started on the future role of government in higher education. A study group of the *Collège de France* concluded that the centralised governmental administration is too rigid to enable higher education institutions to meet the challenges of the future. The *Groupe d'Etude pour la Renovation de l'Université Francaise* has proposed leaving a greater role to market-coordination in French higher education (Neave, 1988b, 360).

The development towards a new governmental strategy can also be found in several Northern American states. In New Jersey the state bureaucracy with respect to state colleges and universities has been greatly reduced with the new legislation of 1986. The legislation included three steps: '(1) establishment of a state college governing board association that serves as an advocate for the autonomy of the colleges and has authority to file suit; (2) authorisation of the colleges to contract and handle their own transactions without going to the treasure: (3) empowerment of the boards of trustees to manage their institutions, including having responsibility for the institution's fiscal operations' (Newman, 1987, 71). Similarly, in Kentucky the House Bill 622 of 1982 (the Universities Management Bill) reversed 40 years of state centralisation and in Wisconsin the governor supported the recommendations of a task force to increase the state university's autonomy (Mingle, 1983; Folger and McGuiness, 1984; Newman, 1987).

The increase of autonomy for higher education institutions, found in several countries, indicates a fundamental change in governmental strategies towards higher education. It shows the loss of confidence in governmental capabilities to centrally plan and control a higher education system. And it may very well point at a growing inclination towards the strategy of self-regulation and the cybernetic perspective of decision-making which is behind that strategy (see Chapter 1).

Teichler (1988) distinguishes three stages in the development of higher education policies in Western industrial societies. The first stage, which occupied the latter half of the 1950s and the early 1960s, shows the establishment of the numerous planning and counseling bodies in the various countries. The second stage (latter half of the 1960s and the early 1970s) brought a search for new and modernised structures for the higher education system. During this stage many governments were provided with increased powers in the area of higher education and the belief in sophisticated governmental planning grew. The third stage, which in most countries started in the beginning of the 1980s is characterised by a shift from 'optimism' regarding the needs and the virtues of educational expansion towards 'pessimism' and renewed scepticism (Husen, 1979). According to Teichler, this third stage also shows a 'collapse of faith in societal planning, both in terms of understanding sufficiently the complexity of higher education and its environment in order to design appropriate innovations as well as in terms of success in carrying through plans: the rising popularity of the term "implementation" as well as the visible retreat from ambitious goals in higher education policies, most clearly support such a description of this stage of higher education policies, as well as reduced hope that educational research might have a strong impact on policies' (Teichler, 1988, 21, 22; see also: Berg and Oestergren, 1977; Cerych, 1980, 1984; Husen and Kogan, 1984; Premfors, 1984).

Teichler (1988) suggests that during the 1980s a new stage of higher education policy is gradually emerging, but that it is still too early to assess the general policy which will come forward during this new stage. It is our opinion that this new stage shows the development of a new governmental attitude with respect to higher education, in which it is acknowledged that the increase of the autonomy of the higher education institutions is of crucial importance.

Besides the increase of autonomy of the higher education institutions, there are two other aspects of the recent changes in government attitudes with respect to higher education that, taken together, appear to refer to the rise of the strategy of self-regulation.

The first of these two aspects is the growing importance of 'a posteriori evaluation'. Neave indicates that in several countries in Western Europe government is using the mechanism of a posteriori evaluation 'to elicit how far goals have been met' (Neave, 1988a, 9). In terms of the cybernetic perspective of decision-making such an a posteriori evaluation can be interpreted as the wish to monitor the general 'critical variables', chosen by government to shape the 'remote control function' of the cybernetic interpretation of decision-making. In this sense a posteriori evaluation is not necessarily a governmental attempt to steer a higher education system by means of 'output' or 'product control'. It can also indicate a crucial aspect of the governmental strategy of self-regulation.

In the recent policy-proposals in some of the countries where the new strategy of self-regulation may be rising, the newly established evaluation systems are still only partly developed. For instance, in Finland it is not yet clear what the roles and authorities will be of on the one hand the Ministry of Education and on the other the higher education institutions (Hölttä, 1988, 98). In Sweden a basic question is whether government will or will not link the annual reporting of the universities and colleges to financial allocation (Bauer, 1988). From the point of view of the strategy of self-regulation, evaluation systems should not be used for direct decisions on financial allocation. Where such a use develops, the traditional governmental strategy of rational planning and control prevails. For the further development of the strategy of self-regulation evaluation systems should rather be a combination of internal self-evaluation (Kells, 1988) and external monitoring (by government) of a limited set of critical systems variables. The budget decisions should be taken at a strategic level and in a political context, taking the results of both the internal self-studies and the external monitoring into account.

Another aspect of the recent changes in the general attitude of government with respect to higher education which may point to a growing interest in the strategy of self-regulation is, what Beer has called, the 'changing of the rules of the game' (see Chapter 1). A higher level system consists of trying to influence the behaviour of the lower level actors by confronting them with a set of general rules. Steering a system in this sense is designing and presenting some general rules that guide the behaviour of the system units.

It appears that several governments in Western countries have claimed to want to operate according to this basic cybernetic idea. These governments want to evoke certain kinds of behaviour in higher education institutions by confronting them with certain rules and guidelines.

A crucial question with regard to this aspect of the strategy of self-regulation concerns the level of restraint which is implied in the rules that are being used by government to influence the higher education institutions. In the concept of the strategy of self-regulation this level of restraint is assumed to be rather low. The rules and guidelines should be broad and general. By no means should they heavily restrain the actors who are supposed to use the autonomy granted to them.

However, the recent policy-changes in the several countries which have taken their first steps towards the strategy of self-regulation do not appear to follow this idea. The new governmental approaches, on the contrary, still contain instruments which can be quite restraining. In the Netherlands, for instance, the Ministry of Education has recently indicated that it will use a 'negative statement of financing' if an institutional activity, which is regarded by government as undesirable, is not modified or stopped (Maassen and Van Vught, 1988, 70). In Finland, government still controls the allocation of academic positions among institutions and disciplines (Hölttä, 1988, 92).

These examples show that, although in some countries the new governmental strategy of self-regulation is certainly rising, government in these countries is not yet willing to really step back. Government sees it as its task to guide the higher education system and, to reach this objective, government still applies rather restraining instruments that often reach even to the level of the basic-level system units. The new governmental approaches to higher education in these countries appear to be a combination of two extreme theoretical conceptions. Elements of the strategy of self-regulation are combined with elements of the strategy of rational planning and control. The result is 'a strange hybrid' (Maassen and Van Vught, 1988, 69) and a 'species of a half-way house between out-and-out dirigism and integral institutional autonomy' (Neave, 1986, 20).

For the future governance of higher education it is of extreme importance to watch the further development of the recent governmental approaches in which some (but not all) of the three basic aspects of the strategy of self-regulation can be distinguished. When these approaches remain as hybrid constructions of opposite theoretical models, we must indeed fear (as Neave (1988a) has suggested) that they only refer to a modern reformulation of the traditional strategy of rational planning and control. However, when the basic ideas of the strategy of self-regulation are accepted, higher education will experience a fundamentally different governmental attitude.

5. The growing governmental influence on the planning of curricula

Governmental interest in the planning of curricula is much more recent than its involvement in higher education affairs in general. Until lately, this last interest was mainly dictated by governments' wish to control the right to award degrees and compliance with minimum standards. This wish stemmed from the responsibility, which in our liberal societies often falls to the State, to see that markets operate efficiently and that consumers - in this case students and graduates - are properly protected. This type of government intervention in the affairs of higher education institutions has varied from one country to another, according to the prevailing political culture. But even where intervention has formally affected curricula - as in France, for example, where government soon came to control curriculum content via national degrees - it was less due to a real interest in their orientation and content than to the desire to establish equality of treatment and conditions for the students enrolling and graduating from the various authorised institutions.

This absence of real governmental interest in the actual content of curricula was particularly evident in the United States and Canada, where private initiative largely contributed to the launching and development of the higher education system. Government intervention, when it emerged, mainly took the form of regulating the right to award degrees. Government's greater or lesser liberality in granting this right also tended to be counterbalanced, as regards its control over curriculum standards, by mechanisms for the accreditation or periodic evaluation of the quality of institutions and of their curricula, the initiative for these mechanisms often being taken by the institutions concerned themselves. This concern to maintain academic standards at a proper level was very evident in the United States, where the right to award university degrees was granted much more liberally by individual states than, for example, by the Canadian provinces (Skolnik, 1987).

The current situation is very different. In the majority, if not all, of our Western countries, government now exercises considerable influence, in many ways, over the actual orientation of course programmes in higher education and even over the content of certain curricula.

Three factors appear to be responsible for the growing governmental interest in the orientation and contents of curricula: the emergence of mass higher education, the theory of human capital and the crisis of the Welfare State. These factors - the first two of which occurred largely at the same time in certain countries - have had the effect of increasingly drawing govennment's attention to the planning of the course programmes in higher education, which had hitherto been the private domain of the institutions.

5.1. *The emergence of mass higher education*

Trow (1974) estimated that an elitist type of higher education becomes mass higher education when at least 15 per cent of the 20 - 24 age group enrol in institutions belonging to that system. The United States and the USSR passed that point immediately after World War II, whereas most Western European countries reached it about 30 years later. The rise in enrolment rates was particularly high during the 1960s and, although it has tended to slow down practically everywhere since then, it has nonetheless considerably increased the university clientele. Especially as, according to Neave's data (1985), the actual size of the 20 - 24 cohorts has increased at the same time, the most populous - apart from some exceptions, including Ireland and France - passing through the higher education system during the 1980s.

The rapid rise in the university clientele resulting from the emergence of mass higher education has made it another 'public good' whose development must be accelerated and which must be made more accessible. All the more since this coincided with the growing acceptance of the right to education, eventually at every level, irrespective of the financial situation of students and their families. This created two tasks which governments have quickly assumed. They had, first, to speed up the quantitative expansion of the university system by suitable overall policies. They also had to find the means for improving accessibility to higher studies for the greatest number, both geographically and financially speaking (scholarships and grants, controlled educational costs, cheap student services, etc.).

These tasks have given birth to a generation of public programmes mainly aimed at increasing the university system's capacity by various means: university building grants, creation of new universities, introduction of new curricula, integration in the higher education system of technical institutions which had not previously enjoyed that status, financing formulas usually based on the number and level of enrolments, etc.

All these measures were aimed above all at expanding the enrolment capacity of the university system as a whole and less, for the moment, at influencing its orientation. However several of the new instruments of intervention had some effects on the planning of course programmes. It is certainly not by chance that the new university curricula created at that time (for example, in the United Kingdom, France and Norway) were generally shorter and more technology-oriented than the traditional university programmes. While making higher education accessible to more students, they confirmed the prime interest of governments for curricula which could contribute directly to economic growth by providing highly skilled professionals and, in the long run, scientific and technological breakthroughs.

5.2. *The human capital theory*

The very early tendency of government to take more interest in certain types of curricula grew stronger with the progress of human capital theory and its application to economic policy. The revival of the concept of 'human capital' goes back to the speech made by Theodore Schultz, at that time President of the American Economic Association, to the latter's annual assembly in 1960. Schultz demonstrated that expenditure for the 'improvement of man' could well be seen as capital expenditure in the same way as is investment in plant and machinery (Schultz, 1961). This paper had the effect of prompting more research and publication on 'human capital' (Kiker, 1971). Experts very soon assessed the positive externalities of every form of education and identified expenditure in this field, notably in higher education, as one of the most profitable investments for economic development (Economic Council of Canada, 1965). This research came at a time when the monetary and fiscal policies inspired by the Keynesian economic analysis were increasingly less able to cure both unemployment and inflation. Governments were therefore quickly attracted to a theory which suggested that they should invest in improving labour forces in order to make factors of production more responsive to the economic situation, and thus solve the inflation/unemployment dilemma more effectively. Educational policies became the preferred weapon for raising the general qualifications of the labour force as well as its mobility and for providing a sufficient number of key qualifications.

The supporters of the human capital theory initially made little distinction between disciplines and fields of study when endeavouring to demonstrate the positive effects of higher education on economic development. Nevertheless, the new trend that their efforts helped to give to economic policy increased the interest which governments had already begun to show in higher education curricula of a professional type, especially in the pure and applied sciences.

The new role of manpower policies for economic equilibrium and development also had the effect, in countries with a federal structure, of arousing central government interest in education in general and higher education in particular. It was thus that in Canada, for example, the federal government - which has no jurisdiction over education in theory but had got involved in the postwar financing of technical and vocational education - endeavoured (and managed) to do likewise in case of higher education. So in Canada two kinds of government, and not just one, have tried to put higher education in general high up on the list of public priorities, with certain types of curricula in particular right at the top of that list. Government interest in these matters has not slackened since. Quite the contrary, as attested by the latest generation of public initiatives adopted to this end concerning support for 'centres of excellence' and research/development.

5.3. *The crisis of the Welfare State*

The public finance crisis experienced by Western industrialised societies since the mid-1970s and the resulting questioning of the Welfare State in many of them have finally had the effect of prompting governments to define their ambitions with regard to higher education. Besides, these developments have stimulated governments to increasingly attempt to influence part of the contents of course programmes if not their general orientation.

The last objective was first inspired by the slowing down of public investment in education made necessary by the state of public finances and public debt. Being thus obliged to husband their resources, governments first took two kinds of initiative which immediately affected and are still affecting curricula. The first concerns the 'differentiation' between institutions, the second is related to the way in which higher education is financed.

The argument in favour of greater differentiation between the various higher education institutes stems from the rationalisation forced on all the partners by budget constraints. This argument leads to trying to persuade each institution to adopt its own distinctive mission and cater more to the special needs arising from its geographical position or the special quality of its resources in certain fields. The aim is to enrich the system and avoid expensive overlapping. 'Differentiation' has become a common '*Leitmotif*' in higher education policy-making. The argument in favour of this procedure is now often accompanied by more or less tempting incentives to persuade institutions to adopt it in their plans and policies. As a result, most higher education systems today comprise an increasing number of institutions which justify some of their curriculum initiatives by their desire, for example, to respond more effectively to the needs of the surrounding community or to use their special skills to the utmost, etc. In short, the argument has borne fruit.

Regarding the funding of higher education most governments have not, as far as we know, fully compensated for inflation and the support has in several cases gradually become less sensitive to the trend of enrolments. The latest tendency is moreover to make funding less 'automatic'. This has been done in a number of ways: by funding based on various performance criteria and reviewed more or less frequently, by increasing the number of special targeted appropriations, by inviting tenders for special purposes, etc. Whatever form it takes, it usually has the effect of giving government an extra tool for influencing the planning of course programmes in the system, if not actually of institutions within it.

It appears that the influence of government on the planning of the orientation and the contents of curricula has been growing considerably during the last decades. In most Western industrialised countries government has come to believe it to be its task to stimulate the higher education system to higher levels of performance, differentiation and societal relevance. And, as a matter of course, it expanded its influence into what had traditionally been the 'private life of higher education' (Trow, 1975).

6. Government regulation and decision-making on curricula

In Chapter 1 government regulation has been described as the efforts of government to steer the decisions and actions of specific actors. It has been indicated that government regulation can be studied in the perspective of decision-making. In this perspective government regulation is understood as the structuring of the decision-making processes of societal actors.

In this paragraph we look at the influences of government regulation on the decision-making processes with regard to curricula. Three subjects are distinguished around which the influence of government regulation on decision-making regarding curricula appears to be centred: the regulation of structures, financial regulation and the regulation of curricula themselves.

6.1. *The regulation of structures*

In nearly all Western industrialised societies governments have felt the need, sometimes frequently, to intervene in order to regulate the structures of the higher education system and of the institutions that belong to it. This need grew stronger with the permanent installation of mass higher education. In countries where universities are private institutions, it resulted in profound evolution in the relationships between the institutions and government whereby the latter, while respecting the universities' autonomy, try to influence their behaviour through a complex system of public advisory boards and 'buffer' organisations. As was indicated above, in many countries where higher education is under State control, the outcome has been a fundamental reform of the system, usually accompanied by regulation of the management of institutions themselves.

Not every aspect of these reforms was aimed directly at influencing curricula. In fact, their special target was often quite different: organisational structures, institutional management and decision-making methods, funding and budgetary control, student admissions, etc. However, nearly all have had a strong, albeit indirect, long-term impact on the decision-making processes regarding curricula.

The case of participation by students and younger members of the teaching staff, and frequently of other groups too, in the university decision-making process is a good illustration of these observations.

Participation is often regarded as having been imposed on higher education by the student agitation of the late 1960s. Indeed, the principle of participation was imbedded in public regulation in several countries where higher education belongs to the public sector. The concept spread from there to become one of the current characteristics of the culture of higher education institutes almost everywhere in the Western world, including systems - such as in the Canadian provinces - where, exceptions apart, the universities are private and accustomed to determine their own internal structures. In fact, the pressures which prompted participatory structures probably originated in the rise of mass higher education. As soon as the massive increase in the number of students enrolled at any given time was matched by a correspondingly significant increase in the number of university teachers (notably young teachers) and in the number of potential graduates joining the labour market, it was inevitable that the universities' traditional structures and the balance of power prevailing in it, as well as the integration of the large number of future graduates into the labour market would be re-examined. In short, the emergence of participation was only a secondary symptom of a whole series of new tensions to which higher education systems were obliged to adjust and which were eventually bound to affect curricula.

And that is what in fact happened. Participation meant the sharing of power within higher education institutions. It has had the effect of more or less making room in decision-making processes in higher education institutes for the new concerns coming from students and from the younger members of the professorate and even, in several systems, for the interests voiced by representatives of the community as a whole. In thus changing the balance between the sources of influence and power within each institution participation has focussed the attention in the processes of decision-making on curricula to factors such as the employability of graduates, the utilitarian content of curricula, service to community, etc. In short, participation has inevitably contributed, although it is difficult to say exactly how much, to innovations such as the considerable expansion of professional or technology-oriented university courses, the importance of regional considerations in institutional development, etc.

Furthermore, initiatives in certain countries to introduce new structures have had still more direct repercussions on decision-making on curricula. This category includes public initiatives which profoundly changed the higher education landscape itself by introducing new elements that had not been there before. Such was the case, for example, when the French government decided to enlarge the first university cycle to include the IUTs. Having been given priority and power, such as choosing their students, which the traditional universities were not allowed to do, the IUTs have expanded rapidly. They have also greatly diversified their curricula, even so far, in response to a ministerial directive instructing them to facilitate longer studies for those of their graduates who wanted them, as to create programmes that build bridges between their own programmes (initially designed as short, self-contained and professional) and more advanced professional programmes. No one can now deny the considerable impact of the IUTs on the range of programmes offered at French first-cycle university level and on the careers chosen by a substantial proportion of students of the relevant age-group.

The creation of regional universities, and of multi-campus universities are other examples of governmental initiatives whose locomotive effects on the orientation of programmes offered were of major importance, especially as regards to the relationship between curriculum planning and the special needs of the regions in which these institutions operate.

6.2. *Financial regulation*

The impact of the oil shocks of 1973 and later years, the reduced governmental budgets and the crisis of the Welfare State are all, as we saw above, factors which have prompted governments to be more selective in their educational investments and to put a tight financial squeeze on higher education systems. This gave rise to a wave of administrative and financial regulations whose effects on the decision-making with regards to curricula were very far from being neutral. Two recent trends are particularly worth pointing out here.

The most criticised effect of the financial and administrative constraints was of course that they made balanced budgets an obsessive and very pressing problem for higher education institutions. The administrators of these institutions had either to cut expenditure as much as possible or search for new sources of income. It was against this background that the universities began to set themselves targets such as canvassing new clienteles, developing closer university/industry ties (especially at a regional level), etc. Indeed, the budget squeeze created the need for a certain university 'entrepreneurship', a new form of institutional management in higher education, very different from the traditional academic culture.

The methods and aims of the new entrepreneurial attitude happened to coincide quite closely with government's preference for the strategy of rational planning and control. The entrepreneurial attitude appeared to respond to the wish of many governments for the needs of society. And the entrepreneurial attitude offered governments the possibility to influence the fundamental decision-making processes in higher education institutions on the design and development of curricula. In this latter connection, canvassing new student clienteles and bringing university and industry closer together have, for example, provided opportunities for new study-programmes; 'co-operative' programmes (a combination of conventional study and on-the-job training), and intensive professional development courses the 'executive version' of the well established Master of Business Administration, etc. In short, institutional leadership has tended to change direction. This is particularly evident in the higher education systems where the institutional leaders are still 'appointed' according to a more or less consultative selection process rather than elected.

This said, various empirical observations give reason to believe that the need for more systematic rationalisation of development possibilities and for improved 'marketing' of the universities are now at the heart of the management processes in most higher education institutions, whatever the processes governing the choice of their leaders is. Indeed, all kinds of institutional support, such as the appointment of university/industry liaison officers, stronger public relations departments, etc., have been created and demonstrate this change of direction practically everywhere. Higher education management tends to become a speciality within the university profession and this has inevitably affected the decision-making on the contents and the orientation of curricula.

Government has also endeavoured to limit its investment in education and to pay closer attention to the return on the investment by manipulating the way in which higher education is funded. Two initiatives must be particularly emphasised in this connection, as they both give government powerful leverage for highly specific intervention in the decision-making processes with regard to the design and development of curricula.

The first is the introduction of very specifically targeted appropriations into the different methods of funding higher education. These can be more or less permanent. In the Canadian province of Ontario, for example, such appropriations now accompany the general operating grant; and most of the specific appropriations are announced as being for at least a few years in order to persuade universities to adopt various initiatives favored by the Ministry. Thus, for the last two years, universities in Ontario have been entitled to a package giving access to grants to facilitate the winding up of out-of-date programmes and the redeployment of the resources thus released to other purposes. In the Netherlands a similar governmental policy exists. In this country universities are encouraged to undertake certain activities in exchange for extra amounts of targeted funding. Recently the Dutch government has announced a financing mechanism which is specifically tailored to stimulating the higher education institutions to develop their specific profiles and missions, and to increase their performance (the 'mission budget') (Maassen and Van Vught, 1988).

'Tendering', which has become increasingly common in, for instance, France over the last few years (while fees and the fixed subsidy per student enrolled have remained almost stationary), is another example of the handling of financial arrangements whereby government makes the higher education institutes do what it wants, while leaving it to the Minister and his advisers themselves to choose the objectives they consider desirable. It was indeed such tendering which provided the opportunity in recent years for the renovation of the curricula for the *Diplome d'Etudes Universitaires Générales* (DEUG) and which gave the go-ahead for several second-cycle programmes leading to a new degree (the *Magistère*). These programmes are highly selective and enable some universities to compete with the *Grandes Ecoles* on their own terms (see Chapter 6).

Whether it involves specific appropriations or tenders, such targeted control of university funding - affecting the main public source of funds for the development of curricula - allows government itself to choose a good many of the programmes or disciplines in which innovations can actually be made, especially in the context of a tight budget and scarce resources.

6.3. *The regulation of curricula*

Government also endeavours to influence curricula. However, it rarely does so directly by ordering specific courses or programmes to be given. It usually takes an indirect approach, proposing that institutions adopt targets - generally accompanied by financial incentives - that it considers particularly suitable. The renovation of the above mentioned DEUGs and the introduction of the *Magistère*-curriculum in France in recent years are examples of this type of intervention.

Nonetheless, it is rare for a government to act in this way of its own accord. In the vast majority of cases its intervention in this area is usually in more or less close consultation with advisory bodies - permanent or specially appointed - which often imply, in one form or another, the participation of representatives of higher education. Those of the bodies which are permanent (such as the (former) British 'University Grants Committee', the *Conseil National de l'Enseignement Supérieur et de la Recherche* in France, the *Conseil des Universités du Québec*, the 'Ontario Council on University Affairs', etc. and their various committees) are commissioned to advise their respective governments on developments in higher education. They are also often given executive or semi-executive functions related to their terms of reference, the most frequent situation in this respect being where the Minister - while reserving the right to decide in the last resort - does in fact usually accept their recommendations. This arrangement makes these bodies the privileged partners of both the government and the higher education institutions. It also gives them considerable influence when governmental policies are introduced, their opinion usually being requested by the Minister on whether projects submitted by the various institutions under specific government policies should be funded.

The advisory bodies have played a key role in several recent cases of government intervention in decision-making processes with regard to curricula. However this has in no way reduced government's influence in this connection. On the contrary, the growing impact of public intervention in the higher education system and the increasingly specific nature of government in this respect appear to have made the advisory bodies more important. Set up to protect the higher education institutions from political and bureaucratic interference and ill-suited to the supervision of higher education curricula and qualifications, the advisory bodies have naturally been obliged, in order to make their approaches to the public authorities effective, to come to terms with the latters' objectives and to take account of them as far as possible in their efforts to maintain the quality of higher education and research. As Southern notices: '. . . . if intermediaries are to be effective in facilitating an appropriate arm's length relationship between government and universities they cannot operate solely on principles or pleas for co-operation; they must be active players in a political process. These bodies must navigate by carefully drawn maps based on accurate perceptions of the converging interests of the governments and universities' (Southern, 1987, 53).

Thus, because they are more and more deeply involved in the process of mediation made necessary by the extent and specific nature of government intervention in higher education, the major intermediary advisory bodies have probably become a 'secular arm' of the State as well as 'buffers' between it and the higher education institutions. In doing so, they rendered the institutions a service by taking their fears and points of view into the heart of the new public policies affecting them. But they are also largely responsible for the fact that a large proportion of the public concerns behind those policies were successfully translated in operational terms. And these operational terms very often indicate a growing influence of government on the decision-making processes regarding the design and development of curricula.

7. Governmental strategies and curriculum innovation

Our overview of the developments in the governance of higher education systems during the 1970s and the 1980s indicates that both the strategy of rational planning and control, and the strategy of self-regulation can be found in higher education governance. The strategy of rational planning and control was definitely the dominant strategy of the 1970s and the first half of the 1980s. The second half of the 1980s shows the cautious rise of the strategy of self-regulation. And although it may still be too early to try to estimate its full effectiveness, the rise of this new strategy gives an important incentive to explore its repercussions.

Both in the strategy of rational planning and control and in the strategy of self-regulation, value is set on the innovative capacities of higher education systems. Higher education systems are expected to contribute to economic growth by providing scientific and technological breakthroughs as well as highly skilled professionals. Higher education systems are expected to perform the indispensable tasks of the most important societal innovator.

In the strategy of rational planning and control the assumption is that the innovative capacities of higher education institutions can be triggered by detailed regulations and comprehensive control mechanisms. In this strategy government sees it as its tasks to steer the higher education institutions towards specific innovations, using powerful instruments. Government sets the innovation priorities; the higher education institutions are expected to adopt and implement them.

In the strategy of self-regulation the assumption is that the enlargement of the institutional autonomy enables higher education institutions to adjust to, or even anticipate, changing societal needs. Higher education institutions are supposed to be able to initiate innovations themselves. Government only has the limited tasks of facilitating these innovations.

Both strategies are thought to be effective in producing a higher level of innovativeness in higher education systems. Both strategies are aiming for the same result. An important question is of course which of these two strategies is more successful. In the following chapter we will try to formulate a preliminary answer to this question.

Regarding the decision-making on higher education curricula we noted an increasing influence of government, both directly and indirectly. Government undeniably influences the orientation and contents of higher education curricula by various means. While it is true that the higher education institutions have managed to keep control over the quality of existing or future curricula in most of our higher education systems, they now have little control over the actual parameters which to a large extent influence the decision-making on these curricula. At institutional levels, innumerable examples can be found of public programmes carrying projects which, in a system solely dominated by the traditional values of higher education, would perhaps have had greater difficulty in obtaining institutional priority. One only has to think of the widespread incorporation of professional and technology-oriented courses in higher education, the new internal balance in a great many institutions between the respective places of 'academic' and 'professional' programmes, the considerable efforts made to recruit new clienteles (often via new courses), etc.

It also seems that with regard to influencing the design and development of higher education curricula, the traditional governmental strategy of rational planning and control prevails. Governments often see themselves as central actors able to steer the orientation and contents of curricula by means of detailed regulation, restricting forms of authorisation and targeted financial incentives.

However, there are also a few small indications found in this field which seem to point to the rise of the strategy of self-regulation. In Sweden, for instance, less governmental influence is reported on the contents of general study programmes (Bauer, 1988). In the Netherlands government has stated that it wants to abolish all regulation with regards to curricula. In this country, government will no longer formulate course requirements and will stop formalising study-programmes.

In the next chapter we will try to explore the effects of the two governmental strategies with respect to the innovation of curricula.

Chapter 4

GOVERNMENTAL STRATEGIES IN PRACTICE
Conclusions from the case-studies

Frans A. van Vught

1. Introduction

In this chapter we will try to systematically bring together and to interpret the findings of the three case-studies on governmental regulation and innovations of higher education curricula, which are presented in Part II of this book. We will relate these findings to the theoretical notions and the practical developments that have been presented in the first three chapters and will try to draw some empirically based conclusions.

In the last paragraphs of this chapter we take up the general question of the appropriateness of governmental instruments and strategies in the context of higher education. We will explore our empirical findings and finally we will sketch a broader picture which, in our opinion, offers an important challenge for higher education policy-making in the 1990s.

2. Innovations of curricula within higher education institutions

Our exploration of the theoretical and empirical literature (Chapter 2) taught us not only that innovations may arise easily and often in higher education institutions, but also that the diffusion of these innovations is sometimes hard to realise. We concluded that the fundamental characteristics of higher education institutions make these institutions in principle low in innovation resistance, especially when innovations are created at the bottom levels of the higher education system. But we also found that internally initiated innovations will only be successful when they are judged to be worthwhile by professional colleagues.

The case-study on the Federal Republic of Germany suggests some empirical support for these conclusions. In the study it is reported that many ambitious and impressive initiatives for innovations were found within the higher education institutions. The introduction of computer science courses and the development of interdisciplinary approaches appear to be particular innovations in German higher education curricula. And very often these innovations are the result of individual initiatives and the cooperation of faculty colleagues.

The innovation processes generally appear to take the form of changes in the *Studienplan* (in which the details of a curriculum are formulated by the faculty), the *Studienordnung* (in which the higher education institution describes the contents of a curriculum) and the *Prüfungsordnung* (in which the institution presents general information to the Ministry of the *Land*). Until 1985 the Ministries of the *Länder* were required to approve a *Studienordnung*. However, owing to a change in the federal *Hochschulrahmengesetz* this no longer is the case. The Ministries of the *Länder* have retained the authority to approve the *Prüfungsordnungen*.

This description already shows that in the Federal Republic of Germany the potential influence of the states (*Länder*) on innovations in the higher education system is substantial. They, in theory, have the possibility to approve or disapprove innovations by means of the *Prüfungsordnung*. In practice, innovations are reported to take place while avoiding or ignoring governmental regulations. Innovations are created within the boundaries of existing orders, by creatively interpreting orders or without seeking formal approval at all.

In France also higher education institutions appear to have an inclination towards innovations. The case-study on France offers several examples of successful innovation processes which were only possible because of the initiatives taken within the higher education institutions. Specific introduction courses and preparation programmes are designed and implemented to assist first year students with certain deficiencies. New courses and even completely new diplomas are developed to be able to explore new professional markets or to meet the needs of industry and/or the local and regional communities.

Although the French governmental strategy towards innovations in higher education is rather restrictive and centralised, it appears that higher education institutions (and especially groups of professional colleagues within these institutions) are nevertheless able to respond to new chances and circumstances. The professionals appear to use the small amount of autonomy which is given to them in the general governmental guidelines for the levels and the contents of study programmes (the *maquettes*) to design curricula which are directed towards felt needs and opportunities.

In the case-study on the Netherlands the innovations are called 'overwhelming'. Both the amount and the intensity of innovations are reported to be rather high. It also is concluded that, compared to most other Western European countries, the decision-making processes at Dutch universities are relatively decentralised and indicate rather limited managerial power at the central level. Taking into account that in this country the faculties have the final say about programmes and curricula (and that a large number of innovations were found) it may be concluded that the internal characteristics of higher education institutions make these institutions indeed inclined towards innovations.

Recently in the Netherlands a new governmental 'steering philosophy' has been developed which leaves the higher education institutions a larger autonomy to develop their own policies than ever before. This new steering philosophy will soon be fully implemented. Compared with the Federal Republic of Germany and France, the role of government in higher education has always been more limited in the Netherlands. However, the introduction of the new steering approach in 1985 means the complete abolition of all direct governmental supervision of curricula. The basic idea behind the new governmental attitude is that institutions of higher education can be expected to make intelligent and pertinent decisions concerning the processes and outcomes of teaching and research, and that therefore government should limit itself to 'steering from a distance'.

This new governmental attitude offers the higher education institutions the possibility to develop new courses and curricula according to their own insights and preferences, as long as they stay within the framework of their 'sectors'. These sectors are the broad substantial categories of fields of study that are assigned to the institutions by government.

It appears that the Dutch higher education institutions tend to be able to use the autonomy that is given to them. The de-regulation will enable the institutions to develop all kinds of administrative and organisational conditions that are supposed to be fruitful for specific curriculum innovations. Besides, the number and the intensity of the innovations may be expected to grow. It can be concluded that when higher education institutions are given more autonomy, they will indeed appear to be quite innovative.

3. Incremental and comprehensive innovations

Another conclusion drawn from the exploration of the literature (Chapter 2) concerned the character of the innovations in higher education institutions. It was assumed that these innovations would mainly be incremental adjustments, originating from developments in professional insights and opinions.

The case-study on the Federal Republic of Germany appears to endorse this statement. The initiatives for the innovation of curricula are mostly taken in dialogue between professional colleagues. The freedom of teaching which is ensured in the German *Grundgesetz* offers these professionals the basic authority to develop the curricula according to their insights. The processes of compromising and consensus-building between professional colleagues may be an important factor in explaining why innovations are, to a considerable extent, incremental adjustments of existing programmes.

It is also important to note, however, that the governmental regulations and especially the procedures of approval which are applied by the Ministries of the *Länder*, appear to encourage the professionals to try to design innovations that fit into the prevailing *Prüfungsordnungen*. The tendency to avoid paperwork and bureaucratic procedures appears to be an important incentive to develop innovations that are mainly adaptations of existing programmes. This of course does not mean that comprehensive innovations are absent. It only indicates a certain tendency towards incremental adjustments.

Important motives for the design of innovations are, on the hand, the perceived needs of industry and the perceived changes on the labour market. On the other hand the developments in science and technology are mentioned as crucial stimuli for innovations. Apparently the internal criteria of science still represent fundamental values when professionals design curricula in German higher education.

In some cases specific external incentives appear to be successful with regard to the creation of innovations. The expressed needs of specific industries and companies and the recommendations of national bodies (e.g. the *Verband Deutscher Elektrotechniker*) especially, appear to be able to incite professionals to design innovations. Occasionally an initiative of the *Facultätentag* (a joint meeting of faculties on the federal level) results in curriculum change.

The case-study on France also shows that initiatives to develop new programmes come to a large extent from the professional scholars within the institutions. In the French higher education system professional opinions about potential new markets for teaching and research and about the local and regional needs appear to be a basic drive in the attempts to develop new courses

Unlike the German study, the French study offers no clear indications that the innovations in the higher education institutions are mainly incremental adjustments. On the contrary, it appears that often completely new programmes are designed, which are rather different from previous programmes.

Also in the case-study on the Netherlands the innovations are mainly the result of the decisions and activities of the professionals within the higher education institutions. In the case-study it is reported that the professionals see themselves as a crucial innovative factor. In the Dutch case it appears to be mainly the internal scientific developments within the disciplines and professions that stimulate the professionals within the higher education institutions to adjust their courses and curricula. However, the changes on the labour market also appear to encourage professionals to create innovations in curricula.

In the Netherlands both incremental adjustments of existing programmes and completely new programmes can be found. The innovations certainly are not limited to small changes of existing programmes. New programmes are regularly designed and implemented.

The impression is that the more comprehensive innovations sometimes are created because of some special incentives provided by government. By using the approach of 'incentive steering' a government explicitly tries to stimulate innovations in certain disciplines or with respect to certain subjects. In the funding scheme specific governmental objectives are translated into rewards and sanctions for the higher education institutions, thus instigating them to create the innovations government judges to be necessary. On the other hand comprehensive innovations also appear to be realised when government does not appear on the scene.

4. The effects of forms of integration

In Chapter 2 (paragraph 4.1.2.) we hypothesised that the mechanisms of integration which can be found in a higher education system have an influence on the potential success of an externally induced innovation. Referring to Clark's distinction of bureaucratic, oligarchic, political and market integration we expected that every specific combination of forms of integration would appear to have its own set of constraining and facilitating factors with regard to innovations.

It appears to be very difficult to draw some clear and valid conclusions on this subject from the case-studies. Although differences between the German, French and Dutch combinations of forms of integration can certainly be seen, it nevertheless is difficult to relate specific innovation constraining and facilitating factors to these combinations.

The case-study on the Federal Republic of Germany underlines the importance of the academic chair in the German higher education system, and thus of the oligarchic form of integration that goes with it. At the same time the study makes it clear that the bureaucratic form of integration is also quite important. And, given the conditions of a bottom-heavy system as well as of a slowly growing openness to certain external needs, the mechanisms of political and market integration may also be expected to have their influences.

In France the emphasis must probably be put on the bureaucratic form of integration. Given the large amount of centralisation in the French higher education system and the amount of detailed regulation, this mechanism may be expected to dominate the combination of integrating forms. On the other hand, it should not be forgotten that in French higher education (as in French society in general) the politicisation of decision-making processes is large. French higher education may on all levels be seen as a composition of many interest groups, watching each other carefully and trying to distribute benefits to their own clienteles.

The Netherlands offers a picture of a careful balance of especially the oligarchic, political and bureaucratic forms of integration, while the influence of market integration is growing. The autonomy of academics is still widely respected in this country, but the democratisation reforms of the beginning of the 1970s have touched their authority. The governmental bureaucracy was, until recently, a crucial mechanism in Dutch higher education. The recent stepping-back of government, as well as the financial stringencies have created an increasing influence for the market form of integration.

Generally speaking, it may be expected that the German combination of forms of integration facilitates the processes of innovation at the lower levels of the higher education system, that the French combination facilitates innovations from the higher levels of the higher education system, and that the Dutch combination of forms of integration is somewhere in between. However, it would take a far more detailed analysis of some decision-making processes in higher education in each of these countries to formulate some more definite conclusions.

5. Academic disciplines and fields as social communities

Chapter 2 (paragraph 4.1.3.) also suggested that innovations in higher education can be studied as specific processes in disciplines and fields, when these are seen as social communities with their own identity, their own history, their own language and their own values and norms. From the work of Elzinga, Kogan, Henkel and others we deduced the assumption that the specific characteristics of a discipline or field might be important factors explaining the level of success or failure of an innovation.

Unfortunately it must again be concluded that the case-studies of Part II of this book do not offer enough detailed information to draw one or more conclusions on this subject. Moreover, the ways in which the case-studies were designed and performed do not seem to bring the detailed differences between academic fields as social communities easily to light.

The approach of analysing disciplines and fields as social communities opens up an important field of study in higher education. In our final paragraph we will combine this approach with the notion of ‘strategy-fit’ in the hope of indicating a fruitful perspective for further research.

6. Congruence with existing values and practices

In the second section of chapter 2 we explored some characteristics of the innovation itself, which may or may not be related to the success of an innovation. We will now make an inventory of the results of the three case-studies regarding these characteristics.

An important conclusion from the analysis of the theoretical and empirical literature was that a governmental approach will be more successful in creating innovations in higher education institutions when such a strategy is in congruence with existing values and practices in the higher education system.

In the Federal Republic of Germany the academic values and practices are widely respected. Von Humbolt's *Lehr- und Lernfreiheit* are still cornerstones of German academic life. However, in governmental policy-making towards higher education the respect for academic values and practices is combined with a rather extensive set of regulations. As was mentioned before, not only the approval procedures, but also the regulations concerning budgets and personnel at the level of the *Länder* make the governmental approach rather restrictive. It may be the case that, although the academic values and practices are respected, the present German governmental attitude nevertheless hampers the innovative capacity of the higher education institutions.

Another factor worth mentioning is the emphasis put on the comparability of programmes. In German higher education policy-making this comparability appears to be of great importance. In the sections 8 and 9 of the *Hochschulrahmengesetz* it is stipulated that the *Länder* must maintain a standard of comparability with regard to disciplines and programmes. Comparability is considered to be an important value, among other things because it is supposed the lead to quality and equality in the higher education system.

It is because of this emphasis on comparability that the *Länder* feel the responsibility to steer and coordinate the activities of the higher education institutions. However, as is indicated in the German case-study, it is questionable whether in practice they succeed in doing so. The basic elements of programmes may be comparable; the differences in the details of the programmes appear to be considerable.

The French case-study proves that the governmental approach to higher education in this country also corresponds with a value which appears to be deeply rooted in the French higher education culture. This value regards the idea that national diplomas meet national standards and, like in Germany, therefore provide equality and quality. Maybe this is the reason why in the French governmental strategy the emphasis is put on the use of rather restrictive instruments.

However, the conclusion can also be drawn that, because of this emphasis on national diplomas, the number of created innovations in curricula is probably smaller than it could have been when a governmental strategy of less restrictive instruments would have been applied. In the French case-study it is indicated that potential innovations are sometimes not realised because of the procedures used by government.

Except for the emphasis on national diplomas and standards the French case-study does not offer clear indications that the French governmental approach is in congruence with existing values and practices in the higher education system. On the contrary, the impression remains that, because of its rather formal character, the governmental strategy is at some distance from the academic values and practices. Perhaps this distance explains why the actors within the higher education institutions seem to be rather uncertain about the chances of approval for their proposals.

The case-study on the Netherlands illustrates that many Dutch scholars are of the opinion that by implementing its far-reaching reforms in the beginning of the 1980s the Dutch government has violated some of the basic academic values and practices. This also may explain why up until now mistrust and bitterness with regard to government is still found in the Dutch higher education institutions.

Generally, the new governmental approach is judged to be more in congruence with the existing values and practices in higher education. The emphasis on deregulation and dialogue is welcomed as an acknowledgement of the basic academic 'way of life' and the enlargement of the institutional autonomy is considered to have a positive influence on the academic forum. As far as this is concerned, the new Dutch governmental strategy towards higher education may be expected to be successful in creating innovations.

However, there is also criticism heard, especially with regard to the governmental approach of 'incentive-steering'. The incentives by government are judged to be too direct and to be too deeply penetrating. The present Dutch governmental strategy comes to the fore as a combination of two extremes. It only partly appears to be in congruence with existing values and practices.

Another conclusion from the exploration of the literature (Chapter 2) implied that a governmental policy towards the creation of a radical innovation in higher education can be successful when such a strategy addresses only a few subjects or a small number of institutions.

The case-study on Germany does not offer clear empirical observations which might be useful to discuss this statement. It is reported that apparently the *Länder* use their authority to approve the *Prüfungsordnungen* as an instrument to prioritise innovation proposals. Perhaps their policies could teach us something about the implementational aspects of radical innovations. Unfortunately these policies could not be studied.

The French case-study also does not enable us to confront the statement about radical innovations with clear empirical observations. In France the governmental strategy towards innovations in higher education is above all a national, centralised and highly formalised strategy. From the information gathered in the French case-study no definite conclusions can be drawn regarding the efforts of government to stimulate certain areas or to influence particular institutions.

However, it has been suggested that the Ministry of Education uses the so-called *Carte de Formation Superieures et de la Recherche* to judge the relevance of the institutions' proposals for curriculum innovation. This Carte is a kind of implicit plan which is designed and revised by the Ministry and which offers a framework to set governmental priorities in terms of perceived national and regional needs. It may be that this instrument is used as suggested in the conclusion drawn from the literature. Unfortunately, as was indicated previously, the French case-study does not provide enough detailed information to draw clear conclusions.

In the study on the Netherlands it is shown that the Dutch government has been rather successful in the implementation of some relatively far-reaching reforms. The introduction of the two-tier structure of university study programmes, the establishment of the system of 'conditional research financing', the comprehensive merger operation of the schools for higher vocational training (*hoger beroepsonderwijs*) and extreme retrenchment operations in the universities are all reforms initiated (and sometimes extorted) by government. These 'corrective policies' may have been successful because government has limited itself to one policy at the time and has not tried to combine all reforms into one comprehensive approach. Nevertheless, it may also be noted that these reforms (and especially the severe budget-cuts) have created mistrust and bitterness in the higher education system. Many actors within the higher education institutions are not convinced of the sincereness of the attempts of government to follow-up these 'corrective policies' with the 'facilitating' approach of 'steering from a distance'.

The present Dutch governmental attitude seems to take the idea of the limited breadth of innovations to heart. The general strategy of deregulation is combined with the introduction of the instrument of the 'mission budget' which is supposed to be used for the encouragement of non-conventional innovations. By reserving a small percentage of the total budget for specific new targets, government hopes to be able to stimulate some extra innovations in the system.

Unfortunately, so far the Dutch government has not yet developed the instrument of the mission-budget in operational terms. The Dutch experiences with 'incentive steering' indicate that this instrument may to a certain extent prove to be effective. Innovations tend to follow government's stimulating efforts. On the other hand these incentives also bring about reactions of mistrust and aloofness.

7. Profitability

Another conclusion from the literature underlined the importance in a governmental policy of the profitability of an innovation for those who are supposed to develop it.

The case-study on the Federal Republic of Germany does not present this issue as something of extreme importance. It is reported in the study that the *Länder* try to stimulate innovation processes through some extra funding. On the other hand it is also concluded that the annual budgets are fossilised because large proportions are allocated by means of the contracts with the professorial chairs. This implies that only a small part of the budget is available for the stimulation of innovations.

The contracts with the professorial chairs are a characteristic aspect of German higher education policy-making. These contracts are used to decide about the allocation of budgets and staff to a specific chair. A crucial implication of this approach is that a reallocation of resources is only possible when a chair becomes vacant.

The issue of the profitability of an innovation apparently is not considered to be fundamental in German higher education policy-making. So far it has not inspired policy-makers to try to change the fossilised budgets and to apply the innovation-oriented instruments of financial incentive.

The case-study on French higher education shows that the governmental approach towards higher education in this country can be characterised to a certain extent as an approach of profitability. The combination of a specific approval-procedure (*habilitation*) and the provision of extra funding for programmes approved with the national diploma, works as an effective incentive for the higher education institutions to design and implement new national diploma programmes. In the French case-study several examples of such innovations are given.

However, the case-study also shows that the *habilitation*-procedure destroys initiatives for curriculum innovations. When proposals do not receive the national diploma status and therefore are not rewarded with extra funding, higher education institutions are forced to try to develop them as university programmes, which often results in forgetting about them altogether. Moreover, proposals are sometimes not developed because the actors within the institutions are pessimistic about their chances to obtain approval by the Ministry. Apparently the centralised and restrictive governmental strategy is only partially successful in addressing the higher education institutions in terms of profitability.

The case-study on the Netherlands offers some clear examples of the use of the idea of profitability in the governmental approach towards higher education. Especially the emphasis on financial incentives shows that the Dutch government intends to address the higher education institutions in terms of profitability. The positive and negative incentives which are used by government to stimulate innovations are considered to be powerful mechanisms of change.

In practice these governmental instruments appear to be rather effective in creating innovations. The governmental contracts and transfers appear to be attractive for higher education institutions. Often these institutions are willing to develop the innovations the incentives try to create.

However, it should also be noted that the incentives are not always understood and that, when they are understood, their effects are sometimes limited because of their prospective discontinuity. Besides, when the incentives are too widely used, or are judged to be too restrictive, the scholars within the higher education institutions regularly decide to ignore them, arguing that it should not be the Minister of Education and Science who decides which innovations are important or necessary, but the academic professionals themselves.

8. Complexity

Regarding the complexity of the innovation, we expected a negative relationship between the level of complexity (defined as the combination of the degree to which an innovation is a departure from existing values and practices with the number of functional areas aimed at by the innovation) and the rate of adoption of an innovation. The more complex an innovation, the less successful that innovation was expected to be in getting adopted.

The German case-study does not offer a clear empirical indication on this subject. The general outcome of the study that many innovations are initiated by individual professionals and in cooperation at the faculty level, and that these innovations more often than not are created within existing frameworks, suggest that the level of complexity of these innovations is not extremely high. Taking into account that apparently many of these innovations are adopted, we may with some prudence conclude that the theoretical expectation is endorsed.

The case-study on France taught us that rather comprehensive innovations that imply important departures from existing practices, are possible in French higher education. Although in this study also, a detailed analysis has not been possible, the impression is that the general theoretical expectation regarding the relationship between the level of complexity of an innovation and its rate of adoption may be falsified.

The case-study on the Netherlands also shows the actual occurrence of innovations which are not only minor. In this study it is reported that the governmental approach of 'incentive steering' is used with mixed success, in the sense that the development of new programmes sometimes does not succeed because of the mistrust within the institutions. An explanation of such a failure can perhaps be found in the level of complexity of the innovation.

9. Observability

The level of observability of an innovation was not judged to be an important factor for the success or failure of an innovation. Rather, we expected this variable to be strategically related to the compatibility and the profitability of an innovation.

Although this issue does not appear to be of great importance in the three reports, the three case-studies provide no reasons for changing the theoretical expectation. An interesting observation in this context is the inclination at the lower levels of the higher education system in the Federal Republic of Germany to minimise the visibility of an innovation that might be judged to exceed the boundaries of existing *Prüfungsordnungen*.

10. Triability

Regarding the concept of triability our exploration of the literature suggested that a governmental strategy is more successful in creating innovations in higher education institutions when in such a strategy attention is paid to the idea of experimentation on a small scale and within a limited time span.

The German case-study reports of experiments, undertaken by some of the *Länder*, with subjects such as a more global budget allocation, a certain amount of deregulation and a change of institutional management structures. It is not clear whether these experiments have also been undertaken to try to create more fruitful conditions for curriculum innovation. Unfortunately we do not have enough information on this matter to draw an empirically based conclusion.

The case-study on France makes it clear that the idea of triability does not play a significant role in the innovation processes in French higher education. The French governmental strategy appears to be too formalised and too regulated to leave room for such experimentation.

The case-study on the Netherlands shows that already in the previous

Dutch legislation the idea of triability was incorporated. If a new field of study was suggested by a higher education institution, the Minister of Education and Science usually approved an experimental phase of 5 to 10 years, after which a final decision was taken.

The present governmental steering conception puts the responsibility for new courses and curricula to a large extent in the hands of the institutions. It is also for the institutions to decide whether they want to experiment with certain innovations before taking a final decision. It may be expected that the higher education institutions will increasingly recognise the advantages of the idea of triability. Confronted with a lump-sum funding and urged to develop their own missions and priorities the institutions will probably incorporate the idea of triability in their policy-processes.

To some extent the idea of triability can also be found in the Dutch governmental approach of incentive steering. The positive incentives provided by government are all temporary. After a certain period the innovations which are stimulated by these incentives are expected to be evaluated. The higher education institutions are then confronted with the decision to take over these innovations using whatever financial resources they might have, or to abandon them. As is indicated in the Dutch case study, this prospect of financial discontinuity appears to limit the effectiveness of the incentive instruments. The higher education institutions do not always want to take the risk of an uncertain future to gain some temporary rewards.

11. Mildly restrictive or firmly compulsive instruments?

In Chapter 1 we presented in some detail the various instruments governments may use when they set themselves the task to influence parts of society. A crucial question which so far has not been answered is of course what instruments may be expected to be successful when government wants to stimulate or create innovations of curricula in higher education.

After discussing the fundamental characteristics of higher education institutions (paragraph 3 of Chapter 2) we suggested that an extreme restriction of the behaviour of professional scholars in higher education institutions may create disillusion and apathy in these institutions. The hypothesis that may be derived from that discussion is that a governmental strategy will be more successful in creating innovations when this strategy is a combination of mildly restrictive instruments rather than of extreme compulsive instruments. What do the three case-studies teach us on this matter?

The case-study on the Federal Republic of Germany makes it clear that in this country a large amount of governmental regulations exists, but that these regulations also leave room for innovative initiatives by the higher education institutions. An important question is whether the governmental regulations should or should not be regarded as an obstacle to innovations in the higher education system.

At the federal level the *Hochschulrahmengesetz* contains general regulations about the form and contents of programmes and courses. Also, general regulations for the development of curricula are given by the *Gemeinsame Kommission für die Koordinierung von Studium und Prüfung*. This committee is a cooperative effort of the standing conference of the Ministers of the eleven *Länder* and of the *Westdeutsche Rektorenkonferenz* (which is a buffer-organisation consisting of representatives of universities, institutions of higher vocational education and colleges of arts). It provides both general regulation (*Algemeine Bestimmungen für Diplomprüfungs-ordnungen*) and regulations directed towards disciplines (*Rahmenordnungen für die Diplomprüfung im Studiengang*). At the level of the *Länder* the regulations concern the *Prüfungsordnungen* (which need the approval of the Ministry of a *Land*) as well as the budget-allocations and the personnel policies.

Although the approval procedures could be classified as mild instruments of authority, it should also be pointed out that the combination of these instruments with decisions on budget-allocation and personnel makes the governmental strategy at the level of the *Länder* rather restrictive. As is reported in the case-study, the professionals within the higher education institutions try to avoid these governmental regulations by developing innovations that fit within already approved programmes. The conclusion may be that the governmental strategy at the level of the *Länder* apparently is perceived as an obstacle for comprehensive innovations in higher education.

Regarding the hypothesis that a governmental strategy of mildly restrictive instruments is more successful in creating innovations than a strategy of extreme compulsive instruments, the French case-study also offers some interesting empirical observations.

It should be noted that the French governmental attitude towards higher education in general is rather interventionistic. The *Loi Savary*, which since 1984 is the central law concerning higher education in France, contains several provisions that indicate a strong preoccupation with the desire to steer the higher education system. This interventionistic attitude can clearly be recognised with regard to the subject of curriculum innovations.

The various instruments which are used by the French government to create innovations indicate that the overall governmental strategy is rather restrictive. The *habilitation* which is an authoritive declaration by government about the acceptability of a programme as a national diploma, may as such perhaps be classified as a rather mild instrument of authority, but the fact that only programmes that have received this certificate are eligible for extra funding makes it clear that government has an effective instrument at its disposal to influence the behaviour of the higher education institutions. Also the *Arretés* (rules and orders) in which government has indicated the minimum standards and contents of course-programmes appear to have a very restrictive effect on the behaviour of the higher education institutions. The *maquettes*, which describe the contents of a programme, are especially experienced as rather mandatory. Besides, the facts that nearly all funds are earmarked and that personnel policies are completely centralised make it clear that government has a strong influence on the higher education system.

It may be concluded from the case-study on France that the innovations of the higher education institutions in this country are to a large extent regulated by government. It may be true that the *Loi Savary* provides the institutions with the right to deliver their own university diplomas (not considered to be national diplomas), but these university diplomas are not entitled to extra governmental funding. It is not surprising, therefore, that the involvement of the institutions with these diplomas is minimal and that most efforts to innovate are directed towards the acquisition of the status of a national diploma.

The French governmental strategy of rather restrictive instruments can be judged to impede the innovative capacity of the higher education institutions in this country. The case-study makes it clear that the higher education institutions experience this strategy as a unnecessary imposition of regulations. They apparently feel obliged to follow these regulations and by doing so feel limited in exploring innovative possibilities. The fact that the partial deregulation of the *maquettes* has been welcomed as an opportunity to develop specific curriculum innovations, is a clear indication that a less restrictive governmental strategy might lead to a larger number of innovations.

In the Netherlands the introduction of the strategy of 'steering from a distance' is a major change in the governmental attitude towards higher education. Instead of traditional detailed rules and orders this new strategy promises a more global form of steering and emphasises 'dialogue'. As regards this dialogue, both the Ministry of Education and Science and the higher education institutions each produce their own policy-plans, which are used in mutual discussions to reach conclusions on policy-decisions and budget-allocations.

As is shown in the case-study on the Netherlands, the Dutch government has decided to concentrate on the instruments of information and financial incentives, instead of on the traditional instruments of authority. Approval procedures, constraints and earmarked budgets are largely abandoned. Rather, government invites the institutions to accept and use their widened responsibilities. The funding takes place by means of a lump-sum.

But government also tries to influence the behaviour of the higher education institutions. The financial instruments especially appear to be used to get the institutions to behave according to the wishes of government. Contracts are offered to create certain programmes; transfers are promised when certain innovations are realised. The instruments of 'cheque book government' (Hood, 1983) are clearly introduced as a supplement to dialogue and deregulation.

At the same time the Dutch government has introduced a system of quality control, consisting of visiting committees of peers, a higher education inspectorate and in the near future probably the use of performance indicators. The objective of the introduction of this system is to supply the necessary information for both system-wide and institution-oriented policy and budget-decisions.

In the case-study on the Netherlands the new governmental strategy is characterised as 'semi-structured'. The core elements of the withdrawal from detailed supervision and the introduction of lump-sum funding are supplemented by incentive steering and the launching of a nation-wide quality control system. This semi-structured strategy is received by the higher education institutions with a combination of enthusiasm and scepticism. The enthusiasm concerns the enlargement of the institutional autonomy. The scepticism goes back to the mistrust and bitterness because of the 'corrective' measures government undertook before the present strategy was introduced.

It may be concluded that the new Dutch governmental strategy towards higher education is a combination of, on the one hand, instruments that are hardly restrictive at all (the instruments of information) and on the other hand, instruments that can be very restrictive (the instruments of financial incentive). Through both these categories of instruments the Dutch government tries to stimulate the innovative capacity of the higher education institutions. From the reactions of the professionals within the institutions, as reported in the case-study, the conclusion may be drawn that the strategy does not hamper the innovative capacity of the higher education system. Leaving scepticism aside, it may even be expected that the strategy might be able to stimulate and enlarge the innovative capacity. However, no final conclusion can be drawn, since the experiences with this new strategy are still quite limited.

The three case-studies appear to endorse the hypothesis that a governmental strategy will be more successful in creating innovations when such a strategy is a combination of mildly restrictive, rather than of extreme compulsive instruments. The fundamental characteristics of the higher education institutions appear to add up to a context in which government cannot execute compulsive actions without also bringing about some negative side-effects of these actions. This brings us back to the general question whether the strategy of rational planning and control or the strategy of self-regulation is the most appropriate when the objective is to enlarge the number of innovations in higher education.

12. Which strategy?

In Chapter 3 we noticed that both the strategy of rational planning and control, and the strategy of self-regulation are relevant approaches to the basic objective set by many governments in the Western world. To be able to contribute to economic growth, the higher education system is expected to provide scientific and technological breakthroughs, and to train highly skilled professionals for future positions on the labour market. The higher education system is expected to be excellent and innovative and government wants to stimulate this innovativeness. For doing so government can, generally speaking, make a choice between the more or less traditional strategy of rational planning and control, and the newly developing strategy of self-regulation.

Throughout this book we have indicated that the two governmental strategies vary in a rather fundamental way with regards to the assumptions they are based on. The strategy of rational planning and control is founded on the basic assumption of the rationalist perspective on decision-making. In every practical decision-making situation it strives after the objective of trying to select the best alternative from a set that should be as complete as possible. But confronted with the limitations of this ideal, in practice the strategy of rational planning and control also denies the ideal of a 'community of discourse' which should lead to a sincere consensus regarding the selection of the best alternative (see paragraph 3.2 of Chapter 1) and it takes its refuge in confidence in a strong centralisation of decision-making processes and a large amount of control over these decision-making processes as well as over the implementation of the chosen policy.

The instruments that appear to be most closely related to the strategy of rational planning and control are the highly restrictive instruments of authority and the instruments of treasure. Both these categories of instruments are used in this strategy to control the behaviour of non-governmental actors in such a way that they comply with the objectives set by government.

The strategy of self-regulation is based on the cybernetic perspective on decision-making. It tries to make use of the self-regulatory capacities of decentralised decision-making units. It limits the role of government to the monitoring of a set of 'critical variables' and to the analysis and, if judged necessary, the influencing of the framework of rules guiding the behaviour of decentralised actors.

In this strategy the appropriate instruments are the instruments of information and the mildly restrictive instruments of authority. The indirect instruments of treasure may be used in this strategy to influence the behavioural patterns of self-regulating actors ('incentive steering').

It may be hypothesised from the case-studies that, when the basic objective is to stimulate the innovativeness of the higher education institutions, the strategy of rational planning and control, generally speaking, is less successful than the strategy of self-regulation. The strategy of rational planning and control appears to be based on assumptions that are at odds with some of the fundamental characteristics of higher education institutions. The strategy of rational planning and control ignores the fundamental features of higher education that are found in characteristics like the high level of professional autonomy, the large organisational fragmentation and the large diffusion of the decision-making power.

The strategy of self-regulation appears to be better suited to the context of higher education. It acknowledges the fundamental characteristics of higher education institutions and it tries to make use of some of these characteristics to stimulate the innovativeness of the whole system of higher education. By limiting itself to only global forms of steering and by putting its confidence in the self-regulatory capacities of the professionals and the basic units of the higher education institutions, this strategy has the potential to become an effective approach to reach the basic objective of many Western nations.

The case-studies of Part II seem to underline this general hypothesis. It may be assumed that, of the approaches taken by the governments of the three countries studied, the national, centralised and highly formalised approach of the French government comes the closest to the general strategy of rational planning and control. On the other hand, it may be expected that the new, decentralised Dutch governmental approach of 'steering from a distance' is most akin to the general strategy of self-regulation. The German governmental approach may be assumed to take an in-between position.

The case-study on France suggests that, although innovations of curricula can certainly be found in this country, the number of actually created innovations is probably less than it could have been when the governmental policies would be less restrictive and less centralised. Apparently potential innovations are not realised because the professionals within the higher education institutions are not always able or willing to accept the conditions set by the governmental strategy. The case-study on the Netherlands illustrates that a decentralised and less formalised governmental approach is judged to be more in congruence with the values and practices of higher education. The professionals tend to welcome such a strategy and they seem to accept the challenge to create innovations within its broad and mildly restrictive framework.

However, the study on the Netherlands also makes it clear that the use of the instruments of treasure in the strategy of self-regulation may create inverted effects. The approach of positive or negative incentive steering may lead to reactions of mistrust, apathy and bitterness. The professionals may wonder whether government is not really using the strategy of rational planning, while only pretending to prefer the strategy of self-regulation. As can be seen from the present situation in the Netherlands, especially when recently some far-reaching reforms have been implemented, such mistrust arises easily.

This leads to the conclusion that in the context of higher education, the influencing of the 'rules of the game', as part of the strategy of self-regulation, should be executed with great prudence and reserve. The professionals within the higher education institutions are extremely sensitive to a superfluous use of power, especially regarding the subjects upon which they think themselves best to be able to decide. When one wants to make use of the self-regulatory capacities of the decentralised decision-making units in a system of higher education, one has to be careful not to destroy these capacities by trying to impose upon the professionals within the system a set of rules which is experienced as being to a large extent at odds with the fundamental system characteristics.

13. Strategy fit, market-coordination and enlightened oversight

With respect to higher education Clark (1983b) especially has asked the question of 'governance fit': 'What governance arrangements are "naturally" generated? What structures of governance help this or that function to operate well? What governance "fits"?' (Clark, 1983b, 27). The author comes to the conclusion that 'fit is a matter of balance among alternative forms for effecting national governance. Too much emphasis in any one direction, for example on state command, produces an imbalance that leads to a "fit" in a different meaning of the term! - a sudden and violent attack of a disorder, a convulsion, an exacerbation of troubles perhaps leading to prolonged sickness' (Clark, 1983b, 27).

It seems that we have been exploring an issue which is very much related to Clark's question of governance fit. More or less like Clark we have asked which governmental strategy fits a higher education system when the basic objective is to stimulate the innovativeness of that system. Our conclusion was that the strategy of self-regulation appears to fit better than the strategy of rational planning and control. At the same time we warned against the use of government instruments that may be judged to be too restrictive in the eyes of the professional actors in a higher education system. We suggested a prudent and reserved use of the instruments of treasury.

Clark argues that differentiation should be the name of the governance game in higher education. He indicates (among other things) that diverse structures accommodate the conflicting tasks of higher education better than simple structures, that diverse structures allow status differentiation and sector diversification and that diverse structures stimulate flexibility and innovation (Clark, 1983b, 31-37). Along the same lines we have tried to show that the strategy of self-regulation (because of its foundation in the cybernetic perspective on decision-making) offers the advantages of flexibility and innovation, of experimenting and robustness, of self-determination and responsibility. At the same time this strategy is relatively low in the costs of information, transaction and administration.

The crucial problems with which the strategy of rational planning and control is confronted in higher education can to a large extent be carried back to the basic differences between this general strategy and the fundamental characteristics of the higher education context. The adherents of the rational planning model tend to see higher education more as an object than as a complex set of subjects (Trow, 1980; Neave, 1985). Besides, they see a higher education system as an object which can be controlled from outside and which can be moulded to the wishes of society and/or government.

It is not surprising therefore that the strategy of rational planning and control sometimes degenerates into a condition of 'policy extravagance' (Lane and Fredriksson, 1983, 242). The authors just mentioned offer a clear illustration of such a case. The Swedish U68 Commission proposed in its 1973 report to bring all existing Swedish institutes of higher education (including all universities) together under the label of *Högskola*. However, in its extreme self-confidence, believing itself to be able to completely reshape and control the Swedish higher education system, the commission overlooked the obvious reaction of the established institutions that such a reform would imply an 'institutional descent'. And the commission was confronted with the rejection of a parliamentary commission, appointed to screen all the U68 Commission proposals, to accept the new label (Lane and Fredrikson, 1983, 243).

The strategy of rational planning and control puts its confidence in centralisation and a large amount of control. But by doing so, it alienates itself from a societal sector like higher education, which above all else is characterised by a large amount of autonomy and differentiation. Speaking of the 'unitary approach' Clark (1983b) formulates the same conclusion: 'Surely what we fear most about the unitary approach is the way it cramps a multiplicity of approaches and increases the likelihood of the arbitrary dictate and the large error. Nearly every time we plan centrally we eliminate some options of the operators. In each reform we add structures that constrain future choices. If we do not want things to escape our eyes, we systemise some more, generating a rule book that clogs formal channels and in turn stimulates underground activity for getting things done' (Clark, 1983b, 38).

It should not be surprising that the strategy of rational planning and control cannot be called a good fit for an innovation-oriented higher education system. The strategy of rational planning and control overlooks the crucial issue of the costs of acquiring knowledge for the sake of creating innovations. It forgets that in a multi-level system general knowledge is usually more economically acquired by higher level decision-making units, while specific knowledge is more easily and more cheaply acquired by lower level units. And it forgets that, by introducing rigid and detailed procedures of hierarchical control, it cuts itself off from the possible knowledge advantages of the lower level decision-making units and thereby loses a large innovative potential. '. . . . the effectiveness of hierarchical subordination varies with the extent to which the subordinate unit has knowledge advantages over the higher unit. In those cases where the subordinate unit has better information, then in terms of the whole decision-making process the knowledge is one place and the power is another; the quality of decisions suffers as a result. Moreover, subordination itself becomes illusory to the extent that the lower level unit can use its knowledge to evade, counteract, or redirect the thrust of orders from its nominal superiors' (Sowell, 1980, 13, 14).

Compared to the strategy of rational planning and control, the strategy of self-regulation seems to offer a better fit. This strategy seems to be better equipped to be used as a general incitement towards innovations in a higher education system. It addresses these systems while taking their fundamental characteristics seriously. It leaves sufficient room for the (semi-)autonomous professionals and basic units and it does not try to coordinate the large variety of a higher education system in a limited set of rules.

Referring to some of the recent changes in higher education governance in Western Europe (see paragraph 2 of Chapter 3), Neave (1988a) sums up some advantages government may try to secure by introducing the strategy of self-regulation in higher education: 'By devolving the responsibility for deciding how overall systems objectives are to be attained, down to the level of the individual establishment, a number of advantages are secured: first, debate is diffused away from the centre and forced to concentrate on the implications it holds for the individual university; second, by creating greater 'tactical latitude', a greater degree of initiative may be stimulated, with the result (hopefully) that the particular university will look to its own efforts rather than seek guidance and interpretation from central government; and third, such a system will give rise to the ability of individual universities - and thus, at an aggregate level, the whole higher education system - to undertake 'fine tuning' in response to local or regional circumstances, in response to changes in both the national and regional labour markets' (Neave, 1988a, 13, 14). Broadening the concept of innovation a little to include a high level of flexibility, adaptivity and robustness, the advantages of the strategy of self-regulation may be thought to cumulate in an increase of the innovativeness of a higher education system. By enlarging the autonomy of the higher education institutions and by limiting itself to monitoring some 'critical' system variables and to (not too often and not too drastically) adapting some general 'rules of the game', government may have found in the strategy of self-regulation an important approach which may both stimulate the innovativeness of the higher education system and secure its basic values and practices.

An important question which remains to be answered, is the one regarding the relationship between the strategy of self-regulation and the mechanism of market-coordination. Concerning the mechanism of market-coordination in higher education the opinions (and emotions) appear to differ widely. There are those who argue that the market offers a crucial mechanism for the development of a higher education system. And there are those who point out that the market cannot be applied to higher education.

To let the opponents of the market come first, let us cite Breneman (1981) who argues that a pure form of market-coordination cannot exist in higher education because of the following reasons:

'- The 'firms' in this industry are not seeking to maximize profits or to minimize costs for a given level of activity . . . .
- The educational services produced by colleges and universities are not priced to the student at marginal cost, average cost, or even full cost . . . .
- The information available to students about colleges can hardly be considered complete (or even adequate) in many cases . . . .
- Some firms in this industry (the state institutions) receive substantial public subsidies, whereas comparable firms (the independent institutions)

do not.' (Breneman, 1981, 25).

Although these arguments do not all have to be completely accepted, it must be concluded that the author has a point: it will be very difficult, if possible, to install a completely market-driven higher education system, even in a country like the United States.

However, the question remains whether the market should be rejected as a mechanism of coordination and development in higher education. The economist Stigler (1984) argues that this should not be the case. He even makes a plea to reconsider the similarities between higher education and the market system. ' . . . . there is a . . . . powerful reason the intellectual might be sympathetic to the marketplace: the organising principles of both areas are the same. An enterprise system is a system of voluntary contract. Neither fraud nor coercion is within the ethics of the market system. Indeed, there is no possibility of coercion in a pure enterprise system because the competition of rivals provides alternatives to every buyer and seller . . . . The intellectual world . . . . is also a voluntary system. Its central credo is that opinions are to be formed from free discussion on the basis of full disclosure of evidence. Fraud and coercion are equally repugnant to the scholar. Freedom of thought is preserved by the open competition of scholars and ideas. Authority, the equivalent of monopoly power, is the great enemy of freedom of inquiry . . . . Just as real markets have some fraud and monopoly, which impair the claims for the marketplace, so the intellectual world has its instances of coercion and deception, with the coercion exercised by claques and fashion. But again these deviants are outside the logic of the system. Both areas, moreover, are democratic. The intellectual believes that every willing and able young person should get a good education whatever his race or financial background. The market believes that every willing and able person should be permitted to enter an industry or occupation, whatever his race or educational background . . . . The analogies could be pursued much further . . . . I shall merely mention, in passing, that both fields pay a fair amount of attention to packaging and advertising, and both fields place an absurdly high value on originality. There are also many minor differences . . . . The basic fact is that the intellectual believes in the free market in ideas and, what is not quite the same thing, in words' (Stigler, 1984, 145-147).

Stigler's argumentation is convincing. But nevertheless (as Stigler himself indicates) we should not close our eyes to possible deficiencies of real market processes in higher education. And it is especially in the context of the strategy of self-regulation that we should be aware of them.

Some of these deficiencies are already being reported as an artefact of the growing importance of the strategy of self-regulation in Western

Europe. In Sweden the increase of the responsiveness of higher education institutions to certain profitable market-needs has led the student associations in this country to formulate an official protest. 'The business ambitions of the institutions are, according to the students, too outspoken. The students claim that the general study programmes on undergraduate level are treated unfairly when the institutions are eager to sell in-service training or further vocational training to companies and enterprises' (Askling, 1988, 5).

In a more general sense, 'vocationalism' (Williams, 1985) or 'vocational shift' (Youll and Brennan, 1988) appears to be an important side-effect of an increasing influence of the mechanism of market-coordination (see also; Boyer and Martin, 1985). Youll and Brennan point out that both in curricula and in research programmes a move can be observed 'towards applied areas in order to win the funds available'. The combination of tight financial budgets and the increase of autonomy may incite individuals and groups in higher education institutions to accept a growing influence of external criteria, leading among other things, to changes in curricula. 'For the most part they do not derive from clearly formulated institutional policies but are opportunistic as staff individuals and departments collectively pursue what they see as their best interests' (Youll and Brennan, 1988, 205).

Vocational shift is an indicator of what Kogan (1988) has indicated as 'the movement from the classic autonomous model towards the responsive, dependent model of the institution's relationship with the society which sustains it' (Kogan, 1988, 14). The rise of the strategy of self-regulation brings an increase of the number of innovations in a higher education system, but it also may bring the retreat of the internalist theory of knowledge (Merton, 1973) in favour of a growing influence of external sponsors, who might (in the extreme case) define the criteria for determining the contents of the processes of teaching and research.

In the United Kingdom higher education institutions are found to be on the move from the classical autonomous position to a position which is more responsive to the external environment. A study undertaken by the Department of Government at Brunel University of the developments in undergraduate teaching in nine British universities and polytechnics concludes that higher education institutions 'are being forced to adjust to changes in the environment. As the need to find sources of external funding increases, higher education institutions tend to become more outward looking, to recognise the influence of the consumer and to identify potential sources of finance. In addition, the higher education institution is responding to external pressures to establish more managerial, central modes of working' (Kogan and Youll, 1988, 165). Another important conclusion from this study is that higher education institutions respond differently to external pressures, depending on their status and history (Kogan and Youll, 1988, 174). This finding underlines the importance of the hypothesis (mentioned in Chapter 2) on the differences in the level of responsiveness of academic disciplines and fields to external influences. This hypothesis suggests that the level of responsiveness will be higher, the less disciplines and fields have developed their paradigms, the less they rely on exclusive languages and techniques and the less clear they are about their criteria of determining academic merit (Henkel, 1988, 185).

The hypothesis on responsiveness to external influences and temptations points to a crucial area of research on the boundaries between higher education studies and the 'science of science'. From the perspective of developing approaches and policies that may be assumed to stimulate excellence and innovativeness in higher education, it would be extremely interesting and relevant to find out how different disciplines and fields in different contexts react to their environment. A special focus could be directed towards the interplay of social (external) and cognitive (internal) factors (Rip, 1981) and to the processes of both academic drift (the tendency in higher education institutions to converge upon the university as the perceived ideal) and epistemic drift ('the phenomenon whereby external pressures and norms begin to take the place of internal cultural values and norms within scientific communities') (Elzinga, 1987, 11, 114-15). This is not the place to develop such a research programme in detail. However, it may be noticed that a further differentiation of the question of 'strategy fit' will be possible when a broader and more detailed knowledge can be acquired about the level of responsiveness of a variety of disciplines and fields in a variety of contexts.

Let us finally return to the issue of market-coordination within the strategy of self-regulation.

An extreme movement in higher education to the responsive, dependent model and a too heavy emphasis on vocationalism must be considered as negative side-effects of an increasing influence of the market. It is for this reason that, next to the preservation of the freedom of open competition of scholars and ideas (which, as Stigler notices, to a large extent is similar to the freedom from fraud and coercion in a market system) the guarding of academic righteousness becomes an important aspect of a governmental strategy towards higher education. A choice for the strategy of self-regulation should not imply a choice for abandoning the academic values and practices that have brought about so many insights and inventions. Also, for the sake of stimulating the innovativeness of higher education, the 'rules of the game' should be designed in such a way that the decentralised decision-making units are not tempted to slip away into opportunism and short-term profit seeking. While the strategy of self-regulation leaves more room for coordination and development by the mechanism of market-coordination, it also calls for what Clark has called 'enlightened oversight' by government (Clark, 1983b, 36). The true challenge for governmental policy-making in higher education in the 1990s is to give shape to such a broad and general, but also effective and legitimised, enlightened oversight.

PART II

CASE STUDIES

Chapter 5

GOVERNMENT AND CURRICULUM INNOVATION IN THE FEDERAL REPUBLIC OF GERMANY

Olaf mc-Daniel, Pierre Gauye and Jacques Guin

1. Introduction

In the field study in the Federal Republic of Germany (FRG), only two of the more than sixty universities were visited. Just two out of eleven *Länder* (states) were involved (Baden-Württenberg and Nordrhein-Westfalen), which implies that in a country in which the *Länder*-policy is highly influential on higher education only a minority of governmentalinstitutions was visited.

All three institutions that operate on the federal level - the Federal Ministry of Education and Science, the Standing Conference of *Länder* Ministers of Education (KMK), and the West-German Rectors' Conference, were incorporated in the case study.

Taking into consideration that only a fraction of the whole system was studied, the findings of this study must be presented with caution. Especially in the Federal Republic of Germany with its independant *Länder*, a wide variety of state regulations and policy-practice can be identified. The validity and representative value, in a statistical and methodological sense, of this study is therefore limited. The results can not be regarded as representative of the day to day policies of all the universities and government institutions.

Also, no institutes of higher vocational education were visited or taken into consideration in the questions that were adressed to the governmental bodies.

Nevertheless, the findings in this chapter reflect on issues that are in the spotlight in the present debates on higher education issues. The findings and analysis, as well as the suggestions for discussion, will, it is hoped, be of help in the future processes of orientation and policy development.

2. Governmental regulations with respect to higher education

2.1. *Federal and state regulations*

The higher education system in the Federal Republic of Germany is, so far as curriculum regulation is concerned, regulated to a high extent. There are regulations on the federal level and on the state level.

On the federal level, the *Hochschulrahmengesetz* (HRG), embodies the framework of the legislation of all eleven *Länder*. It contains general regulations on for example the issues of studies and teaching, research, admission, participation, staff policy, organisation and administration.

In section 8 of the HRG, institutions of higher education are given a permanent task of reviewing and developing - in co-operation with the competent government authorities - the contents and forms of study courses in the light of developments in the arts and sciences and of the practical requirements and changes necessary in the various professions.

Other important sections of the HRG related to the issue of curriculum innovation reflect upon:

* section 9: the coordination of study and examination regulations;
* section 10: the courses of study;
* section 11: study regulations;
* section 15: examinations;
* section 16: examination regulations;
* section 18: academic degrees.

All the *Länder* also have there own 'higher education act' which is the format for development in the various states.

On the federal level, general regulations for curriculum design are given by a joint decision of the *Kultusministerkonferenz* (the standing conference of the ministers of education of the eleven states) prepared in co-operation with the *Westdeutschen Rektorenkonferenz* (a buffer organisation; members are the universities, and representatives of the institutions of higher vocational education and colleges of art). One regulation (*Die Allgemeine Bestimmungen fur Diplomprüfungsordnungen*) has a general content; other regulations (*Rahmenordunung für die Diplomprüfung im Studiengang*) are related to the disciplines.

On the *Länder* level, at the proposal of the universities, *Prüfungsordnungen* related to a subject are under the approval of the *Länder*-ministry. In this document, general information on the curriculum is proposed by the university. In the *Studienordnung*, the university describes the contents of the curriculum more exactly. Due to an amendment of the HRG in the mid eighties, these *Studienordnungen* do not need the approval of the *Länder* ministries. Final details are regulated in the *Studienplan*.

Most of these regulations were created at the end of the sixties. Several interviewees drew attention to the fact that before the late 1960s, only a few curriculum regulations existed. As a result of socio-economic changes in the system (mass enrolment and student unrest) tighter regulations were judged to be as much-needed measures.

The existence of the network of curriculum rules is to a large extent the consequence of sections 8 and 9 of the HRG in which it is stated that the *Länder* must coordinate studies and maintain a standard of comparability between the various *Länder* within the disciplines. This issue of comparability was experienced by the visiting team as a dominant theme in higher education policies in the Federal Republic.

Different arguments for the maintenance of this policy of comparability and its procedures were presented in the interviews. It was felt that comparable curricula in the different institutions for the same disciplines were needed;

a. to serve an informative function to society in general and in particular to employers;
b. to give employers and professional organisations the oppertunity to give advice on the curriculum development;
c. to support the mobility of students;
d. to be a guardian for quality;
e. because the distinction between academic degrees has consequences for salary scales, especially of civil-servants;
f. because federal and *Länder* regulations can prevent frictions within the universities and can reduce the amount of internal regulation in the institution;
g. because comparability can stimulate external democratisation;
h. because comparability also provides protection for the status of graduates throughout the different *Länder* who want to apply for a state job.This prevents the *Länder* from refusing applications from fellow states.

2.2. *The activities of the Länder-ministries*

The present regulations on both curriculum and other factors influencing curriculum renewal (such as planning/budget allocation/personnel policies) authorise the *Länder* to penetrate deeply into the organisation of the university. In the two *Länder* visited a policy tradition has been established in which the balance of power reflects co-operation and dialogue. Still, the authority of the states is potentially larger than is used.

The potential power could raise questions if direct (*Länder*) government involvement in academic affairs on the one hand and more strategical questions (such as priorities, meeting the needs of the future) on the other, are to be carried out in an effective way. In general, a consensus in the interviews was noticed on the statement that the government decisions concerning such higher education issues as the appointment of professors and budget allocation by the *Länder* governments, are taken on a non-expert base, although outside expertise and advice is sometimes engaged. The governmental bodies visited expressed no doubt on the possibility of making their decisions on a rational basis. Specific arguments for involvement of the *Länder* in academic affairs were:

a. budget allocation and 'state-priorities' in the budget allocation system;
b. the potential arbitrating function;
c. judicial control;
d. to act as stimulator (for example, through additional funding);
e. to act as quality guardian;
f. to prevent too many regulations on the lower levels;
g. to correct conflicts of interest.

As far as expert activity in relation to Ministry approvals is concerned, we must distinguish:

a. curricula and appointment of professors, where external advice seems quite often to be requested;
b. budget allocation, where political points of view are dominant.

3. State regulation and curriculum innovation

3.1. *Curriculum innovation in practice*

In the search for factors influential on curriculum innovation, the visiting team was confronted with many ambitious and impressive initiatives to change existing curricula or to set up new ones.

It appeared that, in the current updating of the curricula, the innovation of curricula and the introduction of new activities was often related to the introduction of computer science. Many examples were given in which computer science related subjects were added to the curriculum. Cases were also presented in which interdisciplinary innovation of curricula or research activities were undertaken, mostly extra-departementally organised.

The answers to the direct question whether the network of regulations is a hampering factor in the search for innovation presented a variety of opinions and suggestions. The general feeling was that the present regulatory system has no dominant negative or positive influence on the innovation capacity. Balancing the pros and cons in the answers, the majority of critical remarks refered to the necessary investments in paperwork, often described as bureaucracy, and the length of the procedures, in cases of innovation proposals.

3.2. *Reasons for innovation*

Reasons for a (permanent) curriculum change metioned were:

* adjustment to the labour market;
* adjustment to new developments in science;
* widen spectrum of choice for studies;
* the initiative of the joint meeting of faculties (*Fakultätentag*);
* because other universities adapt their programme;
* initiatives by trade and industry.

3.3. *The proces of innovation*

Education takes place within the Federal and *Länder* government regulations and within the further regulations of the university administration.

The level of detail of the regulations develops from more or less abstract on the Federal level to more concrete on the institutional level. Although formulated generally, sometimes even vaguely, all types of regulations have influence on the innovation process.

Depending on the type of innovation, the regulations can theoretically form a boundary to change.

The following levels of the higher education system are involved in the decision-making process of the different types of curriculum innovation (see table on next page).

The more bodies involved, the more time-consuming the innovation process. Major changes including new interdisciplinairy curriculum activities, require more than just adjustment of the *Studienordnung*.

3.4. *Innovations within regulatory frameworks*

The general impression of the visiting team is that most of the curriculum innovation takes place without alteration of any regulation. The professor, ensured by *Grundgesetz* of having freedom of teaching, is able - mostly in co-operation with the faculty and, if needed, in co-operation with the central university administration - to adjust the contents of the curriculum to meet perceived needs. The fact that the general regulations are superficial and vague enhances the possibilities of change.

Type of innovation	Change of regulations required?	Level involved
1. regularly updating curricula	no	- indiv. prof.* - faculty - university ***
2. introducing new subjects	mostly yes **	- indiv. prof.* - faculty - university *** - Länder **
3. major change in existing curricula	yes	- indiv. prof.* - faculty - university - Länder - WRK/KMK
4. introducing new disciplines	yes	- indiv. prof.* - faculty - university - Länder - WRN/KMK

Key:
* Often the initiative to change curricula is taken by individual professors or groups of professors.
** Depending on the level of fundamentality of the change.
*** The central university administration participates in the discussion if additional funding, or alterations in the teaching commitment are involved.

Three forms of more or less 'evasive' behaviour occur. First, decisions on innovations are in practice often designed to just fit in the formal order, so as not to have to go through the bureaucratic procedures. Secondly, in day to day teaching practice, the regulations are 'stretched out' by creative interpretation of the (vague) rules. This creates a grey area of new, wider, boundaries. And thirdly, changes are carried out without formal or official procedures. During a number of years incremental innovation can be carried out and the changes can, after a few years, already be considered drastic.

Summarising the factors that in practice limit the effects of the bureaucratic procedures on formal curriculum change, we can point at:

a. the vagueness of the regulations;
b. the autonomy of the individual professor;
c. the fact that much innovation is designed so that it just fits within the legal framework;
d. the fact that the regulations are 'stretched-out' by the day-to-day teaching practice: much innovation takes place in the diffuse and grey area of creative interpretation, and combination of formal regulation with the need for regular curriculum adjustment;
e. the fact that incremental innovation is not always formalised.

Most innovation is carried out by a modification of the study plans and study orders. The university has the power to achieve this adaptation without approval by the state, although the state has the right to oppose a study order if it is not in accordance with the examination order. This is, however, a rather formal control.

3.5. *Actors involved in the innovation process*

a) Individuals
Proposals for innovation in the curriculum can have different sources. It was made clear that certain circumstances can improve the atmosphere for innovation. It was drawn to our attention that the most favourable circumstance for change was the inauguration of a new professorial position. The formulation of the tasks for the new professor opens up possibilities for change in both research and education.

b) Faculty level
The initiative for innovation is usually taken at faculty level, in the majority of the cases by the professor(s). The plans can lead to proposals for adjustment of:

* *Prüfungsordnung*;
* *Studienordnung*;
* *Studienplan*.

If the innovation goes beyond the legal framework of the *Rahmenordnung*, initiatives have to be taken on the federal level to discuss the contents of this regulation.

The proposals are subject to discussion in the faculty council. Often a special committee is established to prepare the discussion.

c) Central organs of the university
The Senate (the central administrative council in which representatives of staff and students discuss university policy) has no direct influence on the contents of the curricula, but discusses the proposals for change.

As for the central administrative body (president or rector, pro-rector and the university secretary), the visiting team has the impression that the contents of the innovation are not often discussed at this level, although this may vary from *Land* to *Land*. This body, having ready access to decisions on internal budget allocation, can create some facilities to stimulate innovation. Interesting examples were presented, especially in interdisciplinary fields like environmental science which were established by the joint activity of faculties and rectorate. Still, this power to improve the climate for innovation should not be overestimated; no traditon of strategic management came across to the visiting team. Strategic management and priority setting in relation to the mission of the university as a whole, particularly directed to the faculties, is not day-to-day routine for the central administrative level of the university.

d) Ministry
Study orders had, until recently, to be approved by the Ministry of the *Land*. This rule has been abolished by the federal legislator through the revision of the Framework Act in 1985, as was previously mentioned.

It is a remarkable example of the federal role in innovation, since most of the *Länder* governments were against this amendment. This conception of the *Länder* gives the impression that study orders are of a certain importance for *Länder* policy.

The *Länder* apparently found it important to keep their control over the contents of the curricula. As far as the *Prüfungsordnungen* are concerned, this power remains, and the ministries seem to make use of it.

Difference of opinion was noticeable on the question whether the involvement of the *Länder* is productive or counterproductive of innovation. As far as the appreciation criteria for the *Länder* are concerned, the interviews provided a wide range of possible criteria. The main criteria mentioned were the comparability with other similar examination orders in the country, and the search for a means of shortening the duration of study. These criteria are subject to variation and discussion between the various *Länder*.

The ministries can also examine the scientific value of the proposed curricula. They ask experts to give their opinion, and compare the project with the recommendations of the national faculty conferences (*Fakultätentage*).

The visiting team noticed the use of more politically oriented points of view as well. The importance of the labour market appeared to be considerable. For instance, in one of the universities visited, the proposals for a new course - which was proclaimed to have good research performance in this field - was rejected by the ministry because the proposed alteration would not offer enough opportunity in the labour market.

The procedure for approval of the examination orders can take a long time: up to two or three years according to certain estimations, although faster approval procedures were presented. This time factor, and of course the required paperwork, leads to innovations that preferably fit in the existing regulations.

In the *Länder* policy of prioritising innovation proposals, a concept of the usefulness the disciplines appears to be important. It was felt that the technological fields, in particular, have priority over social sciences, because they provide better access to the labour market for their graduates.

The existence of research projects already undertaken can encourage the state to support new disciplines. External funding or facilities have a stimulating influence as well. An interesting example was the creation of a computer centre which was made possible by the help of an important computer firm in the region. It is obvious that the state tries to make the best use of its financial resources.

As a partial conclusion, we should say that some innovations are much more likely than others to be accepted by the *Länder* government. The utilisation concept is becoming a more and more important theme in the *Länder* government. How influential this aspect is in cases in which no additional funding is required for the proposed innovation could not be estimated, due to the fact that no examples of this kind appeared.

e) The *Fakultätentag*

The role of the *Fakultätentag*, an independant federal disciplinary body co-ordinatied by the WRK and the KMK, seems to differ from discipline to discipline. In enforcing a high degree of conformity of curricula, the *Fakultätentag* could be regarded as a discouragement for substantial innovations.

f) External influences

Industry plays an important role in the conception of new curricula, at least in the fields related to industrial activity. In these cases, there was an interesting process of co-ordinated innovation at federal and *Länder* level, involving several meetings of professors from the whole country. Moreover, the existence of national bodies, whose members can be university professors as well as professional representatives, plays an important role in some disciplines. These bodies, such as the *Fonds der Chemie* or the *Verband Deutscher Elektro Techniker* seem to give substantial incentives to innovation all over the country. Their recommendations are important for the faculties as well as for the ministries. There is a strong link between the private sector and many faculties, and the state often does not oppose the changes worked out in this frame.

Also the financing of research projects by the federal government, the *Länder* or by special bodies, like the *Deutsche Forschungsgemeinschaft*, can influence curriculum innovation. This is due to the close connection between research and teaching as a basic principle of German universities.

Non-academic influences are particularly strong in the field of law. Judges and civil servants, for example, insist on maintaining a great number of disciplines related to their activity, even if the programme becomes overloaded. This can be a positive or negative factor on curriculum innovation.

3.6. *Study reform committees and experiments*

In the seventies, the federal government promoted the instrument of study reform committees for curriculum innovation.

The basic idea of this policy was: innovation through dialogue by universities and government. The attempts attracted a lot of attention and caused a lot of paper-work. They were described during the interviews as a 'large operation with poor success'. Still it was an informal but direct communication line with government, prior to official submission of *Prüfungsordnungen*.

In some cases, references were made to 'experiments' of a different sort such as a more global budget allocation, abolition of certain procedures, the change of internal management structure, and intense change of curricula. The 'experiments' are possible because of the autonomous position of the *Länder*. These cases were presented sometimes as an argument showing that change would lead to an undesired situation, sometimes to reflect on the present steering philosophy. An initiative for discussion was also mentioned in which formal regulations were replaced by a more extempore trouble-shooting system. The proposals were rejected by the *Länder*.

3.7. *The comparability issue*

As mentioned before, the comparability of the curricula between the *Länder* is a very important feature in higher education policy in the FRG. This being of such great importance, the visiting team tried to find out if the purposes mentioned were served.

Although the federal regulations are standard, it could be seen that the diversification of the system and the contents of curricula are greater than would be expected. This, for example, is experienced by students who move from one institution to another. Apparently, the network of regulations itself does not hamper differences in curricula of the same disciplines between the universities, even within the same *Länder*.

These differences make it questionable if the informative function society - the paradigm that all graduates in the same diciplines of different universities have the same qualifications - is carried out in practice. The basic knowledge of the various disciplines is undoubtedly comparable, but the differences, especially in the later parts of the studies, can clearly be substantial. From this aspect it might even be asserted that the comparability concept is to a certain extent misleading. Due to the same diversification the target of stimulating the mobility of students so that students can change from one university to another without losing too much time, is in practice not realised. Not only does a vast majority of students not use the mobility facility, but also in practice there is still a loss of time for the students who do switch to another university.

No indication was found that the curriculum regulations had any effect on the quality of the study; the regulations guarantee nothing more than a vague legal framework of issues that should be taken into consideration.

3.8. *General conclusion*

It is doubtful whether the present system of curriculum regulations serves its purpose. Although in practice it is not experienced as a serious obstacle to innovation, the effectiveness is doubtfull and, furthermore, it might become more and more an obstacle, in the coming period of rapid change and fundamental breakthroughs in science, to giving the universities the incentive to meet the needs of the future.

It was, furthermore, found that the existence of the regulations enhances strategic behaviour of faculties, in the sence that they either express the study contents in the regulations very generally and indistinctly, or neglect the practice of the regulation, for instance, failing to update the contents.

Still, the formal regulations did not seem to hinder innovation too much. It is therefore difficult to draw distinct conclusions on the effect of the regulations on innovation. It could be interesting to bring the concept of comparability of studies in discussion and reflect on the advantages and disadvantages. The choice should be reflected in the future conception of steering. If curriculum regulations were, for the reasons mentioned, required for the future, either as a structural feature or as an instruction, they would probably have to be far more detailed then the present ones.

4. Other factors regarding curriculum innovation

The visiting team has drawn the conclusion that the present regulations have no dominant influence on the potential capacity to innovate curricula. There is, however, a more decisive interference with other factors.

Influential on curriculum innovation - even more influential than the curriculum regulations - the following issues can be distinguished:

a. the budget allocation system which in general lacks incentives for creativity, quality and innovation;
b. the earmarked character of the financial *Länder* contribution and the tight spending regulations;
c. the absence of an evaluation system for teaching;
d. the system of having a guaranteed number of assistants in the appointment contracts of professors;
e. insufficient power for the top level of the university for strategic management.

4.1. *Budget allocation*

The budget allocation is, excluding the external funds in the so called *Drittmittel*, executed by the government. It consists of different parts. First, the part for building and equipment which forms the infra-structural development opportunities of the university. The distribution of this part is a specific politically linked decision. Secondly, the financial support provided for the salaries of the labour-force of the institutions. This part is partly earmarked through the appointment procedure of professors, negotiated directly with the ministry and the nominated professor which has the form of a contract. Thirdly, the support (or the material costs), and fourthly a part in which other income (for instance the so-called *Zusatzmittel*) can be accommodated.

The budget allocation is one of the most important tools of policy for the *Länder* and can therefore be infuential on the incentives to or hampering of (curriculum) innovation.

The observations are:

* there is no direct relation between student enrolment and the budget

allocation, although student numbers have been an important factor from about 1960;

* there is no relation between the quality of teaching or research and the funding procedures, but the influence of reputable hierarchies should not be underestimated;
* there is no relation to output or performance of any other kind;
* the annual budget is partly 'fossilised' because a varying proportion from *Land* to *Land* is allocated, as decided in the individual appointment contracts with the professoriate. This means that necessary reallocations for reasons of innovation are restricted.

4.2. *Staff policy*

Because education is in essence a transfer of kwowledge from teacher to student, and the teacher has a central position in both the execution and the innovation of the curriculum, staff policy is a very important factor. Trying to analyse and explain the difference in staff categories, the visiting team became somewhat confused because:

a. the present situation is a mixture of still active past regulations and current regulations;
b. theory and practice of, for instance, the job-discription of certain categories of personnel differ considerably.

Two staff categories can be distinguished: life time appointment and contract appointment.

a. For teaching staff, some exceptions excluded, only the professors have a life time appointment (cat. C4 and C3).
   The assistants are appointed on a contract basis.
b. There is a wide variety of administrative staff (life time appointment).

Teaching is usually done by the professoriate. Assistants are selected around a 'chair' for research purposes or education. In theory, some categories of assistant are supposed to do research only, but in practice educational tasks are performed as well.
Because budget/staff allocation is so closely related to the 'chair', the only possibility to reallocating resources occurs when a chair becomes vacant.

a. The fact that the chair is empty may be the result of retirement, voluntary leave or the creation of a new chair.
b. The replacement of the professor is discussed in the faculty as well as

on the central level of the university. Interaction between *Land* government and university is the next step. Advice may be asked from the *Fakultätentag*. In the discussion the profile of the new professor is designed. This procedure forces the university to discuss the plausibility of the chair. The discussion can, of course, have the result that no alterations are needed: in that case, the chair can be preserved. Often a revision is proposed to meet future research and educational needs. The discussion of chairs is in practice one of the very few moments, or instruments, in which reconsideration can take place.

c. The renewal of the chair is, finally, an opportunity of renegotiating the personal contract of the former professor with the ministry. This negotiation can affect not only the salary but also the money for basic equipment and his personal staff. These prerogatives can be a recognition for the esteem in which the nominated professor is held.
d. A proposal to fill the vacant position is prepared by the university and normally includes three candidates. The *Land* government decides.

The observations are:

* For the appointment of the professor, there is no permanent academic advisory body to the *Land* government. The choice between the three nominated persons is decided at the political level. The advice of experts is not excluded;
* There could be a lack of future prospects for academics who do not have the possibility of attaining the professioriate, but are nevertheless qualified researchers and/or teachers, because there are few attractive and independent positions in the university other than the professoriate itself;
* In daily practice, a difference between theory and practice of job description is noticeable, expecially with regard to assistants.

4.3. *Internal administration and division of power*

In the university two important levels of power regarding the central issues of the visiting team can be observed.

On the one hand the rectorate and his staff (in the state regulation of Nordrhein-Westfalen: *'dass Rektorate leitet die Universität'*) and on the other the professoriate.

Few counter-powers exist:

* the deans have a co-ordinative role between institutes, but not a real authoritarian function, although in individual cases a more influential position can be established;
* the senate does not seem to be an influential body in the macro-strategic decisions as far as the future development of the university as a

whole is concerned.

In paractice it seems to be difficult to carry out strategic planning in which future mission and future development are discussed.

Faculties have a central role in innovation through the proposal of the *Prüfungsordnungen* and *Studienordnungen*.

It was noticed in some cases, that powers within the university itself can be a hampering factor in innovation. Professors or faculties can block reforms quite efficiently.

4.4. *Lack of quality control and evaluation*

Quality control and quality improvement of teaching (as well as research) performance is a relatively unknown issue in the FRG There is no direct instrumentation that observes (lack of) quality or rewards high standards in the system. Quality control on the performance of professors is rejected by reference to academic freedom. The possible negative side of this system (that is a professor who does not meet the standard in terms of quality or quantity) is accepted.

The visiting team experienced the dominance of professorial academic freedom. It is one of the keystones of the higher education system.

In a high-tech science oriented society in which knowledge expands and becomes obsolete rapidly on the one hand, and budgetary contractions for higher education institutions arise on the other, a more dominant output orientation is expected in the future. From this aspect, reflection on the quality of the higher education system as a whole as well as reflection on the quality of the performance of the scienctific staff - the professoriate included - is conceivable. It is for politics to decide if the supposed advantage of introducing more output-oriented financing systems and a system of quality control will result in a slight reduction in the academic freedom of the universities.

5. Present policy issues

During the study visit, the team observed a number of current policy issues that were to a certain extent related to the main issues of this OECD project, concerning the relationship between regulations and innovation. In this section, a few of these issues are mentioned.

5.1. *The duration of study and the duration of stay*

An important issue in the discussion of higher education is the duration of study, connected with the duration of stay of students. It is generally

argued that the graduation age of men in particular which is mostly more than twenty-five/twenty-six, is too high. In the defence of the present state-controlled regulations, it is argued that abolition of regulations will lead to a further extension of study time. Regulations are thus seen as a control mechanism.
The present system of limiting the duration of study for the majority of the disciplines to eight semesters (the equivalent of four years, in some cases extended by one examination semester) is not successful in reducing the time an average student needs to finish his or her study. The average graduation age is not going down. This is caused by at least two factors:

a. the starting age is, due to compulsory military service for men, around twenty-one years. Taking into consideration that students generally need 1.2 to 1.5 times the actual duration of study to finish their studies, it is no surprise that graduation age is as high as it is;
b. the system of semesters contains a limit on time only, not a limit on workload for students. Reducing the theoretical study time and keeping the workload almost stable cannot contribute to reducing the period of stay at the university.

Further study and discussion on this issue is advisable. Alternatives could be investigated, such as an earlier starting age and an improved system of workload control for students.

5.2. *The numerus clausus decisions*

An important aspect of the higher education policy is the limitation of admission through the system of numerus clausus. It is determined by a complicated procedure and formula how many students are allowed to enrol in the system. Decisions on the number of students are often appealed against in court. Universities are forced to enrol all students unless there is a *numerus clausus* regulation. This force, however, productive with regard to the target of external democratisation, can cause problems in the student staff ratios. Since the enrolment of students is relatively unimportant in budget distribution the factor can be seen as a influence on the possibilities of renewal and quality. Prevention of *numerus clausus* situations could be considered. One helpful instrument could be the introduction of a more student number-oriented financing system.

5.3. *The relationship between the labour market and the universities*

It is noticable that the state of future prospects of students in the labour market reflects the discussion on the curriculum development of the faculties as well as the entrepreneurial activities of the university. Several cases were presented in which, in close discussion with representatives from industry and trade, innovation activities were directed more towards the needs of industry.

The *Länder* governments play an active role in stimulating information exchange, discussion and co-operation between universities and the labour-market.

5.4. *The concept of utilisation and future stress on applied research*

In other countries, as in the Federal Republic, there is a growing interest in further utilisation of higher education facilities. In general this leads to the following policies:

a. emphasis on studies with good prospects for the labour market;
b. closer co-operation between industry and universities regarding research and education;
c. stress on entrepreneurial activities, and growth in the amount of external funding;
d. in some cases, the influence of industry on the curriculum of the university.

5.5. *New demands for higher education*

The visiting team noticed an absence of preparation for chancing education demand in the near future. Not only the decline of student enrolment, but also the entrance of older people with demands other than full-course or full-time curricula and of university graduates needing updated or refreshed knowlegde, will influence the present structure.

It will be a challenge, in co-operation with the established courses offered by the employers, to find an appropriate structure and meet the needs of the future.

5.6. *Policy evaluation*

Especially in the recent past, much effort has been invested in the federal study reform committees. The results of this innovation strategy are, as far as could be judged by the visiting team, disappointing.

Curiously, there was no exact information on the details of succes and failure of the implementation of the products of the study reform commission; an evalution was not considered. Introduction of study reform committees for curriculum innovation on the federal level was, in the opinion of most interviewees, not a succesful strategy for innovation.

Although government is involved in the decision-making process on a large scale, there is limited knowledge of the effects of the policy measures and regulations. It would be advisable to encourage reflection on the effectiveness of the steering concept by means of a more permanent evaluation of policy effects.

Chapter 6

GOVERNMENT AND CURRICULUM INNOVATION IN FRANCE

Denis Carrier and Frans A. van Vught

1. Introduction

The field study in France was mainly undertaken at three universities. At each of these three universities specific innovation processes were identified and analysed.

The visiting team had the opportunity to meet more than forty institutional representatives, among them university presidents, vice-presidents, secretaries general and professors. The team was also able to discuss the various topics with national and regional representatives of government. To all of them the team wishes to express its gratitude.

The results of the analysis, presented in this chapter, are limited. Many details could not be presented. Moreover, the team members' impressions and opinions will have coloured the analysis. Nevertheless, the team hopes that the analysis provides a picture which may be of help in the discussions on innovative strategies in French higher education.

2. The French higher education system

During the last twenty years, the French higher education system has been the object of several reforms, most of them prompted by direct state intervention. For an analysis of the types, processes and effects of innovations in this system, a broad understanding of the recent developments in French higher education is useful. However, in this chapter, only the main characteristics of the system, which are related to academic structures and processes, can be mentioned. Also, only the general aspects of the laws and regulations which pertain to these main characteristics will be dealt with.

2.1. *The 1968 law*

The starting point of the recent transformations of the French system of higher education is described in the *Loi d'Orientation de l'Enseignement Supérieur* (*Loi Faure*), approved by the French parliament in November 1968, following the well known events of May 1968. The main purpose of the law was to reorganise the French university system around three principles :

a. multi-disciplinarity; the old universities were replaced by new ones, of a more manageable size, and structured in such a way that the dialogue between disciplines would have a better chance to flourish;
b. autonomy; the new universities were to have power, through a council composed of elected members who elect a President, to determine their by-laws, their internal structures and their relationships with other institutions, providing that the law and related regulations were respected;
c. participatory management; each new university and its own constituents was to be managed by a council composed of elected members representing the professors, the researchers, the students, the support staff, and the outside community; this council was in particular mandated to elect the President of the university, who would act as its chief executive.

Except for some of its articles, particularly the first two which pertained to the mission of higher education, the *Loi Faure* did not change the structure and the content of the curricula. Neither did it say anything significant about their specific developments. In this regard, the law only determined that the basic academic constituent of each new university would be the Unit of Education and Research (UER: *Unité d'Enseignement et de Recherche*). The UER would be responsible for teaching and research related to a certain discipline or field of studies, at all levels. And it would have to interact with the representatives of the various disciplines and sub-disciplines whose contributions were essential for the implementation and the periodic re-appraisal of these programmes. Apparently, the legislator hoped that these interactions would become the main vehicles for cross-fertilization between disciplines and programmes. The assumption appears to be that in this way the ideal of a multi-disciplinary university could be achieved.

Several by-laws completed eventually the *Loi Faure*, among which were in February 1973, the *Arrêté Général Relatif au Diplôme d'Etudes Universitaires Générales* (DEUG) which sanctioned since then the first university studies cycle of two year duration and, in January 1976, the *Dispositions Relatives au Deuxième cycle des Etudes Universitaires*, which organise the second cycle.

Amended several times, in particular by the *Loi Sauvage* in 1980 (which was only effective for a few months before it was replaced by a new version of the *Loi Faure*), the *Loi Faure* was finally replaced, on January 26, 1984, by the *Loi sur l'Enseignement Supérieur* (known as the *Loi Savary*).

2.2. *The 1984 law*

The *Loi Savary* is much more comprehensive than the *Loi Faure*. First because it pertains to all post-secondary studies, whatever their prime regulator (Ministry of Education or other). Secondly, because it goes much further than the *Loi Faure* in the structural reform of the university system. The *Loi Savary* especially stipulates that:

a. there must be, within each university, two other councils in addition to the Administrative Council (*Conseil d'Administration*): the Scientific Council (*Conseil Scientifique*) (which - in a less specific way - already existed in the *Loi Faure*), and the Curriculum and University Life Council (*Conseil des Etudes et de la Vie Universitaire*). Crucial changes were the participatory election procedures and composition of these councils;
b. the minima and maxima pertaining to the participation in the councils of the various groups concerned should be such that the professoriate should not have the majority, either on the Administrative Council, or on the Curriculum and University Life Council;
c. a National Evaluation Committee (*Comité National d'Evaluation*) is mandated to assess the performance of individual universities and other higher education institutions, with regard to their respective missions and the particular contractual agreements they have agreed upon with the Ministry.

Finally, the *Loi Savary* appears to be much more interventionistic in spirit than the preceding law, especially concerning study programmes. Indeed, several of the provisions of the *Loi Savary* indicate a preoccupation with a clear desire for pedagogical renovations and professional programmes, oriented towards the needs of the labour market and of the regions. As we will see later, these provisions open the door to certain initiatives taken by the Ministry, which generate specific curriculum innovations.

The 1984 law was only partially applied, because it was at the same time challenged by those who opposed its conception of internal structures and processes within the universities, and by those who would have preferred greater and more genuine autonomy for the universities. In 1986 the French government tried to arrive to a more generally accepted solution with a project (*Projet Devaquet*), the adoption of which would have resulted, among other things, in granting more autonomy to individual universities. For instance, the project provided for the right of each university, to select its students according to its own standards, and to increase the universities' resources by raising their academic fees. As is well known, opposition to this project was very strong, and government was forced to abandon it. The result is that the *Loi Savary* is still in force. But it should also be noted that, in July 1987, twenty-seven universities had not yet reorganised themselves internally according to the provisions of that law. Among the three universities which were visited by the study-group only one had readjusted itself to the *Loi Savary*.

The provisions of the *Loi Savary* concerning the university studies regime, as well as the processes applicable to the assessment and accreditation of new programmes (including their staffing and budgeting), have been applied since 1984. It is this regime and these processes which are briefly described below. This description has been reduced to what appears to be the most relevant, to assess the links that might exist between state regulations and curriculum innovations.

2.3. *The university studies diploma structure*

In France, the whole spectrum of university studies is divided into three cycles:

a. a first cycle, of a two years' duration, open to holders of a *baccalauréat* or of an equivalent qualification, and leading to a *Diplôme d'Etudes Universitaires Générales* (DEUG), a *Diplôme Universitaire de Technologie* (DUT), or a *Diplôme d'Etudes Universitaires Scientifiques et Techniques* (DEUST);
b. a second cycle, leading to a *licence* (Bacc + 3) or a *maîtrise* (Bacc. + 4);
c. a third cycle, leading either to a *Diplôme d'Etudes Supérieure Specialisées* (DESS) or a *Diplôme d'Etudes Approfondies* (DEA) after one year, and eventually to a doctorate mentioning the university where the studies have been completed. This *Doctorat* replaces the former state doctorate (*Doctorat d'Etat*) and the third cycle doctorate (*Doctorat de Troisième Cycle*) both having been abolished by the *Loi Savary*.

In the case of the first cycle, the legislator confirmed an interest in sound orientation and supervision of the students, to ensure that as many of them as possible continue their studies through the second cycle, and that those who cannot do so get a first cycle diploma or, at least, some kind of university qualification which will help them to make their living in society. In this regard, the law stipulates (article fourteen) that the students registered for short technological studies programmes (for instance, programmes delivered by the *Instituts Universitaires de Technologie* (IUT) and leading to a DUT, or programmes leading to a DEUST) should, if they wish, have the option of pursuing their studies at the second cycle. The law also indicates that complementary professional training programmes should be implemented for the benefit of students graduating from short professional programmes who do not wish to, or cannot, pursue second cycle studies.

2.4. *National diplomas and university diplomas*

The largest majority by far, of university programmes corresponding to each of the cycles mentioned above reflects a corresponding national *maquette* which describes the contents of the programme. In the aftermath of the *Loi Faure* and its proclamation of university autonomy, a *maquette* has been rendered more flexible and less specific than it was. Indeed, the present *maquettes* usually describe the contents of a programme in very broad terms (for example: the programme must correspond to at least so many hours of teaching, x per cent of them to be selected from among such disciplines or topics, etc.).

These programmes cannot offer a national diploma without being empowered to do so by means of an *habilitation* which is granted by the Minister, on the recommendation of a Commission appointed by him, in which special attention is paid to the availability of resources for such a programme.

Nothwithstanding this general pattern, the *Loi Savary* also provides for the right, granted to individual universities, to organise their own programmes, independently of the national *maquette*, and to deliver their own university diplomas (different from national diplomas). The regulations accompanying the law, however, make it clear that a university is not entitled to new funding (apart from the academic fees it may collect) for programmes leading to such university diplomas. We will see later that the Ministry made an exception to this rule in the case of a new high profile professional programme (called *Magistère*).

2.5. *The Grandes Ecoles*

A special regime exists for a second sector of the French higher education system: the *Grandes Ecoles*. At the time of this study, there were 126 of these *Ecoles* grouped together in the *Conférence des Grandes Ecoles*. The majority of these schools offer various engineering specialities. Approximately 15.000 young professionals graduate from these every year to fill middle and high level technical, executive or advisory positions in the private and public sectors.

The parallel existence of the universities and the *Grandes Ecoles* within the French higher education system has been confirmed by the *Loi Savary*. For the *Ecoles*, this law moreover confirms the right - in contrast to the universities - to apply very strict entrance selection. This is why future applicants to these schools generally choose to follow special preparatory programmes, offered by the *lycées* or, in certain cases, by the universities.

The duration of the programmes of the *Grandes Ecoles* varies from one school to another. The majority deliver a professional degree corresponding to five years of studies after the *baccalauréat* (including the preparatory year(s)).

2.6. *Institutional autonomy or state intervention?*

While affirming the academic, administrative and financial autonomy of individual universities, the *Loi Savary* also includes several provisions suggesting a high level of state interventionism, regarding both the whole system and specific aspects of the day to day operation of individual institutions. Some indications of this interventionism are mentioned below. From the point of view of our analysis these indications are of specific interest.

In addition to what has already been mentioned about the national and the university diplomas, it is relevant to note that, even though the *Doctorat d'Etat* has disappeared and that each doctorate degree should now indicate the name of the particular university where it was completed, an institution wishing to deliver such a programme first has to be empowered to do so. This entitlement is granted by the Minister under conditions specified by him, and after a recommendation from a Commission, which he appoints.

One of these conditions is the relevance of the project in terms of national and regional needs. This, in turn, implies that an assessment of those needs has already been made and that some sort of plan has been developed. Article nineteen of the *Loi Savary* refers to such a plan, by confirming the existence of a *Carte des Formations Supérieures et de la Recherche* which is described as the framework within which decisions are taken (our translation):

> '. . . . pertaining to the geographical location of the establishments, the implementation of second and third cycle programmes of studies and related research activities, to the *habilitations* for the delivery of national diplomas and to the allocation of resources'.

This *Carte des Formations Supérieure et de la Recherche* is determined and revised by the Minister, it being understood that consultations have taken place with the universities, the regional councils, the *Conseil Supérieur de la Recherche et de la Technologie* and the *Conseil National de l'Enseignement Supérieur et de la Recherche* (CNESER).

Another point which it is relevant to note is that, at the first cycle level, the individual universities (in contrast to the IUTs and the *Grandes*

Ecoles) are not free, within the limits of their respective enrolment capacities, to select their students. By law, the universities are obliged to enrol the students who appear at their gates.

Finally, the universities are submitted to a financial regime within which they have little, if any, control over their main resource, i.e. their staff. As the different categories of university personnel are incorporated in the public service, the individual institutions have no real control over the use of the funds corresponding to their salaries and related items, nor over the redeployment of posts which, for one reason or another, become vacant. Furthermore, the rules applicable in the public service are also applied to the universities. The effect of this is that the universities and their academic units must respect all kinds of limits (for instance: the maximum stipends for a part-time lecturer, whatever his/her calibre may be) and criteria (for instance: the admissible and the non-admissible items for reimbursement of travel expenditures) which have originally been devised for quite another set of circumstances. When we try to estimate the propensity of the French higher education system to innovate existing curricula, it is particularly important to take these financial regulations into consideration. They are all the more important in that the *Loi Savary* also stipulates that (our translation):

> 'Their (the universities) teaching, research and documentary activities may be the object of multiyear contracts within the framework of the *Carte des Formations Supérieure* defined in article nineteen. These contracts fix certain obligations for the establishments, and describe the corresponding resources and staff positions granted to them by the State . . . .'

3. Processes of curriculum innovation

From a general point of view, it may be stated that curriculum innovations in the French university system have come from three main avenues. They have been prompted by new goals, to be pursued by the system in the aftermath of the turmoil which characterised the French higher education sector during the last twenty years. They have been the result of the activities of the institutions, using the greater flexibility, introduced in the system since the beginning of the seventies. This flexibility has especially increased in the *maquettes* corresponding to national diplomas. Institutions can now develop particular strengths, and differentiate themselves from their sisters institutions. Finally, innovations undertaken by the institutions have also taken the form of specific initiatives to design and implement a university diploma. An institution may develop and implement a university diploma as an instrument, entirely under its own control, to answer specific needs. An institution may test the vitality of a particular programme for specific markets.

Based on what was perceived during its short visits, the study-group got the impression that these three avenues all were and are still explored by the universities. The study group also had the impression that these three avenues do not present the same level of difficulty. It may very well be because of these differences that the results, in terms of curriculum innovations, are quite unequal.

3.1. *New goals assigned to the universities and curriculum innovations*

To the members of the study-group, who are all foreign students of the recent evolution of the French higher education system, it seems that two goals have been, more than any other, at the forefront of the most noticeable curriculum innovations experienced by the French universities in recent years: the search for a better interface between secondary and university education, and a more systematic involvement of the universities in the applied sciences and technological studies fields.

3.1.1. Interface between secondary and university levels

The enrolment in French universities has increased by more than sixty per cent since 1970; and more than one third of this clientele is normally registered in the first cycle. These data indicate that the objectives related to the counseling of students passing from the secondary to the postsecondary level, as well as to the guidance of new university students, have become more important. Another set of crucial objectives has to do with the increase in the level of students retention.

The prominence of these various goals helps to explain why, starting with the new academic year 1984-85, the Ministry of Education indicated its interest for 'renovated' DEUG programmes. These programmes were expected to better assist students at their entrance at the university level and to permit their reorientation when this would appear to be necessary. Such a reorientation was judged to be especially useful when a gap existed between the type of programmes in which the students were involved at the secondary level and the fields of studies in which they would like to become involved at the university level.

To indicate the importance of the 'renovated' DEUG programmes, the Ministry called for submissions by individual universities for additional support which would be granted under the provisions of article twenty of the Higher Education Law of 1984. This initiative produced some interesting results.

Since the Ministerial initiative, more than fifty DEUG programmes have been 'renovated' by various universities. In all cases, the institutions received additional support from the Ministry to organise additional sections of courses and workshops which would facilitate the assistance of their first year students. It should be noted that this additional support generally takes the form of new staff positions, usually at the lowest level (teachers from *lycées* hired by universities to give basic training in fields where deficiences are noticed in student backgrounds). In some cases, the projects also included a major revision of the curriculum itself, which was often specifically designed to combine the secondary studies which the students had already experienced and the specialised programmes in which they are enroled at the university. This was the case, for instance, at one university which was visited where three different DEUG A programmes (Mathematics/Physics, Mathematics/Physics and some Chemistry, and Mathematics/-Physics/Chemistry) are now offered to first year students, depending on the kind of bachelor's degree they have and the specific university training they are aiming at. The two other universities visited by the study group developed similar projects, and both received additional support for this.

An important positive result of these initiatives seems to be a decrease in the failure rate experienced by students registered in the first cycle. This rate dropped, in all French universities, from 41,1% in 1983-84 to 34,5% in 1984-85.

It has not been possible to assess systematically whether the second objective mentioned above (the re-orientation of the students) has also been reached by the universities. Concerning this issue, the members of the study group were only informed about an experiment, undertaken at one university, and pertaining to a *Formation Scientifique de Base* (FSB). This now offers this programme to students who enter with a non-scientific background degree but who envisage reorienting themselves toward a scientific programme. At the time of our visit, it was still unclear if this new 'programme' should be considered as a new stream within a DEUG programme or as a preparatory year to one of the above-mentioned DEUG A programmes or the DEUG B (Natural and Life Sciences) programme. In fact, the university is of the opinion that the first alternative will prevail. The Ministry, however, did not approve this option, and did not grant any support to the programme. In addition, the Ministry decided that, for student support purposes, the year spent in this programme would be taken into consideration if, after successful completion of the FSB, the student registered in a regular DEUG A or B. The same student would also be eligible for financial support if, instead of registering in a DEUG A or B programme, he reoriented himself towards another (non-scientific) field (for instance, if he registers in a short technological study programme offered by the IUT) (see below).

3.1.2. Integration of applied professional programmes and technological studies

One of the most persistent objectives of the various reforms brought about in the French higher education system during the last twenty years has been the greater involvement of the universities in applied professional programmes - for a long time the *chasse gardée* of the *Grandes Ecoles* - in order to ensure a better link between higher education and the marketplace. This broad objective has been striven for in various forms.

The integration of applied sciences and technological studies within the French higher education system has been one of those forms. This integration began with the creation, in the early seventies, of the *Instituts Universitaires de Technologie* (IUT). The IUTs were created to train highly qualified technicians in a wide variety of fields through short professional programmes. To that effect, they offer a first cycle programme of two years' duration, leading to a *Diplôme Universitaire de Technologie* (DUT). They also accept, in special programmes (of one year), graduates from various DEUG or DEUST programmes who, for some reason do not enrol in the second cycle, and who want to increase their professional qualifications before joining the labour force.

From the perspective of the goal mentioned above, the introduction of these new streams within the first university cycle can certainly be considered a success. The expansion of the IUTs, and the diversification of their offerings imply an important and rather comprehensive innovation in the French higher education system, which is clearly oriented towards the integration of technology and applied sciences.

Enrolment in the IUTs now accounts for approximately five per cent of the entire student body of all French higher education institutions (universities, *Grandes Ecoles*, schools of engineering, business schools, IUTs, etc.). Their presence and their affiliation with the university system broaden considerably the array of university programmes available to graduates from the *lycées*. Besides, they enlarge the overall capacity of the French higher education system, helping to formulate an answer to a variety of training needs.

Finally it is worthwile to note that the goals pursued through the creation and the expansion of the IUTs still appear to be very relevant in the eyes of the Ministry. In recent years the capacity of several IUT departments has been increased and new departments have been created (eight in 1987). The Ministry has committed itself to pursuing this policy in the near future.

Two other recent initiatives reflect the desire to get the French universities more deeply involved in applied professional programmes. The first is the creation of a new first cycle diploma called *Diplôme d'Etudes Universitaires Scientifiques et Techniques* (DEUST). The second concerns the creation of a new type of programme, called *Magistère*. The Ministry has shown its interest in both of them, and granted support to universities which submit projects corresponding to its criteria.

The DEUST is a professional DEUG. Like the latter, this new stream within the first cycle of university studies has a duration of two years and corresponds to a short scientific university programme which is more technological than theoretical in nature. Three of these DEUSTs are organised at one of the universities which were visited (respectively in Biomedical Engineering, Advanced Technologies and Environmental Sciences), each of them including three different sub-options. A DEUST programme in Accounting and Finance has been implemented at one of the other universities visited. At least at one of the three universities visited by the team, the completion of the first year in any one of the DEUST programmes entitles the student to a university diploma called *Certificat d'Aptitude Universitaire Scientifique et Technique* (CAPUST). This diploma permits a student choosing not to pursue further studies to join the labour force with a university recognition of his qualifications. On the other hand, a graduate form a DEUST programme may, under certain conditions, be admitted to a masters' programme in sciences and technology (*Maîtrise en Sciences et Techniques*: MST).

The *Magistère* is a second cycle programme of three years' duration, combining tutorials, case studies and work experience in an industry or a laboratory. The programme is open to students holding a DEUG or an equivalent qualification. The university which offers it can select its students on the basis of their academic records, an examination, an interview or a combination of those. At the time this study was completed, the *Magistère* was still a university rather than a national diploma, although - in order to be funded - a university which planned one had to submit its proposals to the Ministry which, in turn, required the advice of an Advisory Accreditation Committee appointed by the Minister.

Approximately fifty of these *Magistères* have been accepted by the Ministry since the launching of this new diploma in 1985-86. A survey done in the Fall of 1987 shows that this type of curriculum is offered in various universities in a vast array of disciplines and fields of studies, from law *Juristes d'Entreprise* to economics (International Finance, Business Economics, etc.), administration (Marketing, Management Information Systems, etc.), to sciences and engineering (Chemistry, Physics, Computer Sciences, Molecular Engineering, etc.), and even to humanities (including one *Magistère* in Classical Ancient Times).

The DEUST and the *Magistère*, even if they address themselves to a limited number of students, seem to have become instruments by which the universities involve themselves more deeply with applied professional training. More specifically, the *Magistère* helps to reduce the gap between what were considered until the recent past to be the traditional functions of the universities (academic training and fundamental research), and the tasks of the *Grandes Ecoles* (whose programmes were oriented towards the employment needs of the public and private sectors).

Another point of interest, in view of our assessment of the links between state intervention and curriculum innovation, is that the *Magistère* looks like such an attractive proposition that even the *Grandes Ecoles* have reacted to it by creating their own new high profile diploma, called *Mastère*. This programme is open to students with a diploma from a school of engineering or a business school, or holding a DEA. Its duration is at least one year, including 250 hours of instruction and a four months' placement in a private business organisation.

3.2. *Increased differentiation between national diplomas?*

Based on information gathered during the study visit, it appears to the study group that the French universities have perceived the partial deregulation of the national diplomas (more flexible *maquettes*) as an opportunity for the implementation of programmes more specifically knitted around particular strengths and oriented towards local conditions. Although it would be unwise to generalise too much on the basis of limited information, it also seems that the individual institutions are far from being entirely free to implement all the programmes they could design. Let us give some examples in support of this conclusion.

In addition to what has already been mentioned about the 'renovated' DEUGs and the creation of DEUSTs, the three universities which were visited have all implemented innovative programmes in the recent past. Without pretending (or even trying) to provide a complete picture of these innovations, one may call attention to the new DEUG, *licence*, *maîtrise* and DESS programmes in Economic and Social Administration (AES) which were implemented by one of the visited universities starting in the seventies, to the DESS programme in Tropical Botany which the second university launched in co-operation with another university, and to the DESS programme in Sociology of Communications which has been put into place by the third university. The history of these new programmes indicates that they have either been prompted by a particular strength or a particular characteristic of the region, or - more often - by a mixture of these. All three cases provide evidence of the capacity of the university community to adapt itself to new circumstances.

However, it has also become clear that the *habilitation* procedure is such that it does not allow all the proposals to materialise. For instance, one of the universities - despite its geographic location and well-known expertise in these fields - has not been authorised to deliver a DEUG in Arabic Languages and Civilization, nor a DESS in the Management of the Sea Border (*Aménagement du Littoral*).

In these two cases the authority of the Ministry - as the final grantor of the *habilitation* which a university still needs to be able to offer a programme leading to a national diploma - supersedes the propensity of the individual university to innovate.

3.3. *The university diplomas: a non-credible instrument for curriculum*

The three universities visited by the team offer university diplomas: in Political and Administrative Sciences, in Commercial Techniques and in Technological Studies (CAPUST), and in various Applied Foreign Languages and Civilisations as well as in Regional History, Education, Biogeography and Music Therapy. One university appears more involved in these programmes than its two sister institutions, offering twenty first cycle programmes leading to a certificate, and fifteen second cycle programmes leading to a diploma. But there too, the involvement of the institution in these kinds of programmes remains minimal when compared to the resources and effort invested in the standard national diplomas. This minimal involvement is such that one can safely conclude that the ability of universities to create programmes which would lead to their own diplomas does not appear to be a very extensively used vehicle for curriculum innovation in France.

From the information the study group could gather during its visit, it can also be concluded that the French universities are not completely responsible for this situation. Indeed, several factors interact to confirm that obtaining the *habilitation* (granting the national diplomas) remains the cornerstone of the strategy of every institution with respect to curriculum development. Among these factors, the fact that the university diplomas are not eligible for additional funding is of extreme importance.

But perhaps an even more crucial factor is the fact that the principles behind the concept of the national diploma seem to be deeply rooted in the French higher education culture. These principles amplify the idea, widely accepted, that 'national diploma' is equivalent to 'national standards' and provides equality to the holder of such a degree, wherever he or she may have fulfilled its requirements. Whatever the respective importance of these factors, together they explain why, twenty years after the *Loi Faure* and the proclamation of the autonomy of each individual university, the national diploma remains the norm and the university diploma is a second-best possibility which seems to be used mainly when the other route is not available. This conclusion is underlined by the several examples the study group has been informed of concerning programmes which lead to a university diploma but which have been organised in this format only after the *habilitation* for a very similar project (leading to a national diploma) has been turned down by the Ministry.

4. Governmental instruments and curriculum innovation

As was indicated before, the role of government in the French higher education system was - and still is - very important. This role is certainly visible in the processes of curriculum innovation. To be able to get an impression of the characteristics and effects of governmental actions, we will now pay attention to the various instruments government has at its disposal to influence higher education institutions.

4.1. *Laws and regulations*

Traditionally the French higher education system is characterised by various forms of governmental regulations. First, there are the laws, and the rather strange situation which is created by them.

The 1968 law (*Loi Faure*) signalled an increase in the autonomy of the university diplomas (at least in theory). The 1984 law (*Loi Savary*) appeared to leave more room for state interventions, especially concerning the programmes of studies. The *Project Devaquet* (1986), which was eventually abandoned, again implied a greater autonomy for the institutions.

At the time of this study, the *Loi Savary* was in force. However, because of the political developments of the last few years, not all universities have taken the necessary steps to organise themselves according to that law, which has brought about the strange situation that some universities are, formally, not legally authorised.

The *Loi Savary* contains several provisions concerning the development, assessment and authorization of new programmes of studies. As such, it is one of the major governmental instruments. As mentioned before, by using this law, government to a large extent is able to initiate and steer innovations in higher education programmes.

Secondly, besides this law, government uses the instrument of rules and orders (*Arrêtés*). The rules are laid down for all degrees deemed to be of the same level (DEUG, *Licence*, *Maîtrise*). The main purpose of these rules is to define a common framework: minimum number of hours, minimum entrance level, status of teachers, general principles on the checking of knowledge. The ministerial orders contain obligations for the contents of the programmes. These obligations mainly have the character of stipulations about subject balance (for example: forty per cent of the course must deal with the following subjects: contract law, administrative law, commercial law). These *Arrêtés* also give a degree its official title.

Both the rules and the ministerial orders appear to be used by government as general guidelines for the levels and the contents of programmes (*maquettes*). They allow for differences in these levels and contents, while the programmes still bear the same title and still comply with the national rules. This governmental instrument thus gives some autonomy to the universities, especially as far as the details of a programme are concerned. On the other hand, it also makes sure that it is the Ministry which ensures the common obligations.

4.2. *Guidelines and approval procedures*

Two other important governmental instruments are the guidelines and the approval procedures concerning the processes of development, assessment and authorisation of a programme.

To initiate a programme the Ministry can send out a *circulaire*, in which it invites the institutions to bid (*Appels d'Offre*). The *circulaires* usually refer to various detailed guidelines concerning the conditions of the offers.

A university wishing to organise a national diploma must make a *Demande d'Habilitation* (application for approval). On the basis of the national common framework, set out by the rules and the orders, the university draws up its own proposal for the national diploma course. While doing this the university wrestles and juggles with the percentages proposed in the *Arrêtés*. It tries to design a programme within the conditions, while at the same time amplifying its own style and enlightening its own choices. An application for approval therefore bears the stamp of the university which makes it. For this reason there may be great differences between various applications.

When a university wants to organise a university diploma, it may take all the decisions itself. The university may lay down the entrance requirements, the length of the course, the contents of the curriculum, etc.. A university diploma, however, enjoys no subsequent guarantee other than the reputation it gains on the labour market. As was indicated before, this aspect apparently makes a university diploma less attractive than a national diploma. Universities therefore prefer the procedure of the *Demande d'Habilitation*.

Regarding such an application for a national diploma, the crucial step is the submission to the Ministry. After the university's various boards have discussed and approved an application, it is sent to the Ministry where it is examined by three different bodies in succession:

1. A group of experts specialising in the type of course and currently belonging to the discipline regarded as central (mono-disciplinary degree)

or dominant (multi-disciplinary degree). This group usually consists of academics and a few representatives of the socio-economic circles most concerned by the course. The group is able to give an opinion (at this level, there can still be a dialogue with the university to amend the proposal which may shuttle back and forth).
2. The *Conseil National de l'Enseignement Supérieur et de la Recherche* (CNESER) then gives another opinion (this is more concerned with the advisability of approval, with no qualitative view on the proposal itself).
3. The Minister's Private Office then finally takes the decision on the basis of these opinions, but is not obliged to follow them.

In the event of approval, the university is authorised for a given period of time (usually three to five years) to award the national degree on the terms described in the application, i.e. terms chosen by the university itself. During this period the university is bound by this arrangement and may not alter it.

4.3. *Funding*

The French universities are dependent, for the major part of their budgets on governmental funding, although there are at least two other funding resources, namely student fees and contracts with private enterprises (including the *Tax d'Appentisage*, a special tax which obliges private enterprises to spend some resources on education, and which is the only French tax which allows the taxpayer to implement it him/herself).

An important distinction concerning governmental funding of higher education concerns the budget for education and the budget for research. For each of these two budgets a specific allocation system exists.

The funding system for research can be considered as a conditional financing system. Since 1982, universities have had to design four-year research programmes which have to be submitted to government. If approved by a disciplinary committee of the *Centre National de la Recherche Scientific* (CNRS), the universities receive their budget for this programme. This budget is guaranteed for the duration of the programme. Another opportunity for the universities to earn resources is to carry out research contracts for private enterprises. Government does not control this type of funding.

A university budget for educational activities consists of student fees which are paid directly to the university, and of special grants from government. The student fees are fixed by government. Since 1985, they amount to 450 FF per year. The special grants concern three general categories: a contribution per curriculum hour per student per year (dependent on the disciplinary curriculum), a contribution per m2 (different for m2 built upon or not built upon), and the so-called special equipment grants.

It is important to note that the salaries of the university teachers and administrators are directly paid by government. Government acts as the employer of the university teachers and administrators, who have civil servant status. This situation implies that, because these salaries generally take up a large part of the total budget (in the 1988 budget the salaries incorporated 91,8% of the total budget), universities only control a rather limited proportion of their budgets.

Another point worth mentioning is that the governmental grants only apply to programmes that have been submitted to and approved by the Ministry, i.e. authorised national diploma programmes. University diploma programmes are not eligible for governmental funding. The courses of a university diploma programme neither qualify for state grants, nor do they count towards lecturers' official workload or teaching requirements which implies that they have to be paid supplementary hours. For their university diploma programmes the universities have to find special, non-governmental, funds (for instance, by charging comparatively high student fees).

The approval of a national diploma programme releases the resources needed for that programme. The resources are calculated on the basis of the number of students, taking into account the specific educational sector (Sciences, Literature, Law and Economics, Medicine and Pharmacology, etc.) and the number of lecture and practical workhours, laid down as a national norm by ministerial order. The calculated resources are used either to create teaching posts, or to grant supplementary hours which enable the university to pay the teachers who will have to take on this extra work on top of the statutary workload.

It should be noted that since the 1984 law, universities local and regional governments are getting more and more involved in the funding of universities. It is expected that these resources will become more important for the universities in the years to come.

Generally speaking universities also have the opportunity to earn resources by organising (semi-)commercial activities and products (summer courses, contract research, contract courses). Another funding resource is the possibility of private enterprises (sometimes attractive from a tax reduction point of view) making a donation to universities. Regarding the contract activities, universities appear to want to create special organisations and legal circumstances to be able to escape the rather detailed governmental financial regulations.

4.4. *Unintended and disguised steering*

It appears that the relationships between government and the higher education system incorporate some elements of what could be called 'unintended and disguised forms of governmental steering'. In this respect two elements can be mentioned.

First, it appears that the earmarking of governmental funds for specific purposes (e.g. exploitation of buildings) and especially the prohibition on using student fees (which are supposed to be spent for educational purposes) for guest lectures or short-term contract lectures limit the universities in their educational policies. Because of these factors universities are not able to hire extra personnel which, for instance, implies that when enrolments increase, the student-staff ratio will go up and the quality of education may go down. Apparently some governmental regulations, although not specifically meant for this, nevertheless limit the universities in developing their operational educational activities.

Secondly, government appears to hold on to the right to reallocate teaching posts which open up when older faculty members retire. Although this was not clearly stated by the officials met by the study group, it may be the case that the Ministry uses the *Carte des Formations Superieures et de la Recherche* from the *Loi Savary* as a basis on which an implicit governmental policy is executed to create certain specific university profiles. The reallocation of posts may, in these circumstances, be seen as a disguised instrument for reaching this goal.

4.5. *The dominant role of government*

The visiting study group had the opportunity to discuss various processes of innovation at three universities. The group was also able to meet with several representatives of the French government.

It seems to the study group that the representatives both of the higher education institutions and of the French government endorsed the group's hypothesis that the various governmental instruments form the most important factor in the creation of curriculum innovations in French higher education.

The law and regulations (rules and orders), the guidelines and approval procedures, and the funding system, together provide government with the opportunity to steer higher education in accordance with its own ideas and goals.

There is no doubt that the higher education system in France incorporates important stimuli for innovation. Some of those stimuli can be found within the institutions and the professional teaching and research work which is executed there. Some of them can be found in the interactions between the institutions and their environment. And many can be directly related to the governmental instruments mentioned in this chapter.

Really to appreciate the capacity of the whole higher education system to innovate, and to judge the relative influence of these stimuli, one would have to analyse systematically and in great detail the various factors and actors in the system (e.g. the *Carte des Formations Supérieure et de la Recherche*, and the commissions appointed by the Minister to provide advice on specific programmes). Such a thorough analysis is impossible, given the conditions of the project of which this study visit was a part. It may, however, be expected that such an analysis would confirm what nearly everyone whom the study group met suggested: the Ministry is the master of the game.

5. Other factores influencing curriculum innovation

It seems that in France various factors other than governmental instruments can be distinguished which influence the occurance of curriculum innovation in higher education. On the one hand there appear to be factors which stimulate innovations. On the other hand there are factors which hamper innovations. Those factors will be dealt with in this section. The first category will be called positive factors; the second negative factors.

5.1. *Positive factors*

An important factor regarding innovations of studies is certainly the open access of the French higher education system. In principle, everybody holding a *baccalauréat* has the right to enter higher education. However, this open access confronts the institutions of higher education with specific problems. It regularly happens that first year students, although they have a *baccalauréat*, are unable to get through specific courses because of the lack of certain basic knowledge. This has stimulated the universities to develop specific introduction and preparation programmes. An example of such a programme is the previously mentioned *Formation Scientifique de Base* at one of the universities visited. In this programme students are prepared for the DEUG or the DEUST, both first cycle two-year programmes. The FSB implies an extra flexibility, because it gives students the possibility of preparing for an education in the IUT which delivers the *Diplôme Universitaire Technologie* (DUT). The goal of the FSB is to supply students having an insufficient level of knowledge, especially in mathematics, physics and chemistry (usually Bac. D and Bac. F students), with the necessary basic knowledge, so that they can start their studies for DEUG or DEUST. Besides, FSB students are expected to have better chances in getting accepted for the selective IUT programme.

The importance attributed to the open access of the French higher education system has recently resulted in a policy of *delocalisation*. *Delocalisation* implies the creation of 'university outposts' (*Antennes Universitai-*

res) to attract new students. The basic idea is that, to be able to offer the possibility of entering the higher education system to more potential students, new locations (and possibly new programmes) have to be organised. In the near future this new policy (which is still in a pilot stage) may very well become an important factor in stimulating curriculum innovations.

Another positive factor regarding innovations of studies is formed by the new professional markets. It appears that in several professions there is a shortage of specialised personnel. These shortages stimulate institutions of higher education to develop new courses, programmes and diplomas. They also attract students to these innovations. The prospect of an interesting and rewarding job make these new courses and programmes very attractive. Various examples of these types of innovations were found by the study group.

A factor related to the former is formed by the needs of industry. An example of an innovation which is to a large extent the result of this factor is the *Diplome d'Université Technico-Commercial* of one of the universities which were visited. This university diploma has been created as a specialised programme following the first (two-year) cycle. It is directed towards private enterprises, especially those where a combination of technical and commercial capabilities is expected to be needed.
Other examples are the *Mastères* which are offered by an institute within one of the three universities in this study. In general a *Mastère* programme is only accessible for students with a diploma of the *Grandes Ecoles* in engineering or management, or a DEA. The institute mentioned offers *Mastère* programmes in 'Artificial Intelligence and Biological Macromolecules', in 'Fine Organic Chemistry and New Materials' and in 'Plastic Materials and their Processing'.

Another positive factor regarding innovations appears to be the needs of the local and the regional communities. One of the *Mastères* is highly integrated in the development strategy of the region. It is expected that the *Technopole* which is foreseen in this region will be an important market for students finishing their *Mastère de Plasturgie* which has been organised since 1986.

It should be mentioned, however, that the needs of the local and regional communities are not always the most important element in decisions taken by the Ministry to approve or disapprove a new programme. As mentioned before, one of the three universities tried to introduce a programme in the field of 'Foreign languages Applied to Economics', arguing that this programme would contribute to a large extent to the local and regional needs concerning tourism and trade. However, having received the advice of some specialists in the disciplinary fields, the Ministry decided that this programme could not be approved because of its lack of theoretical background.

A factor which is certainly also important is, what might be called the drift towards the *Grandes Ecoles*. The *Grandes Ecoles* form a kind of independent elite sector in the French higher education system. The toplevel graduates who are produced by these schools are highly paid in the job market, and are usually easily accepted in high level positions. A large majority of engineers and managers in the French industry and economy are alumni of the *Grandes Ecoles*. The *Grandes Ecoles* are perceived by many students as a 'ticket to heaven'. However, it is very difficult to get into a *Grande Ecole*; the number of places is limited and the entrance selection is rather stringent.

It sometimes seems that the French universities would like to be in the same position as the *Grandes Ecoles*; only accepting the best students and being independent of government control are stimuli which appear to lead to specific innovations within universities. Concerning the *Magistère de Juriste de Conseil d'Entreprise* (of one of the three visited universities) it is interesting to see that the faculty which is providing this programme, is promoting it by pointing at the model of the *Grandes Ecoles*. It appears that the urge to become an equivalent of the elite sector is an important factor producing innovations in the French university system.

A final positive factor which should be mentioned is the reactive, but often very creative, behaviour of the institutions of higher education. The reactive aspect of this behaviour can be found in the acceptance of the initiatives of government concerning innovations in higher education. It should be noticed, however, that the universities have very little choice. If they were to decide not to agree to governmental initiatives, and try to develop their own university programmes and diplomas, they would not receive sufficient funds. The creative aspect of the behaviour of the institutions comes to the fore when attention is focussed on reactions to governmental initiatives. Various examples of this creativity were found by the study group. The renovations of the first cycle DEUG programme concerning the orientation of students have, in the case of one university, led to innovations in the course structure with a clear emphasis on core courses (*tronc commun*) and a new programme to raise the level of Bac. D and Bac. F students (FSB). At another university a completely new interdisciplinary programme was designed in the field of 'Applied Human Sciences'. In this first-cycle programme, students would have been introduced to basic knowledge in various social sciences. Unfortunately, the programme was only approved for one year, and finally had to be abolished because it could not be followed up by a programme at the level of *licence* and *maîtrise*".

5.2. *Negative factors*

Although many important innovations can be found in the dynamics of the French higher education system, there also seem to be some specific factors which may have hampered innovations.

The study group had the strong feeling that, although at the universities which were visited several initiatives were found to develop university programmes, the basic attitude in French higher education is still very much characterised by an orientation towards national diplomas and approved programmes. French higher education reflects a set of opinions which are deeply rooted in the French culture, and which may very well operate as a factor by which innovations are mitigated. These opinions have regard to the idea that national diplomas meet national standards and therefore provide equality and quality. This same idea influences the behaviour of students, teachers and employers who, for innovations, all look first at the framework given by the Ministry and explore their own needs and ideas only when this framework appears to be too tight.

Other negative factors have to do with the instruments used by government. In particular, the rather rigid financing system (because of the earmarking of budgets) and the centralised personnel policies (civil servant status) limit the universities in their possibilities of formulating innovative educational policies. Nevertheless, it may also be pointed out that at the universities there is still only a rather limited interest in developing plans and strategies for innovations. Perhaps it is a part of the culture mentioned before; perhaps it is an effect of the dominant role of government. The study group, in any case, got the impression that the universities are more reactive than pro-active where curriculum innovations are concerned. When innovations occur, they seem to be the result of individual initiatives or specific proposals from outside. A longer-term innovation plan at the university level is often not available, or only of limited importance.

Another factor worth mentioning is the rather limited competition between universities. Especially the fact that first cycle students have the right of admission to the university in their direct geographical environment but may be refused admittance elsewhere assures universities of an enrolment. Such an assured enrolment however, may also temper the drive to innovate educational programmes which could attract more and/or other groups of students.

When new programmes were designed (as was the case in all three universities visited) these very often appeared to be stimulated by a competition for specific groups of students. The drift towards the *Grandes Ecoles*, mentioned before, can be interpreted as a slowly growing recognition by the universities of the existence of competition. The launching by these *Grandes Ecoles* of the *Mastères* shows, that these institutions have already accepted the idea of competition.

6. Effects of innovations

In this last section an invertory is made of the effects of innnovation processes as they are seen by the study group. This list can only be a subjective overview from the perspective of the visiting team. No effort is made to draw up a comprehensive list of effects. Nevertheless, this inventory may be worthwhile as a basis for further analysis of the processes of innovation in higher education.

A major effect of the various innovations encountered by the study group is the increase of the level of efficiency in the system in general. It was reported, for example that, at one university the renovation of the DEUG progamme resulted in a decrease in the drop-out rate from seventy-five to sixty per cent. This decrease is supposed to be mainly the result of the increase of teaching posts, and the somewhat larger budget for the programme.

However, there are also some problematic consequences related to this efficiency increase. As a result of the decrease in the drop-out rate, the number of students in the second year of the first cycle has grown which leads to problems regarding the organisation and planning of courses and of examinations. Another negative effect which was pointed out several times to the study group, is the introduction of a new category of teachers into the universities. These new teachers are recruited from the schools of secondary education (*lycées*, *collèges*) and are very different from the traditional university professors; they are only there to assist in teaching; they have no research task and cannot be tenured. However, since they also are civil servants their position is rather strong. It will be very difficult to prevent them from becoming a permanent category of higher education personnel.

An effect worth mentioning is the increase of the geographical mobility of students. The highly specialised programmes which are being developed attract students from all over the country. However, it should not be forgotten that this increased mobility mainly occurs at the higher levels of the diploma structure (third cycle). As was pointed out before, the enrolment, especially at the first cycle level, is regionally bound.

A third effect, which was very visible to the study group, derives from the more intense relationships between industry and higher education. In many innovated programmes of the universities visited, the accent was put on applied and technological studies. It could be concluded that the persistent strategy of government of stimulating the universities to increase their involvement in applied professional programmes has been successful.

An effect which was also clear is the increase of the number and intensity of the relationships between the local/regional communities and the university programmes. Several innovations appeared to be the result of consultations with local and/or regional organisations. Very often the programmes resulting from these consultations are directed towards these organisations.

In general, however, innovations in the university programmes, especially because of the first trend mentioned above, appear to be mainly oriented towards applied and technological studies. At the three universities visited the dominant opinion is that these applied and technology oriented programmes have a better chance in getting *habilitation* and are more attractive to students. This opinion may, however, also have the effect that the basic university tasks of furthering science and fostering the cultural heritage disappear in the background. A crucial goal for the French higher education system in the near future may very well be to create a fruitful balance between applied and technology-oriented programmes on the one hand, and the traditional tasks of a university education on the other hand.

Another effect noticed by the study group is the growing competition between universities, especially at the third and second cycle levels. As far as the first cycle is concerned, the universities have to a large extent divided their clientèles. On a national scale, the geographical admittance policy for the first cycle tempers inter-university competition. But at the levels of the second and third cycles, national competition is growing. Programmes with more or less the same contents, and leading to the same diploma, compete with one another for special categories of students.

A last, and important effect noticed by the study group is the increase of diversity within the system of higher education. There are several reasons for this increase in diversity. First, it appears that, within the sometimes rather tight framework of governmental procedures, the universities are nevertheless able to design and implement new national diploma programmes which generally reflect the specific characteristics of the universities. In the previous paragraphs several examples of such new programmes have been given, at all levels of the French higher education system. Secondly, besides these new national diploma programmes, special university programmes have been designed, through which new outflow possibilities have been created. Thirdly, it appears that the new preparatory programmes also create more diversity. Finally, the creation of the *Magistères* and the *Mastères* also contribute to the increase of diversity in the system. The approximately fifty *Magistères* the many *Mastères* offered by the *Grandes Ecoles* have an important diversifying influence on the whole higher education system.

When one tries to consider the effects of curriculum innovations in French higher education, this increase in diversity is an especially important outcome. It may be hypothesised that the French higher education system will further gain in diversity and flexibility, and by this is preparing itself for a future in which higher education will become one of the most important factors contributing to the well-being of society.

Chapter 7

GOVERNMENT AND CURRICULUM INNOVATION IN THE NETHERLANDS

Ulrich Teichler

1. Introduction

For any analysis of changing relationships between the state and institutions of higher education in the 1980s the Netherlands turn out to be a very interesting case. One might argue that the Netherlands are the most interesting case in Western Europe in these respects:

- First, there is not any other Western European country in which government authorities claim a change of the state regulatory system to the extent the Dutch government does. Obviously, the Dutch authorities in charge of higher education believe that a change of the regulatory system regarding higher education is instrumental in bringing about innovation in teaching and research and subsequently in leading to a differentiation of higher education. The Dutch government claims that the underlying philosophy and in fact the trends of the implemented changes of regulations head towards what is called 'de-regulation' in international debates, or has been termed 'steering from a distance' in the Netherlands.
- Second, we note substantial efforts by the Dutch government in the 1980s to realise or at least set guidelines for 'visible' innovations in higher education. The most notable have been those striving for a reduction in the length of university study prior to the first degree, the introduction of a second phase of studies subsequent to the first degree, the inauguration of a funding system of university research which is independent of student numbers and which is closely linked to quality assessment, the upgrading of higher vocational education to non-university higher education as well as the mergers of the previously mostly very small non-university institutions of higher education into medium-size *hogescholen*. Even if not all these aims have been realised, and even if 'visible' reforms are not taken as the sole measure, when innovations taking place gradually or informally are taken into consideration as well, Dutch higher education can certainly be considered very dynamic in the 1980s in comparative perspective.
- Third, the Dutch case is also of interest, because it obviously does not provide a simple lesson regarding the links between state regulation and

innovation in higher education, as a first glance shows. Neither can a hypothesis be confirmed easily that de-regulation leads to innovation, because substantial financial cuts did not easily allow a shift towards 'steering from a distance' and because most of the 'visible' reforms are pushed for by government. Nor did the government emphasis on at least a less direct system of regulation fade away in the course of events; rather, the Ministry of Education and Science claims that policies in the early eighties have helped to pave the way towards the policy of 'steering from a distance' envisaged to get additional momentum in the late 1980s.

The strong emphasis in the Netherlands during the 1980s on changing the state regulatory system regarding higher education as well as the diversity of far-reaching efforts for change under way turned out to be an extraordinarily fruitful basis for the visiting group to draw upon, as far as interesting topics to be observed, wealth of prior information, organisational support for the visit and readiness to respond are concerned. One could hardly imagine any richer preparation and visiting programme.

2. Changes in state regulations

2.1. *Major dimensions of policies and regulations*

The Dutch higher education system shares with most other European countries a historically strong state role as regards higher education. Government provides the basic financial means for higher education; in the Netherlands, this is true to the same extent in both public and private higher education. Laws, ordinances and daily regulations might affect details of staff structure, course programmes, etc. Intermediary organisations do not significantly reduce the regulatory power of the government. Nontheless, European systems of higher education with a strong state regulatory role differed substantially in this respect around the 1980s, i.e. before changes observed in this study had started: the Dutch government left the selection of candidates to be appointed as professor completely to the universities. Individual universities in the Netherlands could easily establish new course programmes as long as they remained within the formal framework of established fields of study, and budget allocation to institutions of higher education was to a much lesser extent earmarked than in France and the Federal Republic of Germany, the two other countries under consideration in this study.

In analysing policies of the Dutch government aimed at changing state regulation regarding higher education, we can distinguish three major dimensions:

- First, we note changes in concepts put forward by government regarding the state regulatory role *vis-à-vis* higher education. Closely linked to these are ways of interaction between government and institutions of higher education, as far as this is shaped by state regulation.
- Second, financial policies played an important role. This applies for mechanisms for the funding of higher education and their regulatory implications on the one hand. On the other hand, retrenchment policies had a substantial impact during the 1980s.
- Third, we address specific policies regarding the educational function of higher education in this report. We note changing regulations regarding the process of establishment or of change or course programmes on the one hand. On the other, policies can be observed aiming directly for certain reforms of the structure and content of course programmes in higher education, or indirectly through reforms of the structure of the higher education system, of the promoting of research, etc.

We can distinguish these dimensions analytically. In practice, however, they interact. If government pursues a policy of very detailed steering in one area, but emphasis a policy of 'steering from a distance' in general, these policies are bound to meet other reactions on the part of the institutions of higher education than just those intended by each single measure.

In presenting the major policies of the Dutch government relevant to explaining the changing state regulatory stystem, we cannot claim to provide a comprehensive and balanced view. For, first, the views and actions within higher education institutions regarding innovation were the major focus of our observation. The state regulatory system only comes in, in so far as it explains the views and actions within institutions of higher education. Second, state regulations regarding higher education in the Netherlands are changing so quickly, and are so complex, that foreign observers cannot fully comprehend it in a short period; as we noticed, we share that problem even with obviously relatively well informed high-level actors in the Dutch higher education system. However, documents and presentations given by government representatives and talks with representatives of intermediary organisations, as well as the perceptions of teaching and administrative staff of institutions of higher education, provided ample information on government policies.

2.2. *Changes in the state regulatory role regarding higher education.*

Representatives of the Dutch Ministry of Education and Science tend to emphasise two principally distinct, but historically somewhat overlapping, phases of the governments' higher education policies in the 1980s:

- In the first stage in the early eighties, 'remedial' or 'corrective' policies dominated. The introduction of the two-stage course structure, the cutting of departments, the merger of former higher vocational schools as well as the reductions of staff were directly aimed at offsetting specific mistakes of the past.
- The second stage was first outlined in 1985 in the White Paper called Higher Education: Autonomy and Quality. The Draft Higher Education and Research Plan published in 1987 is a sequel spelling out in detail policies already envisaged in 1985. A draft of a new Higher Education Law was published soon after the visit of this study group. In this second stage, 'facilitating policies' should dominate.

As a major change, regulation by law, orders and other rules prescribing in detail goals and procedures in higher education should be substituted by a system of 'steering from a distance'. This might be realised by:
- setting at most frameworks for action,
- pursuing government goals, possibly with the help of incentives,
- lump-sum funding,
- resource allocation based on output measures (graduates, dissertations etc.)
- establishment of a system of evaluation and of dialogues related to evaluation,
- establishment of other ways of assessment, such as performance indicators,
- setting a limited number of policy rationals which shape incentive policies, the evaluation process and possibly state intervention, in case higher education institutions fail to take steps on their own.

The move from directive policies towards 'steering from a distance' does not necessarily imply lesser efforts on the part of the government to determine the major goals of higher education. On the contrary, the Dutch government seems to believe that they will have the power to determine the major directions of the higher education system more effectively if higher education institutions are 'steered' less directly than in the past. 'Quality' is conceived by the Dutch government as the most important criterion shaping that indirect steering policy. 'Responsiveness to economic and societal needs' is also taken into consideration. 'Diversity', though of lesser importance, is on the agenda as well. Finally, government might intervene if other issues - not directly related to goals of higher education - are at stake : if institutions of higher education take over functions of which they are not in charge (if a department of economics starts teaching medicine) or if inefficiency is obvious (if, for example, one institution sets up a course programme requiring high investment and corresponding facilities are underutilised at other institutions).

However, it should be noted at this point that governmental policies regarding higher education in the Netherlands in the 1980s cannot be clearly segmented into 'remedial' or 'corrective' policies in the early eighties and 'facilitating' policies in the late eighties, or into 'direct control' on the one hand and 'indirect steering' or 'steering from a distance' on the other. Rather, we note some moves towards 'indirect' steering in the early eighties (for example assessment and decision-making processes regarding 'conditional financing' on the one hand and direct steering in the late eighties (decisions regarding areas of budget cuts 1986/87) on the other. We also observe that all 'remedial' policies have incorporated elements of indirect steering and that all 'facilitating' policies are also based to a certain extent on substantive targets on the part of government.

If there were not such historical overlap of stages, and if there had not been only a gradual difference between dominant policies, the study group would not have been able to analyse at all the consequences of moves towards less direct and less substantive state regulation on views and activities in higher education institutions, or on innovation and diversity in higher education. For the concepts formulated in 1985 were scheduled to start shaping reality in higher education institutions in 1988, i.e. after the visit of the study group in November 1987.

2.3. *Communication between government and institutions of higher education.*

Efforts by the Dutch government to transform the state regulatory system regarding higher education to a considerable extent. The Dutch Ministry of Education and Science seems to have set itself three major directions for change:

a. A reduction in communication on regular administrative and budget issues: Since government wants to surrender detailed and routine supervision, there is less need for communicating guidelines, reporting back and forth etc. As a consequence of this change, government reduced the budget quota assigned for administration within institutions of higher education, arguing that the workload of detailed reporting was diminished.
b. A reduction in communication on goal-setting: The Dutch Ministry of Education and Science terminated the Academic Council, and reduced its roundtable conversations with institutions of higher education and

organisations representing institutions of higher educations. This seems to reflect the view that government either legitimately enforces frames for changes, or leaves major decisions to the institutions of higher education or to an 'output' evaluation.

c. New forms of dialogue between government and institutions of higher education should emerge due to government intention to act, as well be discussed later, both as a frame-setter for changes and as a 'watch-dog' regarding the planning activities of institutions of higher education and the impact of evaluation on institutional planning and policies. Three types of new or increased kinds of activities are already visible:
   - First, institutions of higher education are entrusted by government with finding joint solutions within the frames set by government, and with reporting them jointly to government. Governments' demand that universities should jointly propose a detailed plan for the 1982/1983 financial reductions was a major cause of the establishment of the Association of Co-operating Dutch Universities (*VSNU*), and the Council of Higher Professional Studies (*HBO-Raad*) gained substantial power subsequent to being entrusted by government with stimulating and co-ordinating the process of mergers between non-university institutions of higher education.
   - Second, new academic expert commissions had to be formed which submit their evaluations both to institutions of higher education and to government.
   - Third, institutions of higher education have to set up their own development plans, writing reports as an information base for visiting committees and the inspectorate, reactions on evaluations etc. Most of those activities were expected to start in 1988.

It remains an open question whether the system envisaged will necessitate - contrary to the present design on the part of the government - an additional system of negotiation and goal-setting between government and institutions of higher education. The study group did not focus on that issue, but - as will be explained later - noticed various new areas of potential conflict between government and institutions of higher education in the process of change of the state regulatory system which could support that assumption.

2.4. *Mechanisms for funding higher education*

The system of funding higher education is, obviously, conceived by the Ministry of Education and Science to be the key element in changing the regulatory role of government regarding higher education. In fact, substantial changes in the funding system have been implemented in the 1980s.

Since various Dutch descriptions of those changes seem too closely linked to certain debates and views, we present those major changes in a somewhat different structure:

a. Reduction of 'earmarking' of the budget in favour of global budgets: institutions of higher education are no longer allocated fixed numbers of staff positions or funds for specific facilities, but, rather, are free to decide on their own in those respects. There are various limitations, though, for example, the number of professors and the minimum ratio of 'assistants-in-training' (i.e. salaried doctoral students), the salary scales, the construction budget, etc.
b. Substitution of formula-funding of teaching for bilateral and multilateral negotiations of budgets of individual institutions of higher education: the universities may claim that small fields of study need a larger pool of academic positions than envisaged in the formula, but they cannot demand specific subsidies to their course programme x because historical circumstances have led to establishment of a certain number of positions, or because demand has been higher due to exceptional curricular characteristics. Financing of construction has remained the major exception.
c. Partial dissociation of education and research budgets: research funds allotted to the university through the regulatr budget continue to be calculated on the basis of student numbers and corresponding academic staff numbers only to a limited extent. The bulk is allotted to specific schemes for research funding, as has already been explained ('conditional financing').
d. Substitution of indirect policy measures for direct policy prescriptions, i.e. 'incentives' in funding formulas: the substitution of formula-funding for detailed prescriptions does not necessarily mean that government refrains from pushing very specific policies through the budget. Rather, the Dutch government incorporates specific aims in the funding scheme and thus aims to provide incentives for accepting and implementing those policies. For example, costs for education are no longer calculated according to the number of students (weighted by fields etc.). Rather, costs for 1.35 years propedeutic training for each new student and 4.5 years for each graduate form the basis of calculation in the case of universities. Thus, universities should be pushed to select potential drop-outs very quickly, to avoid drop-out beyond the propedeutic stage, and to keep the enrolment period up to graduate short.
e. Steps towards budget allocation according to results of formal evaluation: the allocation of 'conditional financing' for research on the basis of a nationwide experts' assessment of research plans is interpreted now as the first step toward a strong role for evaluation in all budget decisions.

According to plans partly already enforced and partly still under deliberation at the time of the visit, evaluation of the quality of research by visiting committees of peers, evaluation of education by peers and by an inspectorate of the Ministry, and assessment of institutions according to quantifiable indicators should inform budget decisions.

f. Introduction of 'innovation' or 'mission' budgets: in order to ensure that the mix of generalised budget formulas, of general policies incorporated into the budget, and finally of the criteria and views underlying experts' evaluations and formal indicators do not discourage non-conventional innovations, government reserves a small percentage of the budget for specific new targets. On the one hand, government sets up specific promotion programmes to be partly administered by other agencies (the Academy of Science, the Council of Higher Professional Studies etc.), as is presently the case with microelectronics, post-doctoral studies and research positions for young promising researchers, womens' studies, etc. On the other hand, the individual universities are encouraged to present their specific goals and missions in documents provided for evaluation of teaching and research; in the near future, a certain percentage of subsequent budget decisions should reward specific characteristics and plans.
g. Encouragement of search for income from private sources: in 1987, on average more than ninety per cent of the expenses of higher education institutions were borne by public funds. Government encourages the search for private resources in various ways. It expects, for example, that the establishment of advanced professional courses should be paid for by participants, professional organisations or employers. It also offers specific funds for specific purposes, for example, microelectronic facilities, on condition that these are matched by money both from the general budget of institutions of higher education and from private sources. Further examples could be added.

It does not seem feasible from our point of view to lump all these various changes of regulatory policies regarding funding of higher education consistently together under one heading. Not all of these measures head towards 'output' budgeting or 'indirect steering' or 'formula-based funding'.
It might be added here that the government has proposes further substantial changes in funding: for example, the introduction of education vouchers. Here, however, we do not report models, which are not part of the budget schemes for 1988-92 of the Draft Higher Education and Research Plan published in September 1987.

2.5. *Retrenchment policies*

The new Dutch government coming into power in 1982 began to implement retrenchment policies in higher education which were more visible than corresponding policies in other Western European countries with the exception of Great Britain. In 1982/83, targets were set for budget cuts of eight per cent, and again in 1986/87 for four per cent.

One should note that the cuts started off from a high level. According to comparative statistics presented by the Dutch government, public expenditure on higher education per capital in the Netherlands in the early eighties, was more than twice as high as in France and in the Federal Republic of Germany; student aid in the Netherlands is, moreover, among the highest in Europe. At the same time, however, the overall research and development expenditures as a percentage of the GNP was estimated to be lower than in many Western industrialised societies. The percentage of the correspond-ing age group enrolling at institutions of higher education was thirty-eight in 1984 and thus higher than in France (thirty-four per cent in 1982) and in the Federal Republic of Germany (twenty-seven per cent); however, only one-third of Dutch first-year students were enrolled at universities as opposed to about two-thirds of French and German first-year students.

Higher education expenditure per student decreased both in the Netherlands and in the Federal Republic of Germany from the mid-seventies to the mid-eighties by about thirty per cent in constant prices. But whereas German institutions of higher education experienced small budget increases alongside substantial growth of student numbers, public expenditure on higher education in the Netherlands decreased by sixteen per cent in constant prices from 1980 to 1985 alongside a twelve per cent growth in the total number of students.

In the case of the 1982/83 cuts, the Dutch government conceived their implementation mechanisms to be less prescriptive than regulations usually preferred in the past: government set the target, and demanded that the universities decide in all disciplines which low-quality departments could be closed or cut in size and present a corresponding proposal to the government within a few months. In fact, universities eventually agreed on a proposal of cuts which by and large formed the basis of the cuts finally implemented. In the case of the 1986/87 cuts, government did not repeat this procedure, but rather decided on its own about the disciplines and institutions affected.

2.6. *Regulations regarding the establishment and change of course programmes*

Prior to the changes discussed in this chapter, Dutch university legislation already provided for a much more limited role for government supervision of university studies and degrees than corresponding regulations in France and the Federal Republic of Germany. For each of about 100 fields of study, an Academic Statute was approved by government, which set a mandatory frame for the corresponding course programmes at each university in a relatively broad way. For example, the final examination in economics had to include general economics and industrial economics, whereas all other subjects might be prescribed by the Faculty of the individual university, or might be left open to the students' choice. If a new field of study was suggested by a university, the Minister of Education and Science might approve an experimental phase of five to ten years; after that period the Minister might decide, on the basis of an evaluation, whether a permanent Statute would be enacted.

As a first major change during the 1980s, the Ministry of Education and Science discontinued the traditional practice of universities negotiating with the Ministry the provision of corresponding resources when they intended to establish a new course programme. At most, the Ministry was willing to provide limited resources for a short implementation phase. Otherwise, the institutions of higher education now have to slice the necessary resources out of the available budget and resources, in the hope that by attracting new students the institution may receive additional resources as part of the general budget allocation in the future.

Second, the Ministry put forward plans in 1985 to abolish any direct state supervision of curricula. Instead, teaching and curricula should be regularly evaluated in a generalised nationwide evaluation scheme, whereby the results of evaluation should inform governmental decisions on budget allocation. This system was still under deliberation in 1987.

Third, we note that state regulations regarding studies in the non-university sector should be transformed according to the 1986 legislation from the relatively tight state supervision, typical of secondary education, into something close to that applied to the university sector. Thus, the responsibility of *hogescholen* for the development of curricula and course programmes was dramatically increased the year before this study group visited the Netherlands.

2.7. *Government-induced reforms of studies and related areas*

In the 1980s, the Dutch government initiated various substantial changes in higher education, which were either directed towards studies or affected studies indirectly. The most notable ones were the following:

a. The first major reform was a restructuring of course programmes at universities, which had already been discussed for about a decade, but actually began to be realised in 1982. In order to offset an average duration of study of more than six years, universities had to spell out four-year course programmes in a detailed way. Students were permitted to repeat the propedeutic first-year stage at most once and to prolong the subsequent three-year specialising stage by one year at most. In 1987, it was estimated that the new system had reduced the average duration of studies from six and a half to five and a half years. At the same time a compromise was reached regarding students taking more than six years: they would not be expelled, but rather have to pay much higher tuition fees.

b. The reform of undergraduate education mentioned above has been part of a government proposal to establish a 'two-phase-structure': instead of the merely individualised doctoral training of the past, a system of graduate and professional courses ought to start operating in 1986, taking in about forty per cent of first-degree graduates. The policy had already begun to change in 1984; only three partial elements were realised in 1986. First, medical students had to pursue, as originally envisaged, a fifth and sixth year. Second, students who wanted to become teachers had to take an additional one-year course. Third, a considerable number of academic staff positions were transformed into 'assistants-in-training' positions: persons holding that position are employed by the university and receive about half the salary of junior academic staff at the beginning; they are assigned a small teaching load, and are supposed to spend at least half of their time on postgraduate learning and writing their dissertation. Apart from these three elements, hardly any graduate or professional programmes emerged.

c. As a third major reform, a substantial proportion of personnel (4,500 out of 18,000 academic positions) and material resources of universities was severed from the regular university budget in 1983 and became part of a nationwide system of 'conditional financing' of research: resources are allotted for a period of five years to certain research groups by the Ministry of Education upon recommendation by nationwide disciplinary review panels. In 1987, it was decided that these resources should no longer be allotted to specific large research groups upon proposal, but rather to faculties and department following a nationwide evaluation of research at all universities in a given discipline.

d. Former higher vocational schools were legally up-graded to institutions of higher education by a law addressing specifically this sector of higher education, enacted in 1986. In the 1970s, both the prerequisite of eleven years of schooling and the regular four-year duration of studies had already been implemented. Through the formal upgrading in 1986, the HBO-sector (*hoger beroepsonderwijs*) gained a certain degree of autonomy, although still less than that of the university sector, in establishing curricula and examinations. The decision to confer the title of Baccalaureus to HBO-graduates underscores the new status. The extent of potential change in studies at HBO-institutions envisaged can be most clearly demonstrated by the provi- sion that HBO-graduates might be admitted to graduate and professional studies at universities, and that universities and *hogescholen* might establish second-phase professional courses jointly, whereas at present universities consider a HBO-degree equivalent to one or two years of university study.

e. Concurrently to the formal upgrading process, the more than 400 colleges in the non-university sector (mostly very small) were asked to merge institutionally. About eighty institutions came into being in 1987. This provision set a specific framework for potential change in studies in the process of upgrading: on the one hand, courses or whole course programmes could cross the borderlines of formerly small and specialised educational units. On the other hand, any change in studies during this period of up-grading had to take into consideration economies of scale and potential cuts in academic personnel.

3. The changing role of the central administration of universities

3.1. *Introduction*

The Dutch government policy described above aims to affect the administration of higher education institutions substantially. Institutions of higher education are expected to be alert, wise and rapid decision-makers, impelled by a mix of increased leeway for action on the one hand and on the other by an increased apparatus of incentives, inspections and threat of sanctions.

The extent to which, and the way in which, a change in administration and management at institutions of higher education will take place, will obviously depend on the interaction of four elements:

- The administrative setting of the institutions of higher education: what are the potentials and constraints of the legal frame, the historically grown formal patterns, and the informal elements of administration and management, as regards innovative policies ?
- The conditions set for innovative policies by government: what actions are necessitated, what incentives are provided, what supervision is taking place and what room for manoeuvre is given for institutions of higher education ?
- The substance of the tasks to be achieved by the institutions of higher education: in the context of this study, which focusses on teaching and learning, one has to ask in which way the range of possible and reasonable innovations in studies considered will affect the administrative processes.
- The persons involved: how do they interpret the organisational setting,

the government-set frame and governmental policies as well as the innovative tasks, and how do they act ?

In describing our observations, we face the difficulty of having to address these four dimensions to some extent separately in order to describe it to readers, but concurrently having to show how they interact. We shall describe the situation separately for universities and for the non-university sector, because they differ remarkably in some respects.

3.2. *The administrative setting*

At Dutch universities we note three administrative levels, usually called top, middle and bottom level in the Netherlands: the university, the faculty and the department (*vakgroep*). All levels have their heads, their decision-making bodies, their administrative staff and their legally assigned functions. The guiding principle is that research and studies ought to be supervised on the lowest levels. Upper levels in principle have less say in matters of teaching and research, but more say in co-ordination and in effective resource allocation. As in most other European countries, the university level at Dutch universities has no direct say regarding teaching and research by existing faculties and departments. Influence has traditionally been restricted to control of obvious misuse, to decisions regarding new establishment or closures of units, and finally to indirect steering through resource allocation.

Moreover, the Dutch university administration resembles that of most Western European countries in two respects. First, the rector, the senate and the central administration - whatever the names are in different countries - used to have little power; they rather served as a buffer between government on the one hand and academia on the other, emphasising cohesion, compromise, tradition and ceremonial pride. Second, administrative reforms around 1970 - in the case of the Netherlands the university law enacted in 1971 - partly strengthened executive power on the university level, but partly increased the need to reach broad compromises within institutions of higher education by introducing participation rights for junior academic staff, administrative staff and students. The visiting foreign experts came to the conclusion that the decision-making structures of Dutch universities continue to emphasise compromise, consensus and moderate action on central level more strongly (or managerial power on this level less strongly) than in most other Western European countries. Three features have to be mentioned in this respect:

- There is no individual top executive (president, rector, vice-chancellor etc., but an executive board (*college van bestuur*) of three - at some institutions five - persons: a chairman, a rector and a third person without any specific title. The university council nominates the chairman and the third member for a period of several years. The board of deans nominates the rector for two years. The Ministry of Education and Science formally appoints all three upon nomination. In practice, the Ministry obviously has a strong say as regards the chairman and the third person. Certainly, the top executive in other countries also has to have regard to a balance between academia, administrative rationales, government, public demands etc., but one person is entrust-ed to come up with a solution; in the Netherlands, however, the balance has to be found in a dialogue between top executives.

- A third of the approximately twenty-five or so members of the University Council, which is formally in charge of administrative rules, teaching and researching guidelines, budget allocation, etc., are elected by the teaching staff (professors, senior lecturers and lecturers, not including post-graduate researchers, assistants in training, etc.) by other staff and by students. The fact that teaching staff of various ranks form a common electorate has in practice led to minimal interest among professors in becoming members of the University Council and to the spread to less formalised ways of exerting professorial power.
- The Board of Deans may deliberate various issues, such as general institutional policies, the budget, the appointment of professors, etc. Apart from granting doctorates, it plays an advisory role only, thereby articulating the interests of the range of faculties and at some institutions the views of the professoriate. In practice, it may support or counterbalance views and possible decisions by the university council or by the executive board, but it rarely itself puts forward proposals aiming to set priorities, to establish university-wide initiatives in teaching and research, to reallocate resources substantially, etc.

External members are represented to a lesser extent at the central level at universities than at HBO institutions. At almost all Dutch universities, a few external persons are members of the university council. Notably, the chairman of the executive board will in most cases be neither a professor nor a university administrator, but rather a representative of the public. In the case of the university we visited, he was a former state minister.

There has been debate in the Netherlands as to whether these new higher education policies require more centralised managerial power and a top-down administration. In 1986, some amendments of the University Law led to a reduction in the numbers of members of the university council, and to an increase in the power of the executive board as well as the faculty boards. These changes are interpreted as being small both by those favouring the previous setting and by those favouring a strong executive power.

3.3. *Changing external conditions*

First, the power of the central university level was obviously strengthened by the objectives and procedures set by government for the 1982/83 cuts as well as for the 1983 conditional financing of research. In both cases, universities had to negotiate a solution among themselves, in the former case consisting of cuts and possible mergers, in the latter case of priority research allocation, and they finally had to carry through corresponding cuts and allocations in the annual budget and related decisions such as laying off staff. The need created from above for inter-university co-operation had led to a new power-base at the central level of the universities *vis-à-vis* both government and the faculties.

Second, the central administration became a stronger decision-making power in many issues which government now regulates to a lesser extent than in the past. Notably, the central university level now receives a budget from government which is hardly earmarked at all, but is based on detailed and complicated formulas which might be understood as guidelines for allocation. This, in theory, on the one hand increases the formal right of re-allocation, but on the other hand puts a burden on the central level to justify action if money is channelled in a way substantially differing from that suggested through government formulas, which are not known well, but nevertheless frequently interpreted as guidelines. What the central level can actually do is on the one hand to teach the university the lesson involved in the formulas - making the faculties and departments aware that they gain, if, for example, they discourage prolongation of studies. On the other hand, it can avoid channelling all money through, but rather take a share of the available resources for specific purposes, for example, stimulating new activities, promoting activities requiring inter-faculty-co-operation, supporting programmes at an early stage which are likely to grow in the future, providing resources for areas which had faced a quality decline in the past in order to stimulate an upturn, protecting small unique activities, etc.

Third, the position of the central university level *vis-à-vis* the faculties seems to be strengthened by the introduction of a system of evaluations of research as well as of evaluation of teaching and learning beginning in 1988. For it is strongly involved matters of reporting and providing information, of arrangement of visits, and finally in taking action in response to evaluation. At the time of the visits, it was not yet possible to observe the consequences of those changes.

Fourth, the university level could set up an efficient promotion machinery. Since resources depend to a more obvious extent than in the past on reports which impress not only government, but also the evaluating peers and the public, affecting students' and employers' image of the institution, impressive negotiations and advertisement might be considered to give an edge.

Finally, the substantial financial cuts which universities had to face in the 1980s, may have an impact on the role of the central administration. At this point, the range of financial cuts should be indicated. According to an overview by *VSNU*, almost all disciplines were affected by the 1982/83 retrenchment of eight per cent on average, among them engineering, by seven per cent. Much more strongly affected were medical fields (the most pronounced was dentistry, cut by twenty per cent in the course of the 1982/83 and of the 1986/787 action, but also medicine, cut by ten and five per cent in the same periods respectively, which was identical to social science) and humanities (ten per cent each in both periods). As there were additional smaller cuts, the personnel of the technical university analysed all together had been reduced by about fifteen per cent (in one faculty as much as thirty per cent) during the 1980s. Views seem to vary as to whether the power of the central administration *vis-à-vis* the faculties is likely to grow in the process of implementation of retrenchment within the universities.

3.4. *Activities at university level*

Obviously central university administrations - members of executive boards and other highlevel administrators - of Dutch universities believe that changes in state regulation regarding higher education both necessitate and provide the opportunity for a stronger strategic and administrative role for central administration of the university. In defensive terms, they note - as expressed in a policy paper of the university which we visited - that 'the future of the institution is no longer a fact but will have to be fought for by the institution itself'. This defensive argument plays a strong role, for, first, cuts in the recent past and anticipated future cuts are threatening. Second, hesitation or resistance on the part of the faculties as regards increasing power of the central administration, can best be responded to by emphasising joint dangers.

The central administration seems also to welcome a principal change of state regulation, notwithstanding serious criticism of certain elements. At least the top administrators hail the substantial reduction of 'red tape'. More important, though, they consider stronger power at the central university level desirable. We noted the following major arguments and related activities.

- The university of the past was too decentralised and lacked a corporate identity. It is conceived to be a genuine task of central administration to promote such a sense of identity at the institution of higher education.
- Faculties and departments - it was argued - tend to resist changes in

studies. The central administration of the university we visited believed that it is possible and necessary for the university at large to promote changes of studies desirable across faculties; it claimed that it was the prime force in spreading computerised instruction, and it advocated providing less specialised, more varied and individualised course programmes, more emphasis on modular courses and more learning opportunities in advanced or further education courses.

- Faculties are viewed as too weak in making differential resource allocation for research both in terms of rewarding quality strongly and in reacting to down-turn of certain major areas. The central university administration is the appropriate agent of differential resource allocation. At the university we visited, a programme was established to stimulate innovative research, as will be discussed below.
- The central administration of the university ought to play an important role in exploring and responding to societal demands.
- Under conditions of limited funds, inter-university co-operation is desirable. The university we visited co-operated, first, with other technical universities in formulating a joint plan for engineering in the Netherlands, which envisages both co-operation in some areas and 'division of labour' in other areas. Second, it set up a committee with neighbour universities to explore ways of co-operation, sharing of facilities, etc. A third layer of co-operation is the Association of Co-operative Dutch Universities. Comments from various sources, though, indicate that co-operation in the framework of *VSNU* is not very close; among other factors, the small number of universities and the traditions of state-university communication make it relatively easy for each university to approach government individually.
- The central administration has to take the lead in administrative efficiency, helping the faculty administrations to become more professional and efficient as well as helping the faculties directly regarding complicated administrative issues.

The examples of initiatives actually taken might indicate both the kind of visions and the problems involved. First, the Executive Board of the university we visited had established itself a five-member team of external scholars and experts from firms asked to evaluate research by the university; subsequently, up to ten per cent of all the research money was to be provided for specific programmes in the framework of the university's own innovation programme. This was done prior to governments' decision to introduce nationwide evalutation of research at all faculties. This should not be merely 'seed money' or 'mission money' triggering off activities, but real funding priorities. Some members of the university argued moreover, that the university administration succeeded in convincing others that the commission did not merely want to make sure 'that the rich become richer'. The evaluation was conducted, but the Board succeeded only in setting aside about one per cent of the research budget for that scheme under the conditions of regular budget cuts. Optimism was voiced, though, that more money might be put aside in the future for this internal research promotion scheme.

Second, inter-university negotiations on how to handle the financial cuts had caused substantial conflicts. Secret negotiations by the executive board on closing a department led to termoil when revealed. Activities aimed at establishing a joint advanced course with another university, were not approved by the Ministry. Instead, a joint advanced course had to be established with a non-university-level institution of higher education.

Third, on various occasions the central administration headed for solutions where government policies required actions which faculties considered not to be feasible. When departments considered themselves only able to transform a limited proportion of their regular staff positions into assistants-in-training positions and thus the number of these positions looked rather small for a doctoral programme in each case, the central government pushed through joint doctoral programmes between a few departments, although the departments argued that the advanced training needed had to be distinct.

Nobody at that university claimed that the executive board had been very successful in taking over a strong, genuine institutional policy role in the process of government's move toward less direct supervision. Budget cuts, difficulties in reaching internal agreement on policies and other factors prevented very visible achievements. Members of the executive board we talked to, frequently used metaphors such as the university being an 'archipelago' or being composed of 'castles;'. They also conceived government policy to be inconsistent, in partly strengthening the role of the central administration by reducing direct steering, and partly weakening it by setting new regulations. But they also perceived moderate successes; castles turned out to have 'bridges' as well. One has to take into consideration as well that the nationwide evaluation schemes regarding both research and studies had not yet begun at the time of the visit.

4. The role played by university faculties in innovation of studies

4.1. *Management at faculty level*

The executive power of the faculty is held by a Faculty Board. It comprises three to five members, among them the Dean, elected from the senior teaching staff, and also from a majority of teaching staff. The Faculty

Council consists of at most fifteen members - academic staff (including lower ranks), holding at least half of the seats, as well as students and non-academic staff. A similar structure can be observed at the department level; it should be noted that departments are in many cases relatively large units.

Decision-making regarding individual research projects and individual courses rests with the department. Also, most financial resources are channelled through to the department level. The faculty, however, has the final say about the course programme and research plan. It also decides whether a research contract corresponds to the research programme or, if not, whether the sponsor has to cover all costs, including for example a proportion of a professor's salary.

4.2. *The changing decision-making role of faculties*

Changes in the state regulatory system regarding higher education were unanimously praised by academic staff in one respect: the increased flexibility in utilising the resources available. In the case of engineering, leeway to combine money from different sources in hiring staff or buying equipment was noted. The possibility of providing remuneration beyond fixed salaries to some staff members in order to avoid 'brain drain' to industry was also appreciated; finally, it was reported that it had become easier to hire practitioners as academic staff one day a week, etc.

Different views were expressed as regards the nationwide evaluation of research in each discipline, and of studies beginning to operate in 1988, as already mentioned. Some hoped that this would lead to more reasonable resource allocations, others considered it as an additional mechanism of uncertainty and sudden interventions.

Altogether it is not surprising to find that deans and professors do not welcome the changes in state regulations in the 1980s as a whole. Firstly, government policy is, according to their view, obviously based on the assumption that faculties did not function well in the past in terms of perceiving societal needs and responding to them, in providing efficient course programmes, in conducting good research and in coordinating research. They feel that the blame is put on them; they frequently returned this blame sharply during the course of conversation, in arguing that new government regulations provide evidence of the governments' inability to understand university life, the needs of the students, the skills required in the employment system, etc. Second, it is not surprising to note that the faculties conceive themselves to be the losers by the changes in the regulatory system. In their view, they gain some administrative flexibility, but they lose substantial autonomy *vis-à-vis* the central administration and the multitude of evaluators who are going to approach them. Third, under conditions of retrenchment, they expect losses rather than gains from any new action. Given this state of affairs, one could come to the conclusion that representatives of faculties reacted relatively moderately, and tended to point to some rationales of the changing state regulatory system which they support and some outcomes which they consider positive.

On the basis of the concepts of this study we can argue that we did not want to explore primarily whether faculties are happy with changed conditions imposed on them. We rather needed them as resource persons in order to explore whether innovation has been stimulated by the changing state regulatory system. In this respect we note a mixed picture: the persons interviewed at faculty level point to interesting innovations stimulated thereby, alongside undesirable outcomes, limited effects and innovations neither stimulated nor hampered by it. It was not possible for the visiting team to judge how those elements are distributed. Also, various innovations, such as the allocation of research funds in a way which reflects the results of the formal evaluation of departments, were still underway. Therefore, experience was still lacking at the time this study was undertaken. Yet, links between state regulation and changes in studies can be analysed in some aspects.

4.3. *Views and actions regarding length of study*

One of the major activities regarding studies in which faculties and departments were involved was the reduction of the length of studies as required since 1982. Reactions by faculties we got to know will be described in detail because they show the possibilities and limits of carrying through policies, of setting targets and providing incentives addressing not merely the resources, but also the operation of the higher education system.

All teaching staff we met seemed to agree that some action was needed in order to reduce the length of studies, which had been on average longer than six years. One professor we met pointed out, though, that procedures for reducing the duration of study had implied that the long duration was largely an issue of teaching and learning. Guidance counsellors of the corresponding department had come to the conclusion, however, that in half of the cases of substantial prolongation the causes rested predominantly outside the university. Various means were taken to change curricula, such as 'compressing' certain courses, transferring compulsory areas to electives, emphasising general skills, working abilities and social skill more strongly, reducing the weight placed on specific knowledge, cutting down laboratory work, reducing time allotted to these, etc. The outcome was assessed in conversations as a mix of (a) successful compression and reduction of dispensible course load, (b) the establishment of a norm of about five years, instead of about six years as previously, or of the four years demanded, and (c) of some lowering of standards at the first degree. As regards standards at graduation, it was emphasised on various occasions that this was not just a biased academic perspective, but that employers also see it that way.

As regards length of study, the faculties we visited set targets not in line with government plans and 'incentives'. Five years, instead of about six years in the past, and instead of the four years pushed for by government, was conceived to be the norm for the course programme. It was also generally taken as a normal phenomenon that the majority of students had to take a second year in order to complete successfully the propedeutic phase; at one faculty we were told that only one per cent of the students completed the propedeutic phase after one year. The new de facto target length of study of five years seems to be conceived not infrequently as a reasonable solution, in the light both of academic standards and graduates' job requirements, and as a consequence of the fading away of the readiness on the part of the government to establish a second phase for a considerable proportion of first degree graduates.

It should be added here, that in the case of engineering, studies in the 'second phase' (assistants-in-training, designers-in-training and participants in the professional course programmes) seemed to correspond to about ten per cent of graduates of the 'first phase'. Representatives of engineering fields argued that five years was exactly appropriate in terms of academic standards and labour market requirements; only very few students would have proceeded to a second stage anyway, given the good job perspectives, and the limited manpower demand for engineers trained beyond that level. Some representatives from science, economics and social science fields, however, argued that a first degree after four years could have been appropriate, if about a third to one half of the graduates had the additional opportunity of two years of learning in a second phase. The target of five years was taken as a compromise, when it became clear that cuts did not allow the establishment of a second phase on the basis of available resources, that government was not willing to provide resources for the second stage, and that employers were ready at most to pay some money to advanced course students, but refused to take over institutional costs for second-stage courses - except a few courses in high demand (in telecommunication, etc.).

The governmental funding formula for teaching costs at universities aims to affect the length of study in another way: the stage at which drop-out is supposed primarily to take place. Funding formulas in practice in 1987, and those intended to be realised in the near future at that time, took into account a minimum of staff needed for each field, also certain ratios of academic and non-academic staff, student-academic staff ratios and material costs for teaching in major disciplinary areas, and further ratios of administrative and partial research expenses per student. As regards the number of students calculated, the formula does not refer to the total number of students, but rather provide resources for almost one and a half years of study in the propedeutic phase for beginning students, and for four and a half years of study for each graduate, as already described. Although this is only one element of the calculation of distribution of fixed funds allocated for universities, not, however, a system of increasing or decreasing the overall university budget according to the number of students, it implies an obvious 'incentive': universities fare best financially, if they sort out students at the end of the propedeutic year, discouraging repetition of the first year, and if they do their best in limiting both drop-out and prolongation of studies, once students have successfully completed the propedeutic phase.

At the university analysed, not only was sorting out after one year considered inappropriate by most of the academic staff, as already shown, but a continuous process of sorting out after the successful completion of the propedeutic phase was taken as unavoidable or desirable. Drop-out remained high in science and engineering over the course of study; at the places visited only fifty to sixty per cent of students finally graduated. None of the deans, administrators at faculty level or professors knew details of the 'incentives' regarding length of study and drop-out implied in government funding formulas. They knew, though, the principles, that too much repetition of the propedeutic phase, an overall length of study far beyond four years, and a high drop-out, should be avoided. The only figure repeatedly discussed was the norm obviously emphasised by the central administration of that university, that seventy per cent of those originally beginning to study in that discipline should graduate: this was conceived to be an unreasonable intrusion into teaching and learning. One professor emphasised that this creates a moral conflict between getting along with financial resources at times of retrenchment and keeping standards on the level considered indispensable: 'It is immoral to take students through, if you believe they cannot function as engineers'. Others argued that this leads to a short-sighted lowering of standards which in the long run endangers the market value of graduates. It was also claimed that such a target could only be set, if universities had the power of selecting students themselves upon entry. Criticism was voiced that the targets underlying funding were not in tune with rational ways of shaping curricula and teaching at faculty level. At the same time, it was emphasised that faculties and departments are sufficiently flexible in terms of administration and resources to 'protect' themselves, i.e. keeping students longer than expected and getting along with fewer teaching resources because of higher drop-out than desired. Further action had been taken, though, beyond curricular re-arrangements.

Students were more closely monitored regarding their achievements: those lagging behind were systematically included in counselling activities at an early stage and again at later stages, whereby a change of the field of study or of the institution was frequently recommended.

4.4. *Views and actions regarding other changes in studies*

Sceptical views were voiced as regards the innovative impulses through recent changes of the funding system and through assessment of course programmes. The informal network among Dutch scholars, apparently working very well in a small country, tends to favour, according to the views expressed, a high degree of commonality within a discipline all over the country, and tends to discourage those advertising fancy innovations. At the same time, it was argued that innovation which takes place regularly within the discipline does not depend for such changes on external incentives and pressures; as a typical example, we were presented with details of the substitution of traditional drawing in one engineering programme by CAD. It was obvious, though, that this was not the whole story, as a considerable impact from the changed research funding was expected, and as professors expressed feelings of uneasiness regarding pressures from university-level as regards education.

Research at universities has been viewed as being affected much more strongly by government policies in the eighties than teaching and learning. First, the predominant division of budget allocation between teaching and research seemed to have protected research, as surveys about time allocation of university staff suggest (according to information provided by *VSNU*, total academic staff time allotted to research increased from twenty-five per cent in 1981 to forty-four per cent in 1985, whereas time allotted to teaching decreased from fifty-six to forty-seven per cent). On the other hand, the conditional financing, as well as cuts associated with arguments that other public and private research funds should be acquired, showed that research was more vulnerable to sudden and drastic action. Also, representatives of science and engineering fields argued that adjustments regarding teaching were made easily, whereas cuts in research in many cases strongly affected equipment and thereby had significant effects on research activities. The views varied as to whether cuts harmed high quality research or not, whether a stronger emphasis on fund-raising would stimulate good research or lead to over-emphasis on applied research, and whether regular assessment of research in a given faculty was beneficial for research in the long run or not.

Among recent changes, the new doctoral training system met with most unequivocal criticism on the part of the professors interviewed. About the same number of staff positions as the number of professors had to be converted into assistants-in-training positions, whose holders were counted as two-third staff members, had a teaching load of about thirty per cent of their time, and were paid about half the income of regular teaching staff. Firstly, this led to the fact that more graduates were willing to take over those positions in fields in which employment prospects were dim, thus possibly reinforcing an oversupply of university teachers in those areas in the long run, whereas in highly demanded fields the most talented graduates were less attracted than before to the pursuit of an academic career. Secondly, departments accepting transformation of their positions into assistants-in-training positions had a loss of teaching capacity, which indicates some conflict as regards opting for undergraduate and for graduate education, and may have been forced to dismiss other staff in the process of implementation. Finally, under all these conditions the most likely outcome was a more or less even share of the 'burden' of this transformation among all faculties and departments, which kept the number of assistants-in-training small in most departments. In this case, hardly any stimulation was provided to substitute the traditional individual guidance of doctoral candidates by systematic graduate training. The compromise sought for by the central administration of the university was the establishment of joint graduate courses for broader areas; this - as already reported - met with strong criticism as an administrative act overlooking the different profiles and course requirements of the fields involved.

A certain degree of conflict between the research and the teaching function of universities was seen as emerging from the new state regulation system regarding higher education established in the 1980s. According to the professors' views, an appropriate length of undergraduate study had to be provided partially at the expense of research, because government was pressing for a shorter period of study in their funding model. If cuts were to be made on the ground that student numbers were small or should be reduced, chances of keeping strong research were viewed as slim. A moderate conflict existed regarding resources for undergraduate education and for doctoral programmes, as described. By and large, representatives of faculties and departments believed that they succeeded in keeping those problems within bounds. It was stated repeatedly that research at universities is seen as predominantly serving the students, and that employers and the public conceive the graduates as the main 'product' of the university. What met with more mixed feeling, though, was the impression that both the underlying goals of conditional financing and the economies of scale in doctoral training could lead in the end not only to gradual differentiation of higher education institutions, but also to efforts aimed at establishing a clear-cut division between undergraduate teaching units on the one hand and combined undergraduate teaching, graduate teaching and research units on the other; the limited resources and the small distances between institutions could serve as an argument to establish rigid hierarchies.

4.5. *The role of 'market forces'.*

As already discussed, the Dutch government pursued various strategies in order to bring about innovations in studies. In part, it promoted changes in a directive manner, such as the establishment of doctoral studies by introducing the position of assistants-in-training. In part, it pursued specific goals by means of establishing 'incentives', or a framework to be specified by the institutions of higher education. In part, government expressed its intention to restrain its power and leave it to the institutions of higher education to define new directions themselves. This should be done in part by exploring and responding to social need.

Obviously, these policies have changed the power and functions of potentially 'wise' actors: the central university administration as well as the opinion leaders of the academic disciplines are supposed to have a stronger say, whereas government at least claims its intention to restrain its power, and faculties and departments seem to have lost some of their traditional power. Those having gained power and influence are expected to play an active role in setting goals well. According to the Dutch government, both government 'steering' and the growing responsibility of the institutions of higher education for setting goals and taking action correspondingly, should also make the higher education system more responsive to social needs or to 'market forces', i.e. to demands of students, the employment system or to other societal demands put forward by several 'clients'. Therefore, we tried to explore the role of market forces envisaged and possibly emerging in the frame of the changes of the state regulatory system.

1. One could certainly argue that reduction of direct steering provides room for market regulation. As already emphasised, state regulations regarding studies and exams at Dutch universities are extraordinarily broad and general. Substantial limitations exist at present only if the establishment of a new field of study is envisaged. Government, though, is deliberating the abolishment of all study regulations. There are, however, traditions and stipulations to keep curricular diversity in bound, notably required or voluntary negotiations with 'sister faculties' in the case of major curricular changes or in the case of appointment of new professors. As regards administrative and financial systems, more flexibility was gained concerning the employment of practitioners as teachers in higher education expected to incorporate occupational experiences into course programmes.

2. As regards undergraduate study at universities, the state regulatory system requires faculties to consider individual demand for higher education very carefully, i.e. numbers of students willing to study. For universities have to provide open access in most fields. Also, the funding system of institutions of higher education puts considerable emphasis on student numbers, in spite of changes made to reduce the weight of that factor.

On the other hand, the labour market is not strongly addressed by the government steering system through funding. It mostly plays an indirect role, to the extent that students choose an institution of higher education and their field of study according to labour market signals, and to the extent that the faculty believes the course programme is attractive to the student due to its labour-market orientation. We were told of cases in which the regulatory system seems to create conflicts regarding labour market signals:

- Departments of philosophy must be interested in producing graduates of philosophy rather than encouraging their students to switch after some period to a field promising brighter job prospects.
- Graduates of physics may have better chances of being employed in research and development if they prolong their studies, but the regulatory system encourages the institutions to urge graduation after four years.
- Faculties of economics face financial losses if their students find attractive employment before graduation and drop out after three years.
- Students from those fields which are likely to face serious problems on the labour market do not find a shelter in the university, but rather are pushed out in the same way as students with bright job prospects.

Changes in regulations regarding non-university higher education aim to move the HBO institutions to some extent in the same direction. For the traditional practice of *numerus clausus* at most HBO institutions ought to be substituted by an open admissions policy. On the other hand, links between the non-university sector of higher education and the employment system are so close, that increased administrative flexibility might lead to an even stronger labour market orientation.

3. As regards the 'second phase' of studies, we note a weak emphasis on the labour market. The salary of assistants-in-training is attractive primarily for students from fields of study who otherwise face substantial employment problems; on the other hand graduates from fields in high demand (some engineering fields, etc.) can expect starting salaries even three time as high in other jobs; it turns out to be difficult in some fields to find graduates interested in starting an academic career under

these circumstances. This might in the long run lead to increasing discrepancies between supply of university teachers and student numbers in various fields of study. In medicine, law and teacher training, we observe employment-orientated planning. As regards other private employment sectors, government provides 'seed money' in some cases to establish professional programmes; we heard many voices of scepticism, though, at to whether such programmes will survive once government financial support is withdrawn. Finally, as regards most occupational areas, government takes the view that the consumers (i.e. graduates or employers) should cover the costs completely themselves. This seems to work out only in a few, mostly short, courses in high demand. As we were told, employers tend to argue that government should provide money for the second phase, professionally orientated courses as well.

4. Competition among universities to attract students has not been keen in the past. Given the more or less equal quantity of institutions, the majority of students choose a university near to their home. As formula funding is an incentive for increasing student numbers, as budgets cut in general push for 'survival' strategies and as a demographic decline will affect institutions of higher education in the near future, competition for students might increase. The relatively short distances between most Dutch universities provide room for such competition. Obviously, some relatively new universities are already very active presently in advertising themselves in various ways.

Thus, we note that government policies expect universities to be somewhat more responsive to market forces, and that institutions of higher education might indeed move to some extent in this direction. Again, it is still premature to assess the impact which changed government policies will have in this respect. It is obvious, however, that government does not envisage and that universities are not moving towards, a strongly 'market-driven' system of higher education. For example, universities are by no means expected to recruit as many students as possible to become as diverse as, for example, U.S.-institutions of higher education. On the contrary, government reserves the right to step in if institutions of higher education provide courses considered to be outside their domain, and government emphasises quality of teaching and research more strongly than market forces.

5. The non-university sector

5.1 *Specific conditions of the non-university sector*

From 1986, state regulations regarding the non-university sector became very similar to those regarding the university sector. The HBO law enacted in 1986, provided the non-university sector with more or less the same degree of autonomy as universities used to have. Also, the same basic principle of indirect steering was established: HBO institutions receive a lump-sum which - unlike the fixed sum allotted to each university - is calculated predominantly on the basis of the number of students enrolled. HBO institutions are free to decide how many persons they want to employ, and for what other purposes they want to spend the available resources; they establish and close course programmes and revamp curricula themselves; they employ their staff themselves, etc. As in the university sector, various specific regulations continue to be set, and various exceptions from lump-sum funding remain.

In spite of this basic similarity of the state regulatory system addressed to universities and to the non-university sector, we have to be aware of some fundamental differences which can be observed at present and which may partly be permanent. Four of such differences have to be explained in detail before we discuss experiences gained during the visiting programme.

Before such an explanation is given, a word might be needed regarding the terminology: *hoger beroepsonderwijs* (HBO) was already used as the name, when these institutions were still an undisputed part of secondary education. 'Higher vocational education' would have been an appropriate translation. As the name of the sector was not changed in the process of upgrading, the *HBO-Raad* seems to make up for that by translating it now into 'Higher Professional Education'. The individual institutions themselves adopted the name of *hogeschool* after the merger process - a term used until recently by specialised institutions of the university sector, such as *technische hogeschool*. Since both translations - 'higher vocational' and 'higher professional' - are somewhat misleading, we choose to call them 'HBO institutions', thus avoiding a translation. Similarly, a brochure on 'Higher Education in the Netherlands', published by the Netherlands Ministry of Education and Science in 1988, opted for 'HBO institutes'.

The first difference we should note is that the gap between the traditional system of government steering and the new steering is much wider in the case of the non-university sector than in the case of the university sector. Although HBO institutions are considered as forming a part of the higher education system since the 1970s in government publications, and although some changes of access and course programmes took place in the 1970s, the establishment and supervision of course programmes, the qualification, salaries, appointment and supervision of teaching staff as well as the legal status, the control and the management of the institutions continued to remain like that of secondary schools. Thus, in contrast to the universities, the suddenly increased rights to set curricular and managerial policies themselves would have had the effect of a 'culture shock' *per se*, even if the other changes reported below had not occurred.

Second, the non-university institutions of higher education are now undergoing a period of manifold transitions. The change from close supervision to indirect steering is accompanied by a process of upgrading of studies, institutional upgrading and institutional mergers. The most predetermined one were the institutional mergers. In 1983, the Dutch Ministry of Education and Science decided, in co-operation with the Ministry of Agriculture and Fishery, which is in charge of agricultural institutions, that HBO institutions should merge in order to comprise a minimum number of 600 students per institution and possibly a normal size of about 2,500 students; the mergers should preferably by multidisciplinary in each region, or various institutions of a similar specialisation should merge. The mergers should help to improve administration, to utilise resources more efficiently and allow for the innovations of studies not feasible in small institutional entities. The conditions for implementation of the mergers were similar to those of the retrenchment operation in the university sector in 1982/83: the target was set in a tight frame by government. Small institutions could not remain separate entities, even if they were convinced - as were for example most fine art colleges - that this helped to support the institutional identity and reputation. However, institutions could decide themselves which other institutions they joined in a merger process.

One substantial difference in the case of HBO institutions has to be mentioned, however, namely, that the Ministry of Education and Science entrusted the Council of Higher Professional Education with the co-ordination of the merger process. In this context, the *HBO-Raad* became an extraordinarily powerful 'buffer' organisation by implementing government-regulated actions, providing policy advice to individual institutions and channelling the interests of these institutions of higher education in negotiations with government - partly because the individual HBO institutions, due to the weaker status of the past and the sheer number of them remaining even after the merger, continue to have less access to government and the public than universities. At least in the past and the immediate future, the *de facto* power of individual HBO institutions in choosing their own policies remains overshadowed by such a strong 'buffer' organisation. In 1987, the number of HBO institutions was in fact reduced from almost 400 to about eighty, now having about 2,500 students on average, whereby the number of students per institutions ranges from about 600 to more than 10,000 .

Government did not set any tight framework regarding upgrading of studies and institutional upgrading. As regards prerequisites for admission and length of study, no change was envisaged at all beyond what had already been realised in 1970s. However, expectations for fundamental changes were undoubtedly raised. Whereas HBO graduates in the past were treated by universities in most cases like students having completed one year, or at most two years of university study - about six per cent of university students gained access via HBO institutions - and were mostly paid less than seventy per cent of the salaries of university graduates by large private firms, some provisions recently set by government are obviously aimed at reducing the status difference between universities and the non-university sector. HBO graduates became eligible in principle to enter advanced courses at universities, and universities and HBO institutions might jointly establish advanced professional courses suggesting equality between graduates of both sectors of higher education. A moderate role for HBOs in applied research is encouraged as well. On the other hand the introduction of the 'bachelor' title for HBO graduates in 1986 is a somewhat confusing indicator in this context, for it both underscores the claim of the equivalence of the HBO degree to the English bachelor, and stresses the distinction from the Dutch university degree, which nowadays might also be called Master.

This 'leap' forward expected from HBO institutions is all the more challenging and threatening as well, because upgrading is not accompanied by consistent measures for raising quality in all major relevant aspects. Entry qualifications for HBO teachers continue to be on the level of secondary school teachers, rather than academic staff of university, and salaries continue to be about twenty-five per cent lower than at universities. Although institutions of higher education are gradually being given the right to modify salaries, the lump-sum budget continues according to government plan to be calculated on the assumption that the average salary differences between the two sectors of higher education should not change.

The third major difference remaining between the university sector and the non-university sector as regards the regulatory system concerns the major elements of budgets. HBO institutions are granted a budget calculated for education, whereas the university budget is based on two columns: teaching budget and research budget. This does not mean that universities continue to be provided with much more money for education than HBO institutions; the calculated costs per student at the former are only about one and a half times as high as those at the latter. The main difference is that universities will have two major areas, where rationales about quality, utility for society, consequences of evaluations etc. differ; universities will have broader options in emphasising certain strengths, in helping to cover educational costs from other sources than those provided for that purpose (notably from research funds), and in possibly choosing routes not in line with those pushed by frameworks set in state budgets, or by views presented by evaluators.

The fourth difference is that of institutional governance. Whereas universities are ruled by the academic community or administrators linked to them in each institution, trustees or councils comprising a majority of external representatives have the final say at non-univesity level institutions of higher education.

It should be added at this point that state regulations regarding the non-university higher education sector differed in 1987 from those regarding the university sector in various additional details. In part, this is due to the transitory situation, because the new HBO legislation had just been enacted in 1986. Also, the government funding formulas for HBO institutions in 1987 set less detailed 'incentives' for suggested changes than in the case of universities. The number of students is the most important element in the case of the funding formula for HBO institutions.

5.2. *The complex transition period*

In describing the case of one non-university institution of higher education which we got to know relatively well in the framework of the visiting programme, we can not disentangle the various directions of change the institution is undergoing: curricular upgrading, organisational upgrading, merger, the search for a new management system under conditions of indirect government steering - as have been mentioned in the last section - as well as the change in the persons in charge of the institution, and the strategies emerging for coping with expected cuts. Therefore, we start by first explaining the case in its complexity, and in this context we try to assess the effect of various dimensions of the changing state regulations.

The new *hogeschool* discussed here is the largest merger operation in the Netherlands. Eleven institutions with a total student body of about 13,000 with seventeen major course programmes and fourteen locations in three cities or towns, became one institution. Among the seventeen programmes, our visit primarily addressed the seven engineering areas, which in principle allow curricular integration and joint utilisation to a large extent; in addition, there are programmes in teacher training and fine arts as well as social work and para-medical fields. The merged institutions had been predominantly private, but included some public ones as well.

In the new administrative setting of the HBO institution discussed here, the ultimate decision-making power rests with the Board of Trustees, consisting of eleven members - one representative each of the organisations which ran the predecessor institutions. The members of the executive board (*college van bestuur*) are appointed by the board of trustees. In this specific case, an administrator from the Ministry of Education, an administrator from one university and a person coming from another HBO institution were appointed; not, however, the former principal of one of the predecessor organisations, as suggested by the teaching staff in charge of the various innovations up to the time at which the new executive board took office. In the case of most other HBO institutions, one representative of the predecessor organisations became a member of the new executive board.

A very interesting setting for implementing substantial changes emerged. A core group of former top administrators (principals and vice principals) and key members of the teaching staff, developed detailed plans for a new administrative system, for re-allocation of sites and for curricular innovation during the transitory period following the merger decision and prior to the time at which the new executive board took office.

In this transitory stage, a sorting-out process among the top administrators took place, for it was obvious that the number of administrative positions of this kind had to be reduced. In this case, the Board opted for a reduction from twenty-three to fourteen, not all of which fourteen positions were to be filled by the administrators of the old system. Government facilitated this process through an early retirement scheme for HBO staff starting at the age of fifty-five, whereas sixty is the corresponding age for early retirement in the university sector.

Three features stand out in the administrative system suggested. First, a 'matrix organisation', according to the occupational areas the course programme is prepared for and according to sites (localities). The occupational areas have the final say regarding educational issues. On the other hand, personnel and resource decisions should rest with the heads or committees of each site. Second, a very decentralised distribution of funds and of administrative positions was envisaged. For example, whereas university budgets allocate about eight to ten per cent to the central administration, only about two per cent ought to be reserved for central administration of this new HBO institution. Third, the highest body in decision-making regarding studies is not - as in the case of universities - comprised of members of the institution of higher education, but rather of a committee of five to seven members of each occupational area, of whom the majority are representatives of the employment system; this can be observed now at many HBO institutions.

The model took for granted that the power of the teaching staff and of departmental administration will remain weaker than that of the faculties at universities. One tried, though, to protect teaching staff and administrators at departmental level more against a strong central administration than against direct external influence - by the employment system - on studies. It may well be that this administrative system will not be finally realised; for the time being, however, we note a parallel phenomenon at the university we visitid: the units in charge of teaching want to avoid the change of the steering system leading to strong power for the central administration and to an emphasis on institutional identity, although obviously some need for a common institutional culture was acknowledged.

In addition, a need is felt to establish an efficient administrative apparatus able both to handle the government steering system, i.e. understand the logic of governmental funding policies and implement corresponding arrangements at the institutional level, and to make use of the increased administrative flexibility. In a way, a similar strategy was pursued to that at the university visited: these roles were taken over by persons who had previously worked in the Ministry or were close to the Ministry. One might wonder, though, whether this confidence put in a few insiders might tempt other actors to give up efforts to comprehend the extraordinarily complex governmental funding formulas.

As regards locations, it is obvious that administration is likely to be less costly and more efficient, and that teaching personnel and other facilities can serve a broad range of students and course programmes more easily, if the institution is not dispersed on many small and distant sites. On the other hand, it is obvious that government is not willing to take over costs for new construction or relocation. At the *hogeschool* visited, a plan was put forward to reduce the number of eleven engineering locations to three by means of re-locating a secondary school originally part of one predecessor HBO institution, and by more efficient use of the facilities of the three biggest sites. Plans incorporated one important element of new bugdet flexibility: whereas prior activities were restrained to fiscal years, it was now suggested that a loan could be taken and paid back over several years in order to cover the costs of relocation.

5.3. *State regulation and curricular innovation*

As regards curricula and teaching, an impressive range of discussions as well as detailed plans was presented. Almost all dimensions were under consideration: admission prerequisites, ways of assessment, the courses of the first year *vis-à-vis* those of the subsequent three years, the introduction of shorter course programmes (two or three years), the most suitable timing of the practical period (in the third or fourth year), the degree of specialisation or breadth of the course programmes, incorporation of new technologies, the role of social skills of engineers, etc. It was equally noticeable, though, how much the tone and mood of the presentations differed: professional pride and eagerness on the one hand, anxious efforts on the other, as explicitly stated in one case, to live up with th expectations set by the Ministry.

A considerable part of the discussion regarding new models of course programmes focussed around potential conflicts between educational objectives and pressures to economise:

- The number of courses considered necessary could be provided by fewer teachers through avoidance of courses taken by only a few students, if the various course programmes were less specialised in general or at least had a large number of joint courses. In many areas, though, employers seem to favour - according to the HBO teachers we met - HBO graduates having completed relatively specialised courses. It should be added here, though, that in some areas a preference for less specialised graduates was perceived. Also representatives of a firm we visited expressed their preference for broadly trained engineers.
- In one case, one of the HBO teachers argued that the Ministry itself had impeded the best utilisation of resources by forcing HBOs to dissociate themselves from vocational schools of the same specialisation at a lower level. If that tradition was kept, specialisation on HBO levels would not have been forced to merge with other specialisations on that level. This was in the area of nautical engineering in which government favours closures because of declining manpower demand.
- Concern was voiced about the relatively higher drop-out of students who had completed vocational upper secondary education (HAVO). On the one hand, a rise in admissions standards - about thirty per cent of HBO students have completed academic secondary education - was considered an appropriate solution, but at the same time concern was expressed that one might lose one type of clientele and thereby encounter greater financial pressure.
- A very interesting example of how efforts for innovations interact with the heterogeneous conditions of governmental activities regarding higher education was provided, in the context of efforts to establish a centre for information science and to introduce computer-integrated manufacturing. The institution could receive a third of the initial funds needed for equipment and staff from a 'mission budget' from government monitored by *HBO Raad*, on condition that a third of each was covered by private sponsors and by the regular budget of the *hogeschool*. This could all be realised, but the most difficult burdens, obviously, were the recurrent costs of staff and costs due to maintenance and obsolescence. Those costs could only to some extent be offset by income from parttime training courses, or justified by their quantitative contribution to regular programmes. The argument put forward which should finally save the proposal addressed the overall importance of such courses for the image of the institution: if one refrained from making substantial investments in this

direction, employers would criticise the competence of graduates in the long run, and students would not choose that institution anymore.

One could assess these experiences quite differently. On the one hand, we might argue that the changes in the state regulatory system were successful, because persons responsible for HBO institutions quickly internalised the goal achievement versus efficiency dilemma, and thus will be able to figure out both reasonable and feasible solutions. On the other hand, we might argue that innovative concepts in the process of upgrading were constantly cut short by conditions of retrenchment and were hampered by the multitude of substantial changes which had to be implemented concurrently. In addition, criticism is also voiced that innovations enforced or stimulated do in some respect endanger traditional strength of HBO institutions, such as close links to the community, the communicative environment of small institutions, etc. Possibly all three interpretations are appropriate to some extent. At the time this study was undertaken, it was obviously premature to lean predominantly towards any one such assessment.

The same ambivalence could be observed as regards the role of HBO institutions in comparison to universities, and as regards quality improvement in general. It was obvious that the persons in charge of innovation of studies at the HBO institution visited, did not at all intend to copy universities: they placed their pride in a demanding practical training and the employability of their graduates, several of them conceiving employers to be their stronghold *vis-à-vis* government's demands and retrenchment policies.

On the other hand, they perceived a certain degree of competition between universities and the non-university sector in attracting high school leavers; this was expected to increase in the future as a result of declining age cohorts. According to views expressed at the *HBO Raad*, universities are already believed to be moving into the sectors of the market previously held by HBO institutions; the latter ought to counter this 'in order to guard the excellence of the university sector'.

Efforts to improve the quality of the non-university sector were considered important both in terms of requirements of the employment system and in terms of attracting students, although 'quality' is obviously much less the catch-phrase of debates in the Dutch non-university sector than in the university sector. Applied research funded by firms, some kind of co-operation with universities - for example HBO staff participating in research projects at universities - as well as a few joint professional courses with universities etc., were considered helpful in this respect. The statements 'at present we are not yet an attractive partner for firms' or 'at present we are not yet attractive for the universities' both express a realistic view regarding the present situation and hopes for the future.

Competence and working conditions of the teaching staff could be viewed as a crucial element in this respect, especially because the small number of HBO teaching staff having experienced advanced training beyond a first university degree, as well as the high teaching load of almost thirty hours weekly until 1986, might challenge the claim of quality made by the recent introduction of the title 'bachelor' for HBO graduates. The participants in our conversation were very cautious in expressing hopes of improvement in this respect. The teaching load was in the process of being partially reduced, but was likely to remain more than twenty hours. Some salary differentials might be realised, but only within a very small margin, given the overall tight financial circumstances. There were no indications that career patterns were being introduced as at universities, although the changing tasks in the process of upgrading could suggest such a change. Also, it was argued that substantial further education of the staff could not be afforded. Financial cuts were seen as an obvious obstacle in that respect. It might be added here that the institution had to face a ten per cent budget cut in 1987/88.

The problem of innovation under conditions of increasing administrative flexibility and retrenchment, was summarised by one person in the following way: 'We have more freedom to spend less money'. Notwithstanding, a modest optimism regarding the future of the *hogeschool* could be observed.

6. Concluding observations

1. Altogether, we noted a widespread basic agreement in Dutch higher education institutions regarding some cornerstones of the government's higher education policy: (a) That some reduction of public expenses for higher education has to be accepted. (b) That cuts should be made primarily in low-quality areas and in areas in which oversupply of graduates is obvious. (c) That a reduction of 'red tape' as well as detailed supervision of higher education by government was desirable. (d) That some changes of the regulatory systems ought to be realised in order to stimulate innovation in higher education. Given the usual diversity of socio-political views in a country, given the usual tensions between government and university and given the far-reaching financial cuts implemented in the Netherlands, we were rather surprised to note such an extensive basic agreement in spite of very controversial views concerning the details of higher education.

2. Dutch higher education policies in the 1980s stand out - this statement is justified in comparative perspective - for having an extraordinarily sophisticated and complex agenda regarding changing relationships

between government and institutions of higher education. We noted a widespread feeling of admiration, notwithstanding widespread criticism that the aims and methods do not really show an understanding of functions and the inner life of higher education.

3. The new regulatory system initiated by the Dutch Ministry of Education and Science is a mixture of:
   - substantial reduction of direct supervision and control of administration, and of utilisation of resources,
   - stepping-up of semi-structured interventionist policies, whereby on the one hand a relatively tight frame is set, but on the other hand visible room is left for decision and manoeuvre on the part of the institutions of higher education,
   - the establishment of a system of relatively strong positive and negative sanctions based on a mixture of criteria and procedures, whereby the goals are partly explicitly set by government, partly left open to the diversity of rationales underlying academic evaluation, partly established by institutional policies and partly determined by the market, understood to be the totality of societal forces affecting higher education by means other than direct government action.

   Government claims that it is pursuing a substantial shift from a 'remedial' policy in the early 1980s towards a 'facilitating' policy now emerging.

4. In spite of emphasising growing room left for decision and manoeuvre on the part of the institutions of higher education, the Dutch government seemed to set more specific goals and directly 'steered' more actions for innovation in higher education than many governments of other European countries during the 1980s. Efforts to introduce a two-stage structure of course programmes at universities, to cut low-quality areas at universities in all disciplines with emphasis on areas conceived to produce an oversupply of graduates, to establish a system of 'conditional research funding', to legally upgrade *hoger beroepsonderwijs*, to merge HBO institutions, etc. have to be mentioned in this respect. Also government put much emphasis on cutting areas deemed to be of low quality.

5. It is difficult to present an appropriate labelling of this mixture of different mechanisms. 'De-regulation' or 'increasing autonomy' are mislead-ing, because whereas a reduction of detailed government regulations is obviously underway, it is not so clear whether institutions of higher educations are supposed to have more real say regarding the important issues ranging from the basic criteria for desirable teaching and research towards concrete elements, such as the length of course

programmes. This is not merely a 'theoretical' issue, but rather a very practical one: government might itself have contributed to a confusion in the perception of its policies by using the title *Autonomie en kwaliteit* for the White Paper explaining its *new steering policy*. Probably, the phrase 'steering from a distance' (*sturing op afstand*) is most suitable, because it emphasises changes in procedures as well as the fact that 'steering' does not necessar-ily disappear, if direct control is reduced.

6. We noticed generally a relatively low level of confidence on the part of institutions of higher education regarding the claims of the Ministry of Education and Science that it is willing to reduce directed interventionist activities and actions setting tight frameworks for change, to increase the scope for change and finally to leave the system of positive and negative sanctions very much to the wisdom of institutional policies, academic evaluation and market mechanisms. Views tended to differ as to whether the readiness of government to take action in a controlling manner, was due to a genuine ambivalence of the policy pursued by the Ministry, to the consequences of budget cuts or other superimpositions by parliament or other sectors of government, to the tradition of the bureaucratic apparatus, or whether it was the natural outgrowth of the power of the purse.

7. For various reasons, it turned out to be difficult for the foreign observers to analyse the extent to which the reduction of detailed governmental supervision of Dutch higher education in the 1980s in fact stimulated innovation in studies. First, the number and intensity of specific innovations in higher education tightly or loosely 'steered' by the Dutch government is so overwhelming, that communication with scholars and administrators at institutions of higher education tended to focus more strongly on the impact and the assessment of these specific policies than on the impact of reduced supervision. Second, major moves towards increased room for manoeuvre on the part of the institutions of higher education had been taken recently or were still underway when the foreign experts visited the Netherlands in November 1987. Third, innovations in studies eased or stimulated by reduced direct state regulations cannot be observed easily. For a multitude of dispersed innovations - in many cases concerning the content of course programmes - tends to be less 'visible', than reforms of the whole system steered from 'above' and likely to be structural. But even if they are visible, scholars and administrators involved will hardly attribute those innovations to decreased state regulation.

8. The semi-structured government policies pursued in the 1980s for chang-

ing the Dutch higher education system are - in comparison to widespread 'implementation' approaches, claiming that only moderate changes are likely to be realised and that most far-reaching reform programmes faltered - relatively far-reaching and relatively 'successful', as far as partial achievement of underlying goals is concerned. The length of studies up to completion of the first degree was reduced; however, the 'second phase' was implemented for a much smaller proportion of graduates than initially envisaged. Financial cuts were realised and seem to have affected those departments most strongly which were considered to be academically weak. 'Conditional financing' of research was introduced and upheld after the first phase, although its principles and procedures were substantially changed. Institutions in charge of *hoger beroepsonderwijs* were up-graded, merged to about eighty institutions and internally reorganised. Finally, substantial changes were realised as regards funding and quality assessment of higher education institutions.

9. The core element of the policy of 'steering from a distance' is governments' withdrawal from any detailed supervision of administrative processes and of resource utilisation at the institutions of higher education, and the introduction of lump-sum funding, whereby the formula underlying the lump-sum, ought to transform governmental policies into 'incentives'. This core element is supplemented by more direct steering actions, by the introduction of separate nation wide evaluation systems for research and for curricula, teaching and learning for each discipline, which might again justify specific government actions if the institutions of higher education react insufficiently to these evaluations.

10. In the context of this study we focus on the formal elements of the Dutch state regulatory system regarding higher education; not, however, the underlying goals and specific targets regarding the functions and the performance of higher education. Three characteristics of the formal elements stand out: the emerging Dutch state regulatory system is very forceful, very complex, and constantly revised.

11. One might argue that innovation required in higher education to meet future challenges has to be substantial, thus requiring a system stimulating change forcefully. Under these conditions, a complex system might be necessary, for any simple setting of goals and means would be inappropriate. And if complex and sophisticated mechanisms are needed, our limited state of knowledge about the future as well as about the effects of certain social mechanisms (nobody can blame the Dutch government for this) requires that experience be studied and

subsequently former regulations be revamped. The dilemma we note, though, in the Netherlands is that the regulations are too complex and too rapidly changing: the positive and negative incentives envisaged are thus not understood in most cases, and as far as they are understood, their effects are limited due to their prospective discontinuity. And all this is overshadowed by the mixture of hopes and fears under the conditions of forceful mechanisms.

12. The Dutch government, in designing a new state regulatory system is obviously a strong believer in negative incentives. It did not try to disentangle periods of cuts from those of subsequent innovations, and it did not soften priority-setting in the way, for example, most national research promotion systems do: letting the winner feel it directly and strongly, and the loser indirectly and less strongly. As for the former, we heard the following reaction: 'When a storm comes, I close the window. But the government opens the window'. It is premature to state whether such a policy of negative incentives has worked in the eighties and whether it is likely to work, if eventually the storm is over. Statistics presented about increased productivity in the process of retrenchment may be misleading, because increased numbers of graduates, doctoral dissertations, publications, etc. may be predominantly a result of past growth, and not, as claimed, of recently increasing efficient utilisation of resources.

13. Governmental policies of changing the state regulatory system succeeded in stirring up the central university administration. Top administrators at university level came to the conclusion that a specific identity for an institution is desirable and that the central administration should play an important role in setting priorities, stimulating co-operation, shaping relationships between university and society, and strengthening administrative efficiency. This seems to be true, notwithstanding very divergent reactions on government policies in detail.

    It is a different matter, though, whether university administration succeeded in claiming a strong steering role. We came to the conclusion that it became much more of a visible actor than in the past, but much less than it hoped to be. The strategy of having three (or even more) top executives, limited participation by professors in university councils, and relatively informal channels for departmental and professorial interests, keeps the power of the university administration within bounds. One could consider this to be the outcome of compromises necessitated by government. One could equally well speculate that the king did not choose a crown prince in surrendering a substantial share of his power, but rather transferred some of his powers of control deliberately in part to the university administration, in part to academia and in part to the market, thus keeping an undisputed power of intervention, 'if things go wrong'.

Under conditions of retrenchment, central university administration had the most visible impact in channelling global cuts, whereas there was hardly any room and few resources for visible 'positive' actions. Thus, it is not surprising to note that most academics do not perceive the growing power of the central university administration as a gain of autonomy by the universities.

14. Representatives of university faculties and departments appreciate an increase in administrative flexibility. But they also note that they are blamed by the new state regulatory system as those who have resisted innovation in the past, and that they have lost some degree of autonomy in the process of implementation, and of future changes pending, concern-ing the role of the central level of universities, and concerning evaluation of research and teaching. They strongly express a need to protect studies and research from 'intrusion', whereas stimulation of innovation by government initiatives and by the changing state regulatory system was mentioned to a lesser extent in our conversations.

Various innovations were pointed out, of which some were considered to take place anyway and not be affected by changing policies at all, other took place 'in spite' of changing policies, some were attributed to specific targeted government policies, some were viewed as the consequence of less direct steering, and finally some could be regarded as a compromise between governmental and institutional intentions. As far as governmental actions in this respect were concerned, some were considered reasonable innovations and other detrimental. Of course, those views expressed reflect specific perceptions and interests of administrators and scholars at faculties and departments, but it might be justified to state that there are obviously various sources of innovation. Changing state regulation of higher education is one of those sources. In the framework of our visit, we cannot establish in detail the relative weight of various factors in stimulating innovations.

15. Although the state regulatory system regarding non-university higher education in the Netherlands recently became quite similar to that regarding the university sector, the current situation is dramatically different because the non-university sector is undergoing much more substantial changes. First, past government supervision of HBO institutions resembled that of secondary schools; thus, introduction of 'steering from a distance' implies substantial change in the administrative system. Second, non-university institutions of higher education are

undergoing a period of manifold transitions: a change in the steering system is accompanied by processes of up-grading of studies, institutional up-grading and institutional mergers of small schools towards mostly medium-size colleges. Changes are obviously both challenging and bewildering. The future will show whether this is a fortunate occurrence of parallel changes, or an overburdening of simultaneous requirements for change.

Beyond the transitory period, some substantial differences remain between HBO institutions and universities. On the one hand, the *hogeschool* will have only one money-stream related to educational tasks, whereas both the authority of the university as regards research and the existence of various money streams increases leeway for universities to take educational initia- tives, including those not in tune with the government's 'incentives'. On the other hand, potential for initiatives on the part of the HBO institutions does not rest to that extent on the relationships between state and higher education, because of a visible triangular relationship, which includes the employment system as well. The strong role of representatives of the employers in decision-making in the university sector, underscores that triangular setting.

As regards studies in the non-university sector, the range of potential innovations presently discussed is incredibly far-reaching. Almost anything seems to be open to reform: admission standards and prerequisites, length of course programmes, sequence of individual courses, the role the practical period plays, degree of specialisation or breadth, new technologies and new societal tasks of graduates, etc. Obviously, changed conditions were stimulating concepts. It is difficult, though, to predict how substantial the changes are which one can expect. Constant interactions between educational and resource-related arguments might indicate that the university sector adapted to the objectives of the system of 'steering from a distance'. On the other hand, this might also show that most of the concepts will be shelved by the tightening of resources. In addition, substantial curricular innovation is certainly restricted by the fact that the teaching staff in the non-university sector is not granted any substantial positive incentive - except for the status gain of the institution per se and some limited opportunities for research - in this period of dramatic change: salaries remain more or less the same, reduction of teaching load is likely to remain small, resources for recurrent training are not available, qualification standards for the teaching staff remained unchanged in the process of upgrading, a substantial reduction in the number of teachers in this sector is pending. The success of the various activities seems to be left to a surprising extent to a mix of identification with institutional upgrading, intrinsic motivation and negative incentives embedded in budget cuts and the threat of losing one's position. Notwithstanding, a modest optimism could be observed.

16. As already emphasised, it is very difficult for foreign observers to draw conclusions from this experience in the Netherlands on the relationships between a reduction of direct state regulation of higher education and innovations taking place in higher education. Specific historical conditions never get close to a quasi-experimental setting. The foreign observers felt strongly, though, that the potential for a move towards less direct steering towards stimulating initiatives on the part of higher education institutions, could be explored more fully,
    - if the power structure at the central university level was less diffused,
    - if the implementation of reduced direct state 'steering' was set in motion without such an amount and intensity of concurrent direct steering in some respects,
    - if the efforts of indirect government steering were more transparent and more stable over time,
    - if government's safeguards against possible 'wrong' use of the increased leeway for institutions of higher education to search for solutions on their own, were less manifold and less forceful,
    - if more visible positive incentives were realised in the case of the dramatic dramatic changes the non-university sector is experiencing,
    - if new initiatives were not overshadowed to such an extent by financial cuts.

Our observations took place in the midst of a period of change. Some major elements of the new regulatory system were recently implemented or are just underway. Government also argues that the specific mixture of strong direct government action and indirect steering prevailing in the last few years, will give way to a new mixture of weak direct and initial steering alongside incentives for institutions to take action in the light of outcome indicators and evaluations. It will be interesting to observe in the near future,

- whether a relatively consistent steering system of that kind will emerge or whether government will continue to step in constantly on other occasions and for other reasons than foreseen in that concept of steering,
- whether the mix of increased flexibility and complex mechanisms of positive and negative sanctions will have predominantly stimulating effects, or will be too threatening and thus lead predominantly to self-protecting activities of preservation of the status quo,
- whether the emphasis placed on negative incentives will work as expec-

ted or will rather lead to confusion and blockades,
- how the non-university sector will react to so many concurrent changes.

In spite of various difficulties in getting a comprehensive picture of innovations in studies and in establishing in detail the role state regulations regarding higher education played in this respect, and in spite of diverse views, noted in the Netherlands as well as among foreign observers, in assessing the quality and desirability of the respective innovations, we may undoubtedly state that obviously Dutch higher education in the 1980s is very much 'on the move', and the Dutch governmental policy of 'steering from a distance' does not play only a moderate role concerning innovations in studies. It remains open, though, whether the Dutch government has influenced innovation of studies more strongly through directives or through moves towards de-regulation.

Bibliography

Ackoff, R.L., and Emery, F.E. , (1972), *On Purposeful Systems*, New York, Atherton

Aldrich, H.E., (1979), *Organizations and Environments*, Englewood Cliffs, Prentice-Hall

Allison, Gr.T., (1971), *Essence of Decision*, Boston, Little Brown

Ashby, W.R., (1952), *A Design for a Brain*, New York, John Wiley

Askling, B., (1988), *External Influences on Swedish Higher Education Curricula*, Paris, Organisation for Economic Cooperation and Development

Bailey, G.G., and O'Connor, R.J., (1975), ' Operationalizing Incrementalism', *Public Administration Review*, Vol. 35

Baldridge, J.V., (1971), *Power and Conflict in the University*, New York, John Wiley

Banfield, E.C., (1959), 'Ends and Means in Planning', *International Social Science Journal*, Vol. 11

Barret, S.C., and Fudge, C., (eds.), (1981), *Policy and Action, essays on the implementation of public policy*, London, Methuen

Bauer, M., (1988), 'Evaluation in Swedish Higher Education: recent trends and the outlines of a model', *European Journal of Higher Education*, Vol. 23

Becher, T., (1987), *British Higher Education*, London, Allen & Unwin

Becher, T., and Kogan, M., (1980), *Process and Structure in Higher Education*, London, Heinemann

Beer, St., (1975), *Platform for Change*, New York, John Wiley

Benne, K.D., (1962), Deliberate Changing as the Facilitation of Growth, in: Bennis, W.G., Benne, K.D., and Chin, R. (eds.) *The Planning of Change I*, New York, Holt, Rinehart & Winston

Berdahl, R., (1983), Coordinating Structures: the UGC and U.S. State Coordinating Agencies, in: Shattock, M., (ed.), *The Structure and Governance of Higher Education*, Guildford, Society for Research into Higher Education

Berg, B., and Oestergren, B., (1977), *Innovations and Innovation Processes in Higher Education*, Stockholm, National Board of Universities and Colleges

Bienaymé, A., (1984), 'The New Reform in French Higher Education', *European Journal of Higher Education*, Vol. 19

Bok, D., (1986), *Higher Learning*, Cambridge, Mass., Harvard University Press

Bolan, R.S., and Nutall, R.L., (1975), *Urban Planning and Politics*, Lexington, Lexington Books

Botkin, J., and Dimancescu, D., (1986), *The New Alliance: America's Research and Development Consortia*, Cambridge, Mass., Ballinger

Boyer, E.L., and Martin, W.B., (1985), *The Role and Function of Universities*, Paris, Organisation for Economic Cooperation and Development

Boys, Chr.J., Brennan, J., Henkel, M., Kirkland, J., Kogan, M., and Youll, P., (1988), *Higher Education and the Preparation for Work*, London, Jessica Kingsley

Braybrooke, D., and Lindblom, Ch.E., (1970), *A Strategy of Decision, policy evaluation as a social process*, (orig. 1963), New York, Free Press

Breneman, D., (1981), Strategies for the 1980's in: Mingle, J.R. (ed.), *The Challenges of Retrenchment*, San Francisco, Jossey-Bass

Camhis, M., (1979), *Planning Theory and Philosophy*, London, Tavistock

Cerych, L., (1980), 'Retreat from Ambitious Goals?', *European Journal of Higher Education*, Vol. 15

Cerych, L., (1984), The Policy Perspective, in: Clark, B.R., (ed.), *Perspectives on Higher Education*, Berkeley, University of California Press

Cerych, L., and Sabatier, P., (1986), *Great Expectations and Mixed Performance: the implementation of higher education reforms in Europe*, Trentham, Trentham Books

Cerych, L., Furth, D., and Papadopoulos, G., (1974), Overall Issues in the Development of Future Structures of Post-Secondary Education, in: OECD, *Policies for Higher Education*, Paris, Organisation for Economic Cooperation and Development.

Clark, B.R., (1977), Problems of Access in the Context of Academic Structures in: Burn, B.B., (ed.), *Access, Systems, Youth and Employment*, New York, International Council for Educational Development

Clark, B.R., (1983a), *The Higher Education System*, Berkeley, University of California Press

Clark, B.R., (1983b), Governing the Higher Education System in: Shattock, M., (ed.), *The Structure and Governance of Higher Education*, Guilford, Society for Research into Higher Education

Clark, B.R., (ed.), (1984), *Perspectives on Higher Education*, Berkeley, University of California Press

Collingridge, D., (1982), *Critical Decision Making, a new theory of social choice*, London, Frances Pinter

Cyert, R.M., and March, J.G., (1963), *A Behavioral Theory of the Firm*, Englewood Cliffs, Prentice-Hall

Dahl, R.A., and Lindblom, Ch.E., (1976), *Politics, Economics and Welfare*, (orig. 1953), Chicago, University of Chicago Press

Davidoff, P., (1965), 'Advocacy and Pluralism in Planning', *Journal of the American Institute of Planners*, Vol. 31

Davis, R.H., Strand, R., Alexander, L.T., and Norrul Hussain, M., (1982), 'The Impact of Organizational and Innovation Variables on Instructional Innovation in Higher Education', *Journal of Higher Education*, Vol. 53

Dennison, J.D., (1987), Colleges and Governments - An Evolving Relationship: Government Intervention into the Operations of Community Colleges in Canada 1964-1986, in: Watson, C., (ed.), *Governments and Higher Education, the legitimacy of intervention*, Toronto, Higher Education Group, The Ontario Institute for Studies in Education

Dill, D.D., and Friedman, Ch.P., (1979), 'An Analysis of Frameworks for Research on Innovation and Change in Higher Education', *Review of Educational Research*, Vol. 3

Downs, G.W., and Mohr, L.B., (1976), 'Conceptual Issues in the Study of Innovation', *Administrative Science Quarterly*, Vol. 21

Dunsire, A., (1978), *Implementation in a Bureaucracy*, Oxford, Martin Robinson

Economic Council of Canada, (1965), *Earning and Education*, Ottawa, D.B.S.

Elster, J., (1983), *Sour Grapes: studies in the subversion of rationality*, Cambridge, Cambridge University Press

Elzinga, A., (1985), Research Bureaucracy and the Drift of Epistemic Criteria, in: Wittrock, Bj., and Elzinga, A., (eds.), *The University Research System*, Stockholm, Almqvist & Wiksel

Elzinga, A., (1987), Internal and External Regulations in Research and Higher Education Systems in: Elzinga, A., et al., *Disciplinary Perspectives on Higher Education Research*, Stockholm, Group for the Study of Higher Education and Research Policy, University of Stockholm

Etzioni, A., (1967), 'Mixed Scanning, a 'third' approAch to decision-making,' *Public Administration Review*, Vol. 27

Etzioni, A., (1968), *The Active Society*, London, Collier MacMillan

Faludi, A. (ed.), (1973a), *A Reader in Planning Theory*, Oxford, Pergamon Press

Faludi, A., (1973b), *Planning Theory*, Oxford, Pergamon Press

Faludi, A., (1986), *Critical Rationalism and Planning Methodology*, London, Pion

Folger, J.K., and McGuiness, A.C., (1984), *Catalog of Changes: Incentives for Quality and Management Flexibility in Higher Education*, Denver, Education Commission of the States

Friedmann, J., (1973), *Retracking America, a theory of transactive planning*, Garden City, Anchor Press & Doubleday

Furth, D., (1973), Short-Cycle Higher Education: some basic considerations, in: OECD, *Short-Cycle Higher Education*, Paris, Organisation for Economic Cooperation and Development

Hage, J., and Aiken, M., (1967), 'Program Change and Organizational Properties: a comparative analysis', *American Journal of Sciology*, Vol. 72

Hage, J., and Aiken, M., (1970), *Social Change in Complex Organizations*, New York, Random House

Hardy, C., Langley, A., Mintzberg, H., and Rose, J., (1983), 'Strategy Formulation in the University Setting', *Review of Higher Education*, Vol. 4

Harman, G., (1987), The Australian Experience, Governments and Tertiary Education: Increased Centralization at Four Levels, in: Watson, C., (ed.), *Governments and Higher Education, the legitimacy of intervention*, Toronto, Higher Education Group, The Ontario Institute for Studies in Education

Hefferlin, J.B., (1969), *Dynamics of Academic Reform*, San Francisco, Jossey-Bass

Henkel, M., (1988), Responsiveness of the Subject in our Study: a theoretical perspective, in: Boys, Chr.J., et al., *Higher Education and the Preparation for Work*, London, Jessica Kingsley

Hermanns, H., and Teichler, U., (1983), Integration of Higher Education; concepts and models in: Hermans, H., Teichler, U., and Wasser, H., (eds.), *The Compleat University*, Cambridge, Mass., Schenkman

Hermanns, H., Teichler, U., and Wasser, H. (eds.), (1983), *The Compleat University*, Cambridge, Mass., Schenkman

Hölttä, S., (1988), 'Recent Changes in the Finnish Higher Education System', *European Journal of Higher Education*, Vol. 23

Hood, Chr. C.(1983), *The Tools of Government*, London, MacMillan

Husén, T., (1979), *The School in Question*, London, Oxford University Press, Husén, T. and Kogan, M., (eds.), (1984), *Educational Research and Policy: how do they relate*, Oxford, Pergamon Press

Husén, T., Kogam, M., (eds.), (1984), *Educational Research and Policy: how do they relate*, Oxford, Pergamon Press

Jantsch, E., (1972), *Technological Planning and Social Futures*, London, Casell/ Associated Business Programmes

Kahn, A.E., (1971), *The Economics of Regulation: principles and institutions*, 2 vols., New York, John Wiley

Kells, H.R., (1988), *Self-Study Processes*, (third ed.), New York, MacMillan

Kerr, Cl., (1982), *The Uses of the University*, (third ed.), Cambridge, Mass., Harvard University Press

Kerr, Cl., (1987), 'A Critical Age in the University World: accumulated heritage versus modern imperatives', *European Journal of Education*, Vol. 22

Kiker, B.F., (1971), *Investment in Human Capital*, New York, Columbia University Press

Kogan, M., (1987), The British Experience, in: Watson, C., (ed.), *Governments and Higher Education, the legitimacy of intervention*, Toronto, Higher Education Group, The Ontario Institute for Studies in Education

Kogan, M., (1988), The Nature and Content of Our Study, in: Boys, Chr.J., et al., *Higher Education and the Preparation for Work*, London, Jessica Kingsley

Kogan, M., and Kogan, D., (1983), *The Attack on Higher Education*, London, Kogan Page

Kogan, M., and Youll, P., (1988), Themes: The Changing Role of Higher Education Institutions, in: Boys, Chr.J., et al., *Higher Education and the Preparation for Work*, London, Jessica Kingsley

Lamoure-Rentepoulon, J., and Lamoure, J., (1988), 'French University Education: a brief overview, 1984-1987', *European Journal of Education*, Vol. 23

Lane, J.E., (1984), Possibility and Desirability of Higher Education Reform, in: Premfors, R., (ed.), *Higher Education Organization*, Stockholm Almqvist & Wiksell

Lane, J.E., and Fredriksson, B., (1983), *Higher Education and Public Administration*, Stockholm, Almqvist & Wiksell

Levine, A., (1980), *Why Innovation Fails: the institutionalization and termination of innovation in higher education*, Albany, State University of New York Press

Lewin, K., (1957), *Field Theory in Social Sciences*, New York, Harper & Row

Lindblom, Ch.E., (1959), 'The Science of 'Muddling Through", *Public Administration Review*, Vol. 19

Lindblom, Ch.E., (1965), *Intelligence of Democracy*, New York, Free Press

Lindquist, J., (1974), 'Political Linkage: the academic innovation process', *Journal of Higher Education*, Vol. 45

Maassen, P.A.M., and Van Vught, F.A., (1988), 'An Intriguing Janus-head: the two faces of the new governmental strategy for higher education in the Netherlands', *European Journal of Education*, Vol. 23

Maclure, S., (1987), The Political Context of Higher Education, in: Becher, T., (ed.), *British Higher Education*, London, Allen & Unwin

Mannheim, K., (1968), *Ideology and Utopia*, London, Routledge and Kegan Paul

McGuiness Jr., A., (1986), *The Search for More Effective State Policy Leadership in Higher Education*, Denver, Education Commission of the States, Working Paper, PS-86-1

Merton, R.K., (1973), *The Sociology of Science*, Chicago, University of Chicago Press

Meyerson, M., (1956), 'Building the Middle-Range Bridge for Comprehensive Planning', *Journal of the American Institute of Planners*, Vol. 22

Meyerson, M., and Banfield, E.C., (1955), *Politics, Planning and the Public Interest*, Glencoe, Free Press

Mingle, J.R., (1983), *Management Flexibility and State Regulation in Higher Education*, Atlanta, Southern Regional Education Board

Mingle, J.R. (ed.), (1981), *Challenges of Retrenchment*, San Francisco, Jossey-Bass

Mintzberg, H., (1979), *The Structuring of Organizations*, Englewood Cliffs, Prentice-Hall

Mitnick, B.M., (1980), *The Political Economy of Regulation; creating, designing and removing regulatory reforms*, New York, Columbia University Press

Neave, G., (1983), The Dynamics of Integration in Non-Integrated Systems of Higher Education in Western Europe, in: Hermans, H., Teichler, U., and Wasser, H., (ed.), *The Compleat University*, Cambridge, Mass., Schenkman

Neave, G., (1985), 'Higher Education in a Period of Consolidation: 1975-1985', *European Journal of Education*, Vol. 20

Neave, G., (1986), 'On Shifting Sands: changing priorities and perspectives in European higher education from 1984 to 1986', *European Journal of Education*, Vol. 21

Neave, G., (1988a), 'On the Cultivation of Quality, Efficiency and Enterprise: an overview of recent trends in higher education in Western Europe, 1986-1988', *European Journal of Education*, Vol. 23

Neave, G., (1988b), 'The Reform of French Higher Educarion, or the Ox and the Toad: A Fabulous Tale', *Higher Education Quarterly*, Vol. 42

Newman, F., (1987), *Choosing Quality, reducing conflict between the State and the University*, Denver, Education Commission of the States

O.E.C.D., (1973), *Short-Cycle Higher Education: a search for identity*, Paris, Organisation for Economic Cooperation and Development

O.E.C.D., (1974), *Policies for Higher Education*, Paris, Organisation for Economic Cooperation and Development

Pedró, F., (1988), 'Higher Education in Spain: setting the conditions for an Evaluative State', *European Journal of Education*, Vol. 23

Polanyi, M., (1962), 'The Republic of Science: its political and economic theory', *Minerva*, Vol. 1

Popper, K.R., (1966), *The Open Society and Its Enemies*, London, Routledge and Kegan Paul

Premfors, R., (1984), *Higher Education Organization*, Stockholm, Almqvist & Wiksell

Premfors, R., (1984), Implementation Strategies in Higher Education, in: Premfors, R., (ed.), *Higher Education Organization*, Stockholm, Almqvist & Wiskell

Pressman, J.L., and Wildavsky, A.B., (1973), *Implementation*, Berkeley, University of California Press

Rea, K., (1987), The Political-Economic Record, in: Watson, C., (ed.), *Governments and Higher Education, the legitimacy of intervention,* Toronto, Higher Education Group, The Ontario Institute for Studies in Education

Rein, M., and Rabinovitz, F., (1978), Implementation: a theoretical perspective, in: Burnham, W.D., and Weinberg, W.W., (eds.), *American Politics and Public Policy*, Cambridge, Mass., MIT Press

Rip, A., (1981), 'A Cognitive Approach to Science Policy', *Research Policy*, Vol. 10

Rogers, E.M., and Shoemaker, F.F., (1971), *Communication of Innovations*, New York, Free Press

Russell, B., (1971), *A History of Western Philosophy*, (second ed.), London, George Allen & Unwin

Schäfer, W., (1983), *Finalization in Science, the social orientation of scientific progress*, Dordrecht, Reidel

Schulman, P.R., (1975), 'Nonincremental Policy Making; notes toward an alternative paradigm', *Political Science Review*, Vol. 69

Schultz, Th.W., (1981), 'Investment in Human Capital', *American Economic Review*, Vol. 51

Shattock, M., (ed.), (1983), *The Structure and Governance of Higher Education*, Guildford, Society for Research into Higher Education

Simon, H.A., (1969), *The Sciences of the Artificial*, Cambridge, Mass., MIT Press

Simon, H.A., (1976), *Administrative Behavior: a study of decision-making processes in administrative organization*, (third ed.), New York, Free Press

Skolnik, M.L., (1987), State Control of Degree Granting: the establishment of a public monopoly in Canada, in: Watson, C., (ed.), *Governments and Higher Education, the legitimacy of intervention,* Toronto, Higher Education Group, The Ontario Institute for Studies in Education

Solesbury, W., (1974), *Policy in Urban Planning*, Oxford, Pergamon Press

Southern, L., (1987), Politics and Its Limits on Government, intermediaries and universities, in: Watson, C., (ed.), *Governments and Higher Education, the legitimacy of intervention,* Toronto, Higher Education Group, The Ontario Institute for Studies in Education

Sowell, Th., (1980), *Knowledge and Decisions*, New York, Basic Books

Steinbruner, J.D., (1974), *The Cybernetic Theory of Decision: new dimensions of political analysis*, Princeton, Princeton University Press

Stigler, G.J., (1975), *The Citizen and the State: essays on regulation*, Chicago, University of Chicago Press

Stigler, G.J., (1984), *The Intellectual and the Marketplace*, Cambridge, Mass., Harvard University Press

Taylor, D.D., (1989), *Restructuring Australian Higher Education, the eight-year cycle*, Melbourne, Victoria College

Teichler, U., (1987), *Higher Education in the Federal Republic of Germany*, Kassel, Wissenschaftliches Zentrum für Berufs- und Hochschulforschung, Gesamthochschule Kassel

Teichler, U., (1988), *Changing Patterns of the Higher Education System: the experience of three decades*, London, Jessica Kingsley

Trow, M., (1974), Problems in the Transition from Elite to Mass Higher Education, *Policies for Higher Education*, Paris, Organisation for Economic Cooperation and Development

Trow, M., (1980), *Dilemma's of Higher Education in the 1980's and 1990's*, Montreal, Conference of Learned Societies

Trow, M., (1975), 'The Public and Private Lives of Higher Education', *Daedalus*, Vol. 95

Trow, M., (1984), The Analysis of Status, in: Clark, B.R., (ed.), *Perspectives on Higher Education*, Berkeley, University of California Press

Van Gunsteren, H.R., (1976), *The Quest for Control*, New York, John Wiley

Van Meter, D., and Van Horn, C., (1975), 'The Policy Implementation Process, a conceptual framework', *Administration and Society*, Vol.6

Van Vught, F.A., (1987), 'Pitfalls of Forecasting: fundamental problems for the methodology of forecasting from the philosophy of Science', *Futures, the Journal of Forecasting and Planning*, Vol. 19

Van Vught, F.A., (1988), 'A New Atonomy in European Higher Education? An exploration and analysis of the strategy of self-regulation in higher education governance', *International Journal of Institutional Management in Higher Education*, Vol.12

Van Vught, F.A., (1989), 'State Regulations and Innovations in Higher Education', *Higher Education Management*, Vol. 2

Vilanueva, J., (1984), 'Spain: restructuring, reform and research policy', *European Journal of Education*, Vol. 19

Watson, C., (1987), *Governments and Higher Education, the legitimacy of intervention*, Toronto, Higher Education Group, The Ontario Institute for Studies in Education

Weick, K.F., (1976), 'Educational Organizations as Loosely Coupled Systems', *Administrative Science Quarterly*, Vol. 21

Weinrich, H., (1971), Diskurs, Didaktik und die Diktatur des Sitzfleiches, in: Habermas, J., and Luhman, N., (hrsg.), *Theorie der Gesellschaft oder Sozialtechnologie. Wass leistet die Systemforschung? Theorie-Diskussion*, Frankfurt, Suhrkamp

Wielemans, W., (1988), 'The Labour Market as the Driving Force of Belgian Higher Education', *European Journal of Education*, Vol. 23

Wiener, N., (1948), *Cybernetics: or control and communication in the animal and the machine*, Cambridge, Mass., MIT Press

Wiener, N., (1967), *The Human Use of Human Beings; cybernetics and society*, New York, Avon

Wildavsky, A., (1974), *The Politics of the Budgetary Process*, Boston, Little Brown

Williams, G., (1985), 'Graduate Employment and Vocationalism in Higher Education', *European Journal of Education*, Vol. 20

Wittrock, Bj., and Elzinga, A. (eds.), (1985), *The University Research System*, Stochholm, Almqvist & Wiksell

Youll, P., and Brennan, J., (1988), Higher Educcation and Responsiveness: Our Main Conclusions, in: Boys, Chr.J., et al., *Higher Education and the Preparation for Work*, London, Jessica Kingsley

Zaltman, G., Duncan G., and Holbek, J., (1973), *Innovations and Organisations* , New York, John Wiley

About the authors

Denis Carrier is Professor of Economics and Assistant Vice-Rector (Academic) of the University of Ottawa, Ontario, Canada.

Pierre Gauye is Public Notary in Sion, Valais, Switzerland.

Jacques Guin is Professor of Economics and Director of the Faculty of Economic and Social Administration of the University of Montpellier I, France.

Olaf mc-Daniel is Project-Manager for the Directorate General for Higher Education and Scientific Research of the Ministry of Education and Science, Zoetermeer, the Netherlands.

Ulrich Teichler is Professor at the Centre for Research on Higher Education and Work, Comprehensive University of Kassel, Federal Republic of Germany, and Professor of Education and Social Policy Northwestern University, Evanston, Illinois, USA.

Frans van Vught is Professor of Public Administration and director of the Centre for Higher Education Policy Studies (CHEPS), University of Twente, Enschede, the Netherlands.

INDEX

Index